Hsin Chen

Adopting Emerging Integration Technologies in Organisations

Hsin Chen

Adopting Emerging Integration Technologies in Organisations

Case Studies in IT Industry

VDM Verlag Dr. Müller

Impressum/Imprint (nur für Deutschland/ only for Germany)
Bibliografische Information der Deutschen Nationalbibliothek: Die Deutsche Nationalbibliothek verzeichnet diese Publikation in der Deutschen Nationalbibliografie; detaillierte bibliografische Daten sind im Internet über http://dnb.d-nb.de abrufbar.
Alle in diesem Buch genannten Marken und Produktnamen unterliegen warenzeichen-, marken- oder patentrechtlichem Schutz bzw. sind Warenzeichen oder eingetragene Warenzeichen der jeweiligen Inhaber. Die Wiedergabe von Marken, Produktnamen, Gebrauchsnamen, Handelsnamen, Warenbezeichnungen u.s.w. in diesem Werk berechtigt auch ohne besondere Kennzeichnung nicht zu der Annahme, dass solche Namen im Sinne der Warenzeichen- und Markenschutzgesetzgebung als frei zu betrachten wären und daher von jedermann benutzt werden dürften.

Coverbild: www.purestockx.com

Verlag: VDM Verlag Dr. Müller Aktiengesellschaft & Co. KG
Dudweiler Landstr. 99, 66123 Saarbrücken, Deutschland
Telefon +49 681 9100-698, Telefax +49 681 9100-988, Email: info@vdm-verlag.de
Zugl.: London, Brunel University, Diss., 2005

Herstellung in Deutschland:
Schaltungsdienst Lange o.H.G., Berlin
Books on Demand GmbH, Norderstedt
Reha GmbH, Saarbrücken
Amazon Distribution GmbH, Leipzig
ISBN: 978-3-639-25575-1

Imprint (only for USA, GB)
Bibliographic information published by the Deutsche Nationalbibliothek: The Deutsche Nationalbibliothek lists this publication in the Deutsche Nationalbibliografie; detailed bibliographic data are available in the Internet at http://dnb.d-nb.de .
Any brand names and product names mentioned in this book are subject to trademark, brand or patent protection and are trademarks or registered trademarks of their respective holders. The use of brand names, product names, common names, trade names, product descriptions etc. even without a particular marking in this works is in no way to be construed to mean that such names may be regarded as unrestricted in respect of trademark and brand protection legislation and could thus be used by anyone.

Cover image: www.purestockx.com

Publisher:
VDM Verlag Dr. Müller Aktiengesellschaft & Co. KG
Dudweiler Landstr. 99, 66123 Saarbrücken, Germany
Phone +49 681 9100-698, Fax +49 681 9100-988, Email: info@vdm-publishing.com

Printed in the U.S.A.
Printed in the U.K. by (see last page)
ISBN: 978-3-639-25575-1

Hsin Chen

Adopting Emerging Integration Technologies
in Organisations

Abstract

A review of the innovation and diffusion literature indicates a considerable amount of research, where attention is given to a range of features which may support integration technologies adoption. However, some literature suggests that the findings derived from the study of large enterprises cannot be generalised and applied in SMEs due to the distinct characteristics of SMEs. Although the adoption of integration technologies is recognised in the normative literature as being different between large and small companies, the literature on its adoption by SMEs remains limited. Nevertheless, among the existing works, there are lacks of studies emphasised the reasons why SMEs and large companies take the decision to adopt integration technologies, which focus specifically on the different factors. Thus, this presents a research issue, and is investigated in this research.

This thesis identifies the significant differences in the way that SMEs and large companies approach integration technologies based on the existing literature, theoretical diffusion theories, and resource-based theory. In doing so, the parameters that can be used to explain the adoption of integration technologies in SMEs and large firms are identified, which are *nature of organisations*, *company size*, *integration needs, adoption factors for SMEs and large organisations, and time*. Additionally, adoption factors are found, and are classified into three categories: *adoption factors explicit to SMEs*, *adoption factors explicit to large organisations*, and *common factors*. Based on this, a conceptual model is introduced to explain the factors that influence the different adoption factors between SMEs and large organisations.

The empirical contexts of the research are one project on integration technologies adoption, and four case studies on a large firm and three SMEs, which are analysed using an interpretive and qualitative research approach. The evidence suggests that the empirical data complement the identified dimensions: *nature, integration needs, company size* and *time*. The empirical data also inform that the current integration technologies adoption factors reported in the literature can be classified into *common factors*, *factors explicit to SMEs*, and *factors explicit to large firms* to support a more comprehensive view on this area. Additional factor like perceived future prospect has been considered by the researcher as a factor that influences integration technologies in large organisations. The findings of this research can be useful to guide analysts, and researchers in determining critical aspects of the complex issues involved for integration technologies adoption, and presenting suggestions for further valid research.

Table of Contents

List of Figures

List of Tables

Chapter1: Introduction

Summary

The research presented in this thesis is concerned with the adoption of integration technologies in SMEs and large organisations. More specifically, the aim of the research is to analyse comparatively the adoption of integration technologies between SMEs and large organisations. To set the scene for the subsequent analysis, this chapter begins with an introductory discussion of the relevant background areas, followed by an overview of the theoretical background framing the current research. The detailed aims and objectives of the research are presented next. The chapter ends by outlining the thesis structure to assist the reader in positioning each subsequent chapter within the overall research framework.

1.1 Introduction

Integration problems are not a new issue, and have existed since Information Systems (IS) moved from traditional centralised architectures to distributed architectures. These problems affect all types of organisations, including Small and Medium-Sized Enterprises (SMEs). The incompatible disparate systems are complex and difficult to manage and have caused several problems for organisations. For instance, each individual application needed to store and handle its own data, since applications do not share data or services, resulting in an increased redundancy of data and system functionality. Since each application was based on a different platform or operating system, organisations need more experts to support and maintain all these applications. This has resulted in high operational costs. Hence, enterprises are seeking new ways to integrate their applications, and these which consist of incompatible and disparate applications can improve their performance and efficiency by such integration. Linthicum (1999) suggests that organisations are able to integrate their applications and data sources to have a distinct competitive advantage, such as the strategic utilisation of company data and technology for greater efficiency and profit.

Prior studies on integration technologies in small businesses have primarily focused on the use of Electronic Data Interchange (EDI). In this study, the researcher will be examining the adoption of integration technologies (including emerging integration technologies like Web Services), and will take into consideration the differences between SMEs and large companies, which the researcher believes have so far not been studied in-depth. The primary objective of this study is to identify the state of the application of various integration technologies and the factors that influence the adoption of these technologies between SMEs and large organisations. While most prior studies on integration technologies adoption have focused on large corporations, this research recognises the importance of integration technologies and realises the difficulties involved in its effective adoption by SMEs.

The study begins with the observation that integration technologies have not been widely adopted by SMEs. This research intends to offer an in-depth study of the adoption of integration technologies by examining the factors that affect organisations' adoption decisions by analysing comparatively the differences between SMEs and large organisations. In doing so, the innovation diffusion theory, suggested by Rogers (1995), with the support of the resource-based theory of Conner and Prahalad (1996), will be the main theoretical foundations of this work, and will be carried out by following an interpretive research approach.

Thus, the main purpose of this thesis is to analyse comparatively the adoption of integration technologies between SMEs and large organisations. This chapter serves as an introduction to the research that has led to this thesis. In the first section, the motivation for the research is presented. Specifically, the adoption of integration technologies by SMEs, and their increasing need for awareness, were the starting point for examining the adoption practices. The limitations of the current research will be explained next. In section 1.4, the research aim and objectives will be defined, whereas sections 1.5 and 1.6 will provide an introduction to the methodology and contributions of this research. Finally, section 1.7 will provide an overview of the thesis, summarising the context of each chapter.

1.2 Motivation for Researching the Adoption of Integration Technologies by SMEs

In recent years, businesses have had to operate in a diverse environment. They interact with a wide variety of clients, both inside and outside the enterprise, and rely on disparate systems and processes to power their business activities. In this kind of environment, businesses face an integration challenge. Themistocleous (2002) claimed that, in the majority of cases, the IT infrastructures are incompatible. This has caused intra and inter-organisational incompatibility and created an inherent barrier for information sharing. Organisations that consist of incompatible and heterogeneous applications can improve their performance and efficiency by integrating them. Before the emergence of Enterprise Application Integration (EAI) technology, many organisations connected their IS on a point-to-point basis. As the number of systems grew, such interconnections became more complex and difficult to manage, as changes to any single application required changes to all those applications that shared information.

EAI can be used to overcome this problem because EAI developed a central integration infrastructure where each application is connected (Kaye, 2003). When an application requires changes, the rest of the system is rarely affected, as it is not interconnected with that application. Only applications that require changes and their connection to the central integration infrastructure are altered (Themistocleous, 2002). In doing so, EAI allows organisations to anticipate and react to customers requirements, collaborate with suppliers and partners, identify and exploit new opportunities quickly and effectively, reduce maintenance efforts, as well as increasing flexibility and competitive advantages (Daniel, 2003; Linthicum, 1999; Poon and Swatman, 1999). Since many large organisations have adopted integration technologies to solve their technical difficulties caused by the incompatibility of their systems, the competitive pressure might be set to increase in SMEs. For these reasons, SMEs are under increasing pressure to employ integration technologies to support their IS integration and help maintain their competitive positions, or simply to survive (Thong, 2001). This clearly indicates that SMEs have motivations towards the adoption of integration technologies to support their IS internally, as well as externally.

Although the advantages of adopting and implementing integration technologies are reported to be substantial, most SMEs ignore the idea, according to the normative literature. This will be demonstrated in the next sections.

1.3 Evidence of Low Integration Technologies Adoption in SMEs

Despite the benefits that IS integration and practices can offer to SMEs, little attention has been paid towards the adoption of integration software among such enterprises (Hughes et al., 2003; Tagliavini et al., 2002). There are many explanations for this, such as the resources available, the need for integration, and the low levels of integration in SMEs' existing systems. Other reasons include (1) lack of in-house IT development skills, (2) few affordable turnkey solutions, (3) lack of external pressure to encourage or assist SMEs with integration, (4) concern over the economic costs, and (5) lack of technical knowledge (Cragg and King, 1993a; Daniel, 2003; Iacovou et al., 1995; Poon and Swatman, 1999). While large businesses might suffer from many of the same constraints, the effect on small businesses is more significant. The skills, time and staff necessary for planning are not major issues in large businesses, yet these same issues represent most of the difficulties in small businesses (Thong, 1999).

A review of the literature on the adoption of integration technologies indicates that many studies have focused on different aspects of EDI, EAI and Web Services adoption. For example, Banerjee and Golhar (1994) examined the positive and negative impacts of various factors on the EDI selection decision alone, to assess the impact of EDI on an organisation's employees. Hart and Saunders (1998) studied the role of power and trust in EDI adoption and use. The study also evaluated the differences between proactive and reactive firms, in terms of the extent of adaptation, external connectivity with trading partners, and the integration of EDI information. More recently, Themistocleous (2002) studied the adoption of EAI in multinational organisations, with several adoption factors being identified, such as the benefits, barriers, costs, internal and external pressures, IT sophistication, IT infrastructure, and support. Wu and Sawy (2003) studied Web Services as a special case of IT industry innovation. They first reviewed two key issues at the innovation level of analysis: the type of innovation and innovation characteristics. Then they developed a 3-layer nested-stage model as a road map for studying Web Service innovation. Zhang and Huang (2004) proposed a Web Service adoption model by applying the diffusion theory and security-related research to technology adoption. Chen (2003) developed a framework for analysing the driving forces for the adoption of Web Services, based on a literature review, a technical information analysis, and field and Web-based case studies.

All these studies, however, focused mainly on large businesses. Some literature suggested that due to the different technology adoption patterns between SMEs and larger companies, research findings regarding the larger business should not be generalised and imposed on small organisations as well (DeLone, 1988; Ein-Dor and Segev, 1978; Iacovou et al., 1995; Kuan and Chau, 2001; Raymond, 1985). Since small businesses possess certain unique characteristics, when compared to large businesses, the general applicability of the studies on integration technologies' adoption in large organisations and small businesses may be questionable (Kuan and Chau, 2001). Thus, a better understanding of the ways in which SMEs adopt integration technologies is necessary because the research in this area is proved to be limited, with SMEs requiring answers to many issues.

1.4 Characteristics of SMEs

There is confusion around the globe regarding the definition and classification of SMEs. Small to medium-sized enterprises in some countries are classified into micro, small, or medium enterprises (European Commission, 2003). The three parameters generally applied by most countries, singly or in combination are: (1) capital investment in plant and machinery, (2) the number of employees, and (3) the volume of production or turnover of business. The definition may vary among countries or institutions, based on the differences in economic levels or the wealth of the countries (i.e. there is no single, uniformly acceptable definition of a small company) (Storey, 1994). The definitions of SMEs in different regions are defined and summarised in Table 1.1.

Table 1.1 Summary of SME Definitions

	Micro	Small	Medium
United States (Holmes and Gibson, 2001)	Headcount = up to 20	Headcount = up to 100	Headcount = up to 500
Japan (JSBRI, 2002)	Headcount = up to 20 in Mining & manufacturing and other industries Headcount = up to 5 in Commerce and Service industries	Headcount = up to 100 in wholesale Capitalisation = up to 30 million Yen Headcount = up to 50 in retail Capitalisation = up to 10 million Yen Headcount = up to 300 in industry Capitalization = up to 100 million Yen	
European Union (Commission, 2003)	Headcount = up to 10 Turnover = up to 2 million euros Balance Sheet Total = up to 2 million euros	Headcount = 11 to 50 Turnover = up to 10 million euros Balance Sheet Total = up to 10 million euros	Headcount = 51 to 250 Turnover = up to 50 million euros Balance Sheet Total = up to 43 million euros
Developing and Transition Countries (Gibson, 2001)	Headcount = 11 to 150 Sales = up to US$ 5 million		

SMEs account for over 90% of operating businesses in many countries, and are vital for the global economy, as they (1) generate new jobs, (2) generate local economic activity, (3) create local wealth, (4) create new ideas, (5) introduce new products and services, (6) diversify the private sector, and (7) stabilise the private sector (Bannock and Daly, 1994; Bridge et al., 1998; Brouthers et al., 1998; Burns, 2001; Deakins and Freel, 2003). Thus, it is important that the integration of IS will be embraced by the smaller companies, as well the need for more rigorous and relevant research into this important sector of the economy (Bannock and Daly, 1994; Thong, 2001). This will eventually have an impact on SME productivity, market access, and competitiveness, as well as on the economy in general (Walczuch et al., 2000).

With the rise of e-commerce-based technology and the decrease in the cost of IS, SMEs have the potential to take advantage of the same technology that large business have access to (Daniel, 2003). However, due to the inherent differences between small and large businesses, research findings based on large businesses can not be generalised to small businesses (Pollard and Hayne, 1998; Poon and Swatman, 1999; Wang et al.,

2003). According to Ein-Dor and Segev (1978), an organisation's size is directly associated with us Management Information Systems (MIS) success, and proposed research findings regarding the large business MIS environment can not be generalised to small organisations. DeLone (1981) also reported that firms of different sizes manage their computer operations differently. Iacovou et al.(1995) claimed that smaller organisations have been shown to have different technological adoption patterns than larger ones. In accordance with these considerations, to investigate the adoption of integration technologies in SMEs, it is initially vital to identify those SME characteristics which make them distinct from other types of organisations. Therefore, to better understand the characteristics of SMEs, they will be discussed respectively in relation to their Management, Structure, Marketing, Finance, Human Resources (HR), Research and Development (R&D), and IT.

- **Management**

  According to Burns (2001) and Klandt (1993), many SMEs are family-owned businesses with a management style generally: (1) more flexible in time, work and money, (2) higher in employee motivation, (3) faster in decision-making processes, and (4) suffering more from conflict. Some other analysts also claimed that the supervision and management styles in smaller companies are more immediate, direct and easier, i.e. less costly than larger companies (Brown *et al.*, 1990; Curran *et al.*, 1986). As a result, working rules can be varied, with opportunities arising for employees to participate in several kinds of work (Bridge *et al.*, 1998; Burns, 2001; Storey, 1994). The culture of a small enterprise is tied in with the needs, desires and abilities of its owner (Bridge *et al.*, 1998). According to Deakins and Freel (2003) and Wang *et al.* (2003), owner-managers in SMEs have a strong need for independence. For example, the owners of SMEs often like controlling their own destiny and doing things differently. Burns (2001) reported that the owners of SMEs are highly self-motivated, and often see money as a sign of achievement for the successful entrepreneur. This shows that the owners of SMEs usually have more power than the employees, and are reluctant to share their powers (Bridge *et al.*, 1998; Goss, 1991; Storey, 1994). Thus, decision-making in SMEs leans more towards a centralised approach (i.e. in the form of sole proprietorship), which is less formal and more personalised (Carter and Evan, 2000). Centralisation produces quick decisions and full control of the management, and can be an advantage when reacting to market opportunities in a changing world, i.e. reacting quickly to change (Carter and Evan, 2000). However, Bridge *et al.* (1998) claimed that centralised decision making in SMEs can sometimes be irrational, with the information available to decision makers in SMEs often inaccurate, incomplete, and time-bound, more so than in other organisations. This is due to their heavy reliance on information gathered from personal contacts and the lack of resources in SMEs, such as the management skills of their owners that are sometimes unlikely to encourage rational evaluations.

- **Structure**

Bridge *et al* (1998) and Storey (1994) reported that SMEs tend to have a flexible and simple organisational structure. Pollard and Hayne (1998) also suggested that small organisations are likely to have fewer problems, in terms of organisational politics, since there are only a few stakeholders involved. Hence, the structure of SMEs is simpler than in larger organisations. Moreover, when there is less of a business load, employees can undertake all sorts of different work (i.e. labour-intensive). When there is an urgent need, as requested by the owners, then employees in small businesses are usually more willing to make accommodations for the request and work longer hours if necessary (Deakins and Freel, 2003; Storey, 1994), thus resulting in a more flexible structure for SMEs. However, problem solving is usually regarded by organisations as a higher requirement than that of efficiency (Bridge *et al.*, 1998).

- **Marketing**

Unlike large organisations where they have a formal and systematic marketing strategy, SMEs tend to target markets through self-selection, the recommendations of customers, and their owner-manager's marketing competency (Carter and Evan, 2000). They seem to give marketing a low priority compared to the other functions of their businesses. According to Storey (1994), some problems have risen for SMEs when they come to marketing. Firstly, most small businesses are dependent on a small number of customers and they tend to trade only in a limited geographical area. Secondly, since SMEs have limited financial sources and human resources, they can not afford to spend a high percentage of their income on marketing. Fuller (1994) claimed that since SMEs are lacking in planning efforts, their marketing is usually not planned properly.

- **Finance**

Small companies find it difficult to obtain certain financial[1] sources and face difficulties raising particular types of finance, such as long-term loans, due to the fact

---

[1] The internal financial sources for SME include savings, re-mortgages, or maybe money raised from family and family friends. As for the external sources, which include banks, equity from

that smaller companies have little equity in the form of share capital, which results in their being rated in the high risk category (Deakins and Freel, 2003; Rothwell and Zegveld, 1982; Storey, 1994). For this reason, SMEs usually find it difficult to obtain lower interest rates on their loans, as lending to small companies is perceived as high-risk by the banks (Deakins and Freel, 2003; Storey, 1994). As a result, SMEs tend to obtain loans from the private sector as an alternative (Deakins and Freel, 2003). For example, raising finance like informal venture capital from business angels[2].

- **Human Resources**

SMEs are usually lacking in technological knowledge when compared to larger companies due to their considerable informal employment strategies and certain recruitment difficulties (Atkinson and Storey, 1993; Marlow, 2000). According to Scott *et al.* (1989) and Storey (1994), semi-skilled and unskilled manual workers constitute 44% of all employment in SMEs. This is due to the turnover of staff and the average employment wages in SMEs generally being below larger companies, as well as the issue for smaller companies which do not offer similar remuneration packages or promotional hierarchies like those available in larger companies (Bolton, 1971; Marlow, 2000). However, working in a small group and an informal employment style can result in fewer communication problems, as owners and employees can easily communicate, thus, providing a better environment for the employee than is possible in most large companies (Bolton, 1971; Curran *et al.*, 1986; Storey, 1994).

In relation to training, although formal workforce training is more likely to take place in small to medium-sized companies than in micro-sized companies, informal training is nevertheless still employed by most SMEs (CSBRC, 1992). According to Cambridge Small Business Research, small to medium-sized companies are much more likely to use some form of external training than micro-sized companies. According to Storey (1994), the emphasis in SMEs is to sell the products, rather than to train. Townroe and Mallalieu (1993) also reported that entrepreneurs had no real desire for training. The employers in small companies are reluctant to invest, as well as to participate in training, as they think that they do not require more training to do their jobs better (Creedy and Whitfield, 1988; Storey, 1994).

---

venture capitalists and informal investors and short-term trade credit, leasing, hire-purchase and factoring.

[2] Business angels are private, high net-worth individuals who make direct investments in unquoted companies in which they have no family connection.

- **R&D**

Rothwell and Zegveld (1982) suggested that many SMEs do not engage in formal R&D (probably less than 5% of enterprises employing under 200 people actually perform formal R&D). Carter and Evan (2000) also reported that due to the lack of financial resources and expertise in IT, SMEs usually do not develop IS on their own. Instead, they rely more on standardised and off-the-shelf software packages and normally seek external support for their IT problems, such as friends, vendors or consultants. For these reasons, the emphasis of SME R&D work is in upgrading, not innovating (i.e. modification of the existing products instead of innovation). Although studies suggest that SMEs are much less likely to conduct R&D than large companies, due to the resource constraints, they do so more efficiently, and introduce new products to the marketplace faster than the bigger companies (Burns, 2001). This is due to SMEs' fundamentally behavioural advantages, the internal organisation activities, and their responsiveness to the changing environment, e.g. flexibility and speed (Deakins and Freel, 2003). SMEs are likely to provide something marginally different to the competition, and often go for the low cost options for their innovations, such as their products or services, thus finding a market niche. For example, direct selling via the Internet offers similar advantages to other organisations through the virtual organisation (Burns, 2001).

- **IT**

IT is becoming more affordable, powerful and accessible, due to the fact that computers have become widely available as usability and ease of use have increased and their price has dropped. These all enable small businesses to take advantage of the strategic possibilities that IT offers, as IT used to be perceived as an expensive investment for most SMEs (Pollard and Hayne, 1998). As a result, the adoption rate of IT in SMEs has increased (Carter and Evan, 2000; Levy *et al.*, 2003). Smith (1999) described that most SMEs use IT as a tool to support specific organisational tasks like accounting, networking and some administrative works, but some SMEs are still using very basic forms of technologies, such as phones, answering machines and faxes. Nowadays, with the rise of IT, it is not only being viewed by SMEs as a tool to support their internal organisational tasks, but also as a communication tool to transfer information across organisational boundaries (Poon and Jevons, 1999). Therefore, much attention to Inter-organisational Information Systems (IOS) has increased in SMEs to reach new levels of efficiency and effectiveness in satisfying their external customers (Hughes *et al.*, 2003). For example, the Electronic Data Interchange (EDI).

From the discussion above and the review of the literature, it has been found that the characteristics of SMEs have both strengths and weaknesses. These strengths and weaknesses might be the important determinant factors which influence SMEs' decisions on whether they adopt integration technologies. Therefore, to understand better these strengths and weaknesses, they are summarised in Table 1.2 in terms of their Management, Structure, Marketing, Finance, HR, R&D and IT.

Small organisations have long been found to be different from large organisations in the IS context, as they are not a simple scaled-down model of large organisations (Raymond, 1985). In general, small businesses face greater risks in IS implementation and the use of IT than larger businesses because of inadequate resources, limited knowledge, a lack of 'know-how' about IS, and several other constraints, as mentioned above (Cragg and King, 1993b; Cragg and Zinatelli, 1995; Iacovou et al., 1995). Therefore, SMEs are likely to be less prepared and less able to change. Managers in SMEs have also been characterised as having reservations about the adoption and use of information systems (Chang and Powell, 1998; Thong, 2001).

1.5 Adopting Integration Technologies by SMEs

Despite the lack of literature and the reservations about SMEs' adopting integration technologies, they have not always obviated the benefits and successes that such organisations can achieve from IS. In the past, SMEs tended to use IS as tools to automate standard administrative functions, e.g. accounting, budgeting and inventory control, etc.. Until recently, there is a growing volume of literature that is addressing the issues of SMEs' using IS to gain a competitive advantage (Pollard and Hayne, 1998). According to Lin et al. (1993), the increasing interest in the strategic use of IS by SMEs is based on three factors: (1) increased adoption of IS and its effective use by competitors

Table 1.2 Summary of Strengths and Weaknesses of SME Characteristics

Dimension	Strengths	Weaknesses
Management	• Close relationship between employees and owners • Strong motivation for success • More flexibility in time, work and money. • Close relationship between customer and supplier • Decision-making process faster, centralised, less formal, and more personalised • Owners highly self-motivated • React to change quickly	• Owners in SMEs have strong need for independence • Owner main person in control • Money sign of achievement to successful entrepreneur • Decision-making can sometimes be irrational • Lack of systematic management style like large organisations
Structure	• Flexible • Simple • Non-differentiated • Not as bureaucratic as larger organisations	• Too simple and flexible, in another way means lack of organised structure
Marketing	• Less investment in marketing means more investment in something else	• SMEs can not afford to spend a high percentage of income on marketing • Limited abilities to employ marketing specialists • Lack of planning efforts • Over-reliance on owner-manager's marketing competency
Finance	• Financial sources usually from family capital, therefore avoiding paying interest	• Lack of financial resources, as SMEs find it difficult to obtain financial sources • Difficult to obtain lower interest rates on loans • Sometimes obtain loans from private sector, so might end up paying too much interest
HR	• Informal employment style, thus resulting in easier communication • Close relationship between employees and owners, resulting in better working environment	• Physical working conditions can sometimes be inferior • Turnover of staff and average employment wages generally lower than large companies • Informal training normally engaged • Lack of skilled employees
R&D	• Often go for cost-saving options for innovations • Often find ways of networking with customers and suppliers so as to cut costs and lead times • Innovation activities are relatively routineised and scale economies • SMEs flexible and willing to try new approaches	• Do not engage in formal R&D • Usually rely more on standardised and off-the-shelf software packages • Usually seek external support for IT problems due to lack of know-how and technological knowledge
IT	• Most SMEs use IT as tools to support specific organisational tasks • Use IT to enhance competitiveness	• Some SMEs still using very basic forms of technologies such as phone, answering machine and fax • IT infrastructure and ability not as advanced as large organisations • Due to SMEs' lack of financial resources they can not afford expensive IT

(2) decrease in the cost of IS so that it is accessible to SMEs, and (3) ability for IS to allow SMEs to mask their size from external partners. For these reasons, some SMEs turn to the adoption of integrated IS as a new strategy to improve their competitiveness.

The literature has shown that some SMEs adopt ERP and EDI to automate and integrate their business processes, even though there are a few prior studies that focus on EDI and ERP in small businesses. These studies include Chen and Williams (1998), Chwelos et al. (2001), Daniel (2003), Hughes et al. (2003), Iacovou et al. (1995), Kuan and Chau (2001), Ravarini et al. (2000) and Tagliavini et al.,(2002), Tuunainen (1998), and Waarts et al.,(2002). Before the emergence of EAI and Web Services, ERP and EDI technologies have been used by most organisations to automate their business processes. EDI is a relatively old version of integration technology, when compared to EAI and Web services, which aims to improve and automate the business processes by replacing time-consuming physical flows with automatic and end-to-end information flows. ERP systems can be also considered as an integration technology, or software, which is often used by companies to integrate and automate their internal business processes, although it is not an integration technology.

In the 1990s, ERP systems were introduced as an integrated software solution to help manage a company's resources and integrate all business functions, such as planning and inventory/materials management (Gibson et al., 1999). Although ERP packages offered advantages to enterprises, they have not achieved many of their anticipated benefits. The complexity of ERP, the non-flexible nature of ERP solutions, and the conflict between the ERP systems and the business strategy has caused problems. Since ERP packages are not designed to tie up with other autonomous applications, it can not therefore adequately support organisations to integrate their applications (Schonefeld and Vering, 2000; Themistocleous et al., 2001b). As a result, autonomous and heterogeneous applications co-exist in companies with ERP systems, with the integration problem not having been addressed. Therefore, the use of an ERP system is no longer a support or lead for a competitive advantage for organisations.

EDI may be most easily understood as the replacement of paper-based purchasing orders routines with electronic equivalents (Clarke, 1998). It is an electronic communication between trading partners with structured business messages that conform to common standards from one computer application to another (Edwards, 1997). While EDI has long played an important role in enabling the electronic exchange of business documents, with many SMEs adopting it, it does not adequately support intra- organisational integration, and nor fully automate the business processes (French, 2002). Nonetheless, with its lack of flexibility on file formats (i.e. the same file format is needed), and its high risk of data loss (i.e. during the exchange), as several types of data conversions are involved, labour inspection is required (Iacovou et al., 1995). This makes it an inflexible integration technology, so the business processes are only partially automated when EDI is used. Hence, there is a need to integrate IS with new technologies to fully automate business processes.

EAI and Web services are new integration technologies that might be used for intra-organisational and inter-organisational IS integration. Unlike the integration technology, such as EDI, that EAI and Web services attempt to fully automate and integrate business processes, as well as achieving the objectives of Business-to-Business integration in real-time. In doing so, EAI uses technology like message brokers, to help support process integration, whereas Web services use a set of protocols (open resources) to allow the software to interconnect with other software over the web. Hence, integration can be achieved in a more manageable and flexible way through the use of EAI and Web services. These might be used to support the efficient incorporation of IS, but the literature related to the adoption of these technologies by SMEs has not been comprehensively studied and investigated. This points to a need for an effective adoption of integration technologies by SMEs, especially in the area of EAI and Web Services being adopted by SMEs.

1.6 The Use of Emerging Integration Technologies That Support IS Integration

EAI encompasses technologies that enable business processes and data to speak to one another across applications, integrating many individual systems into a seamless whole (Linthicum, 1999). EAI aimed at modernising, consolidating, and coordinating the computer applications in an enterprise. Typically, an enterprise has existing legacy applications and databases, and wants to continue to use them while adding or migrating to a new set of applications that exploit the Internet, e-commerce, extranets, and other new technologies. Thus, application integration results in supporting an efficient integration. EAI provides a common framework for integrating incompatible and distributed systems, as well as making it faster and easier to tie together applications, so that they can be integrated into business processes. However, the most common problems with EAI are the high investment costs, and particular complexity and flexibility concerns (Charlesworth and Jones, 2003; Zahavi, 1999). Some analysts have pointed out that EAI solutions are expensive and have long implementation timeframes (Darin, 2002).

Web services enable EAI, without having to pay for expensive and extensive development efforts, and also make it easier to integrate software with other pieces of software (Charlesworth et al., 2002; Davery, 2003). Web services provide access and a set of protocols to remote application services over the Web (Coyle, 2002; Linthicum, 2001). Web Services encompass a set of standards, such as the Simple Object Access Protocol (SOAP), Web services Description (WSDL), Universal Description Discovery and Integration (UDDI), Extensible Markup Language (XML), and the Hyper Text Transfer Protocol (HTTP). The role of these standards is important, because Web Services support applications are written in different languages, and operate on different platforms to communicate and exchange data via the Internet (Intranet/extranet) (Linthicum, 2004; Newcomer, 2002).

Clearly, there is a significant difference between Web Services and traditional integration technologies (e.g. middleware) regarding the way they interconnect applications. Traditionally, systems are connected on a point-to-point basis, which involves developing a unique customised integration solution that can link together the existing solutions. As the number of systems grow, such integration becomes more complex and difficult to manage, as changes to any single application will influence all applications that share the information (Sanchez et al., 2002). Also, the number of interconnections required has increased rapidly. In many cases, each application has to be interconnected with all the others (Iyer et al., 2003). Themistocleous et al.(2001a) estimated that for x applications, a total of $x*(x-1)/2$ interconnections are required when each application is interconnected with the other applications. In the case of Web Services, the applications are not linked to each other but are connected through a centralised integration service (Web Services). Thus, the number of connections is equal to the number of applications (x). This clearly shows that the number of interconnections is much smaller when using Web Services. As a result, Web Services are comparatively easy and inexpensive to implement, thus facilitating a wide variety of business processes (Manes, 2003).

Although Web services seem to have a prosperous future, there are still some drawbacks concerning them, such as (1) lack of security protocols and standards (Banks, 2003; Wong, 2002), (2) lack of user-interface encapsulation mechanisms (Samtani and Sadhwani, 2002), (3) concern over transaction distribution management (Charlesworth et al., 2002), (4) there are not many large-scale implementation examples available at present (Aponovich, 2002), and (5) the risk of changing standards (Aponovich, 2002). Web services have been predicted by many researchers as a new integration solution for SMEs, but the advantages, limitations, risks, impact and costs regarding the adoption of Web services by SMEs still remain unclear at this stage, so further research is therefore essential to identify all these issues.

1.7 Research Aim and Objectives

1.7.1 Research Aim

In the previous sections, it was argued that although integration technologies offer several advantages to organisations, SMEs seem reluctant to use integration technologies and practices. According to various studies, the rate of adoption for both ERP and EDI by SMEs has been slow compared to large organisations (Hughes et al., 2003; Tagliavini et al., 2002). Research has also shown that SMEs hesitate to invest in integration technologies due to a lack of necessary knowledge and a lack of external pressure to encourage or assist SMEs with the integration (Daniel, 2003; Poon and Swatman, 1999). As well as this, it was also argued that although there is literature about the adoption of integration technologies by SMEs, many studies have mainly focused on large businesses. Due to the different technology adoption patterns between SMEs and larger companies, as suggested in the literature, the general applicability of the adoption of integration technologies for small businesses is questionable. This research attempts to address these challenges and issues by comparatively analysing and studying the factors between SMEs and large companies, in terms of their adoption of integration technologies. As a result, the aim of this thesis is:

To investigate the adoption of integration technologies by a comparative
analysis of SMEs and larger companies.

1.7.2 Research Objectives

To address the aim of this project and to provide answers to the above mentioned research issues, a number of specific objectives, which will be analysed hereunder, have been set out to clarify the issues.

- To conduct a literature review in the area of integration technologies and the issues related to its adoption in SMEs and large organisations. In doing so, it will identify research issues regarding the adoption of integration technologies for further investigation.

- To analyse and assess the relevant information, theories and characteristics of SMEs. In doing so, it will identify the useful criteria related to SMEs' characteristics and the relevant theories that are often used to study the adoption of integration by SMEs.

- To investigate the issues and approaches associated with the adoption of integration technologies by SMEs and large organisations. In doing so, it will identify how, why and in what ways the integration technologies have been adopted by SMEs and large organisations.

- To study the relevant existing models and frameworks of the adoption of integration technologies between SMEs and large organisations. In doing so, it will develop a framework for the adoption of integration technologies based on a comparative analysis between SMEs and large organisations that might be used as a decision-making tool.

These research objectives that are derived from the research motivation are related, as will be shown in Chapter 2, to the gaps in the previous and current research in the areas of integration technologies adoption by SMEs and large organisations. In addressing the research issues, this thesis will demonstrate the importance of the use of integration technologies by SMEs to support their IS, and the differences between SMEs and large organisations in terms of their adoption of integration technologies.

1.8 Introduction to Research Methodology

The underlying research epistemology of this research is interpretive. An interpretive epistemology is appropriate for the research context under investigation. Firstly, as was described in the previous sections, there are several adoption factors, adoption models and integration technology characteristics that are related to the adoption of integration technologies by SMEs and large organisations, making a fruitful field for an interpretive study. Secondly, the close involvement of the researcher with the phenomena under investigation has made the separation between the phenomena and the values difficult to delineate. Therefore, an interpretive approach for the analysis of the research findings was deemed more appropriate (Walsham, 1995). Additionally, a qualitative research methodology was selected for this thesis, as this approach is more suitable for understanding people within their social and cultural contexts. As the adoption of integration technologies by SMEs is a relatively new phenomenon, qualitative research seems to be more appropriate for collecting the views of SMEs, and understanding the complex socioeconomic environment of this phenomenon.

Finally, concerning the research strategy, the case study approach has been selected for this research. Case studies are gaining importance in IS research, and play a dominant part in the research methods used in the IS field (Orlikowski and Baroudi, 1991; Stake, 2000). There are different types of case study, namely exploratory, descriptive and explanatory, depending on whether they are used to answer "what", "how" and "why" research questions, respectively (Yin, 1994). Based on this taxonomy, this study can be classified as being exploratory, as the research questions presented in section 1.6.2 are of the "what" type. The methodology and research design of this thesis will be discussed in further detail in Chapter 4.

1.9 Structure of Thesis

This thesis consists of seven chapters, with each chapter providing various important issues for this research. The thesis outline is explained in this section with a summary of each chapter (see Figure 1.1).

Chapter 1: Introduction

This chapter provides a detailed analysis of the research aims and objectives, and a description of the origins, and scope.   The thesis outline is introduced here as well.

Chapter 2: Content of Adoption of Integration Technologies in SME and Large Firms

Having provided a brief introduction to the area of research and established the scope, the thesis then begins to review the literature on integration technologies, integration problems, benefits and barriers. This chapter also investigates the issues associated with the adoption of integration technologies in SMEs and large organisations, and the theories applied to studying the adoption of integration technologies by SMEs. The existing models of adopting integration technologies in SMEs and larger companies are also investigated and studied here. After reviewing the normative literature relating to the adoption of integration technologies in SMEs and large organisations, some research issues will also be identified in this chapter, which require further investigation, they will be discussed in Chapter 3.

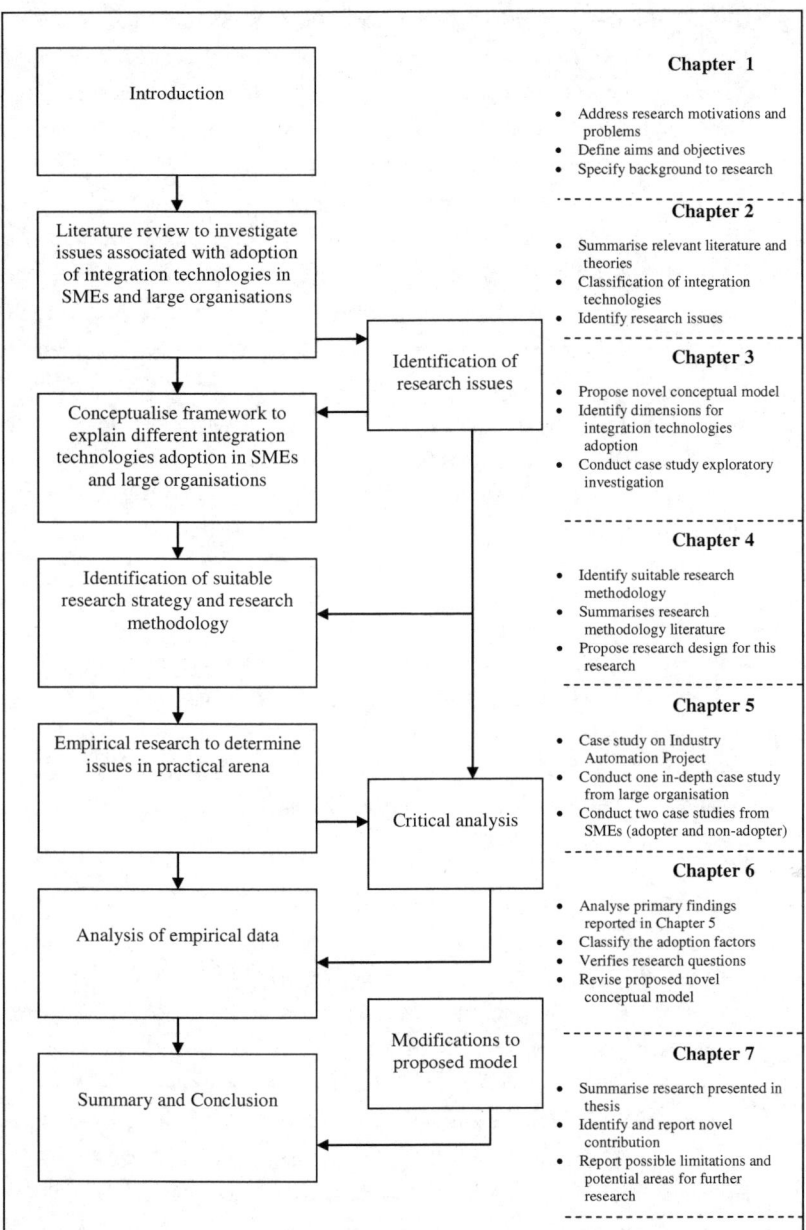

Figure 1.1 Thesis Outline

Chapter 3: Investigation of Integration Technologies in SME and Large Firms

Based on the literature review in Chapter 2, a set of research questions were identified, with the researcher building a conceptual model to address them. In addition, a case study exploratory investigation in the form of survey study is performed by the author to support the identification of the research questions and the analysis. In doing so, the author first identifies the parameters that can be used to explain the different integration technologies adoption between SMEs and large organisations. These parameters are: nature of organisations, integration needs, company size, adoption factors for SMEs, adoption factors for large organisations and time. Thereafter, the author further analyses whether SMEs and large organisations focus on different factors when taking decisions for the adoption of integration technologies. In doing so, resulting in the classification of the adoption factors into three categories: adoption factors explicitly for SMEs, adoption factors explicitly for large organisations and common factors. Based on the identified parameters and the adoption factors classification, a novel conceptual model is introduced which can be used to explain the different integration technology adoption factors focused on by SMEs and large organisations.

Chapter 4: Research Design

Chapters 2 and 3 discussed the background of this research and identified certain issues. In order to undertake the research that focuses on these issues, the research methodology have been discussed and followed. The reasoning behind the research methods is also stated within this chapter. The various research philosophies and methodologies are stated and provided here, as will their suitability for this research. The research problems are also defined in this chapter.

Chapter 5: Issues in Practice – Case studies

Having obtained an understanding of all the relevant issues for this research, this chapter provides a detailed description of the case studies studied for this research. The first case study is the Industry Automation Project. The Industry Automation Project that served as one of the empirical basis for this research is briefly described as well as how this research has emerged working along with it. The follow-up research, which involves four more case studies: one large organisation and three SMEs (adopter and non-adopters) are reported. These include the background to the organisations and describe and analyses the main issues including: (1) case companies' integration problems, (2) case companies' motivations to integration technologies adoption, (3) case companies' perceptions regarding integration technologies benefits and barriers, and (4) the analysis of the parameters for the adoption of integration technologies in SMEs and large organisations.

Chapter 6: Research Findings

Based on the case studies and the research findings reported in Chapter 5, Chapter 6 further analyses the empirical data, and revises the conceptual model proposed in Chapter 3. The revised model for the adoption of integration technologies between SMEs and large organisations can be used as a decision-making tool for SMEs and large organisations.

Chapter 7: Summary and Conclusion

In this chapter the conclusion derived from the findings will be discussed together with an evaluation report of the research work as a whole. This chapter also contains the possible limitations of the research and describes potential areas of further research, and make some recommendations. The novel contributions are also identified in this chapter. This chapter ends with a closing statement.

Chapter 2: Background Research Material

Summary

It was found in Chapter 1 that little academic attention has been paid to the adoption of integration technologies by SMEs. The body of literature suggests that the findings derived from the study of large enterprises can not be generalised and applied to SMEs due to their nature and characteristics. There are many explanations for this, such as the resources available, the need for integration, and the level of integration in SME systems. In an attempt to study this area, Chapter 2 reviews the normative literature related to this area to locate the research gaps for further research.

2.1 Introduction

The research area related to the adoption of integration technologies by SMEs has been neglected in academic literature, as discussed in Chapter 1, Section 1.3. Based on the issues introduced in Chapter 1, this chapter further investigates them by presenting a critical review of the relevant literature related to the adoption of integration technologies by SMEs and large organisations. In doing so, this chapter provides the background theory for this adoption, of which is used in carrying out the research presented later.

The chapter begins by identifying and explaining the integration technologies that might be used by SMEs to support their IS integration. Next, a description and analysis of the existing work related to the adoption of integration technologies by SMEs and large organisations are presented, with a view to positioning this research in relation to this work. Additionally, research studies related to the theories applied to study the adoption of information systems and integration technologies by SMEs will be analysed to examine further the issues related to this topic.

This chapter is structured as follows. In the next section, the integration technologies that can support SMEs' IS integration are defined and discussed. These technologies are then evaluated, based on their strengths and weaknesses, to gain better understanding of them. Sections 4 and 5 present an analysis of the current research on the adoption of integration technologies by SMEs and large companies, respectively, and focus on an analysis of the factors that influence their adoption decisions. Section 6 investigates the innovation diffusion theories and resources-based theories used to examine the current research on the adoption of integration technologies by SMEs. Finally, conclusions from this chapter and an introduction to Chapter 3 are presented in Section 7.

2.2 Review of Integration Technologies

After years of different technological acquisitions, companies have inevitably ended up with disparate systems spread throughout their different units. In this kind of environment, businesses face an integration challenge. The common integration problems/challenges identified by the researcher from the existing literature are shown in Table 2.1 below.

Table 2.1 Summary of the Integration Problems

Integration Problems	Description
Semantic Interoperability	Nowadays, integration technology has become widely available. Any computer system (with at least one interface, human or otherwise, can share data with any other computer system. Often, integration choices are so abundant as to be confusing. Each computer system in an interoperability scenario possesses its own view of reality that includes domain representations, semantic particularities, knowledge structures, and programmatic constraints that limit communication (Pollock, 2001).
Cost	As managing IT becomes more complex, due to the rapid pace of change and the emergence of new and sometimes competing industry 'standards', simplicity becomes more difficult to achieve. This makes initial integration slow, and ongoing maintenance difficult, which in turn makes integration expensive, i.e. large initial costs and even larger implementation costs (Pender, 2000).
Trading Partner Relationship	The importance of forming new relationships with trading partners, while maintaining existing ones, has become crucial to maintaining a solid level of competitiveness. By trading with multiple partners, businesses are faced with an increasing array of disparate data formats, communication needs and process requirements. In order to satisfy the needs of their partners, businesses must be able to respond to these needs and do so in a quick, reliable and secure fashion or risk losing the opportunity (Mozhdehi, 2001).
Message Security	Protecting the message content from being intercepted (confidentiality) or illegally modified (integrity) are primary security concerns (Atkinson *et al.*, 2002). Various security schemes are being developed that attempt to address these requirements. Endpoints need to validate the identity of the users or programs accessing the service to ensure that rogue entities do not get hold of sensitive or proprietary information and resources (Murray, 2003a).
Process Management	Supply-chain processes are very complex and highly dynamic. Most integration vendors can consume or generate Web services, but the problem arises when building lots of Web services. What is needed is some kind of management capability to bind those pieces together appropriately (Harreld, 2002).
Integration Standards	Too many standards exist such as XML, RosettaNet, ebXML, and the OAG specification, etc. (Linthicum, 2001).
Legacy Application Connectivity	Most data are managed by existing application systems that are not necessarily designed to be integrated. Many companies are afraid to alter the legacy systems. They fear they will compromise the underlying functionality they depend on so heavily.

As the number of systems grew, such integration became more complex and difficult to manage, as changes to any single application required changes to all the interconnected applications that shared the information. Without a scalable approach to integration, many organisations found their IT infrastructures difficult to manage, impeding the implementation of new technologies (Sanchez et al., 2002). To overcome these problems, organisations seek ways to integrate their IT infrastructures, as they believe this might help them to increase their competitiveness by cutting down their overall operational and labour costs, as well as to increase efficiency (Morphy, 2003). Companies need to integrate their IT infrastructures to anticipate and react to customers requirements, collaborate with suppliers and partners, and identify and exploit new opportunities quickly and effectively. Such integrated IT infrastructures are flexible, maintainable and scalable.

However, integration is not a simple task, which demands enterprises to continuously invest in their information systems, as most organisations continue to struggle with the integration challenge, especially SMEs. It is expected that there are more barriers to the adoption of integration technologies in SMEs than there are for large businesses. This is partly due to the high capital investment costs and the skilled manpower required to implement and operate integration technologies, and partly due to SMEs' characteristic limitations, as mentioned in Chapter 1, Table 1.2. Despite the difficulties SMEs might face when integrating their information systems, it was found in Chapter 1 that more and more SMEs are under increasing pressure to employ integration technologies. The reasons for this are (1) to maintain their competitive positions, (2) simply to survive, or (3) to anticipate the benefits that integration technologies would bring about.

There are various integration technologies, such as EDI, EAI, Middleware and Web Services, which might be used to bridge their systems together. To better understand this area, the following section reviews the literature on integration technologies and tries to understand in what ways these integration technologies might be used to support organisations' IS integration.

2.2.1 Middleware

Middleware is a technology that allows one entity to communicate with another entity, or entities. Linthicum (2004) define middleware as "any type of software that facilitates communication between two or more software systems" (p. 116). Middleware can be as simple as a raw communication pipe running between applications, such as Java's Remote Method Invocation (RMI), or as sophisticated as information sharing and logic-execution mechanisms such as Transaction Processing (TP) monitors. Nowadays, middleware, is viewed as a technology that allows us to move information between multiple enterprises (Linthicum, 2004). There are different types of middleware each solving its own set of problems (Linthicum, 2004; Ruh et al., 2000). These types of middleware include: Remote Procedure Call (RPC), message-oriented middleware, distributed objects, database-oriented middleware, transaction-oriented middleware, and Transaction Process (TP) monitors. Themistocleous (2002) has already summarised and discussed these different types of middleware in detail, to which readers are now referred. In this section, the author briefly describes the basic concept of middleware technology, instead of the details of the technical issues, which are reported in Appendix B.

2.2.2   ERP

Before the advent of ERP application suites, each business function was typically supported by a separate software package. For example, finance departments had accounting packages, HR and manufacturing departments had isolated systems tailored to their unique needs, and so on. In most cases, these applications replaced purely manual (i.e. paper-based) systems, so in that sense, anything was an improvement. Over time, these single-department applications grew without regard for their peer applications in other departments. Indeed, not all departments were automated, with little thought given to automating entire companies.

As the applications improved, they increasingly supported functions at the periphery, where data flowed into and out of their departments. However, as they varied greatly in terms of technology and structure (i.e. they were heterogeneous), it was difficult to link one department's system to others. The department-specific applications and their associated databases became data silos with some typical data integration paths (Kaye, 2003). Instead of requiring separate systems in each department, ERP promises to build a single integrated system based on separate modules for each department or function.

ERP is a strategic tool that helps a company by integrating is business processes and the available IT resources into one integrated solution (Chung and Snyder, 2000; Zeng et al., 2003). Upon the implementation of an ERP system, organisations are able to: (1) integrate all parts of the organisation so that it has more control over its operation, hence reducing operating costs, (2) help increase operational efficiency by connecting and integrating all business processes, so that people use less time to perform tasks, and (3) provide users with more and faster access to the information, which improves the time and information required for decision making (Beretta, 2002; Gupta, 2000; Shang and Seddon, 2000b; Willis and Willis-Brown, 2002; Zeng et al., 2003).

Despite the normative literature reporting that ERP systems have solved problems in terms of data integrity by unifying incompatible applications on a common database, several applications still co-exist alongside ERP (Gupta, 2000; Hagel and Brown, 2001; Schonefeld and Vering, 2000; Themistocleous et al., 2001a; Willis and Willis-Brown, 2002). Kaye (2003) also reported that ERP package tends to be silos (i.e. isolated from other systems). This means that it is difficult to link ERP systems to other applications (Themistocleous et al., 2001b). Thus, ERP packages could not solve 100% of all business automation needs, and cannot be seen as a reliable solution to integration problems, so there is therefore a need to integrate the ERP solutions with other applications. As integration problems still exist in companies, other integration technologies have emerged (EDI, EAI and Web Services) that can be used to address this problem more effectively by supporting organisations to integrate their intra and inter-organisational IS[3].

2.2.3 EDI

EDI is an integration technology which can be used by organisations to integrate their business processes and support their Inter-Organisational Systems (IOS) (Angeles, 2000; Hughes et al., 2003). EDI allows for the exchange of information between computers in different organisations in a standard format, regardless of size, make or location (Kappelman et al., 1996; Robson, 1994). There are many types of EDI. Some of them like the traditional type, trading partners, are typically connected to a Value Added Network (VAN) to exchange EDI documents on a store and forward basis (Ratnasingam, 1998). Other types of EDI include Web EDI, Extensible Mark-Up Language (XML) EDI, and Internet EDI which use Internet for communication. VANs provide a mailbox service that sorts EDI documents from a sender's to the receiver's mailbox, thus allowing the receiver to pick an EDI document when convenient. In addition, VANs also provide other services, such as translating flat files from the subscriber's application into EDI formatted documents, interfacing with other VANS and supporting various telecommunications modes and data transfer (Kalakota and Whinston, 1996). Upon the implementation of EDI, organisations are able to speed up transactions, reduce paper work, improve inventory control, and provide quick access to information (Barua and Lee, 1997; Brousseau, 1994; Charlesworth et al., 2002a; Gaugler et al., 1996; Zinner, 1999).

However, the traditional EDI, based on standards like UN/EDIFACT, requires dedicated software to translate and integrate business data, as well as mostly relying on closed proprietary networks such as VANs and private messaging networks which are both characterised by relatively high costs and limited connectivity. Other limitations of EDI are: (1) it is difficult to obtain the co-operation of trading partners, since most of them are SMEs (Kappelman et al., 1996), (2) a lack of flexibility on file formats, i.e. the same file format is needed (Iacovou et al., 1995), and (3) a high risk of data loss, i.e. during the exchange, several types of data conversions are involved. These have led organisations to turn to other more advanced and flexible integration technologies such as XML, when

---

[3] Information systems are classified in normative literature into intra-organisational and inter-organisational. Inter-organisational systems are telecommunication-based computer systems used by two or more organisations for the purpose of exchanging information that support a business application or process, whereas intra-organisational system exchanges information at an enterprise level.

compared with the restrictions of EDIFACT protocols, as Internet communication based on XML standards is more flexible and offers a better way to adjust technology support for business processes (Hughes et al., 2003; Pawar and Driva, 2000).

According to Raghunathan and Yeh (2001) and Poon and Swatman (1999), traditional IOS, primarily in the form of EDI, tended only to support inter-organisational transactions, whereas Internet-based IOS, while supporting transactions, is also capable of supporting a wide range of business functions, and hence provides the organisations with greater flexibility. Hence, EDI technologies are slowly being replaced by e-business technologies (i.e. standard Internet protocols and infrastructure replaced the proprietary VANs), as programming and scripting support are now based on open de facto standards such as HyperText Mark-up Language (HTML), JavaServer Pages (JSP), JAVA, Enterprise Java Beans (EJB), and C++ (Sommer, 2003). Thus, other integrative technology has emerged, such as EAI.

2.2.4 EAI

EAI acts as software data translators that take information from, for example, Enterprise ERP and convert it into formats that other applications can understand (Linthicum, 1999). EAI software typically runs on dedicated servers, often called hubs or brokers (Kaye, 2003; Ruh et al., 2001). EAI also allows the enterprise to greatly simplify interactions among enterprise applications by adopting a standard approach to integration, replacing hundreds or thousands of ad hoc integration designs (Linthicum, 1999; Ruh et al., 2001). In other words, EAI develops a central integration infrastructure where each application is connected with an integration infrastructure (Kaye, 2003; Themistocleous, 2002). Because of this, traditional point-to-point interconnections are eliminated. Since EAI solutions are based on a centralised integration infrastructure, when an application requires changes, the rest of the system is rarely affected, as it is not interconnected with the application that requires those changes. Only those applications that requires, changes and their connection to the central integration infrastructure are altered, resulting in a reduced maintenance effort and increased flexibility (Themistocleous, 2002).

By employing EAI effectively, an enterprise can leverage its existing assets to provide new products and services, to improve its relationships with customers, suppliers, and other stakeholders, as well as to streamline its operations (Edwards and Newing, 2000; Ruh et al., 2001). Moreover, as Zahavi (1999) suggested, EAI incorporates enterprise and cross-enterprise applications. From this conceptual viewpoint, unlike EDI, EAI can therefore lead to integrated intra and inter-organisational systems. By enabling all these capabilities, Ruh et al. (2000) claimed, EAI can help an enterprise create a competitive advantage. However, the high investment costs and the complexity associated with EAI have caused much concern for many organisations, especially SMEs (Charlesworth et al., 2002a; Duke et al., 1999). According to Charlesworth and Jones (2003), integration technologies need to be "dumbed-down" to communicate effectively the benefits and issues at the most appropriate level within the organisation. As a result, newer integration technology, such as Web Services, was introduced and is claimed by many researchers as providing a relatively easy, fast and cheap enterprise application integration solution (Charlesworth and Jones, 2003; Davery, 2003; Wu and Sawy, 2003).

Nevertheless, EAI and Web Services use a similar concept of a universal integration technology supported by adapters for each application (Kaye, 2003). The most important difference, though, is that Web Services technology is based on open standards and is designed to run over the less expensive and more flexible medium of the Web (see Figure 2.1). Similar to other integration technologies like XML, Enterprise Java Beans (EJB) and CORBA, etc., which can be used to support EAI technology, Web Services are another.

2.2.5   Web Services

Web services are the least mature set of integrative technologies. Web Services refers to any service that is available over the Internet, where it is possible to interact with one another via a standardised XML messaging system, and is not tied to any one operating system or programming language (Cerami, 2002). In general, Web Services are about connecting systems of diverse types. The role of today's World Wide Web (WWW) has transformed to what is now regarded as an intermediate platform which allows for interactive access to documents and applications. Such success is due to the users, who typically work through Web browsers, audio players, or other interactive front-end systems. The Web can grow significantly in power and scope if it is extended to support communication between applications, from one program to another. To this end, Web

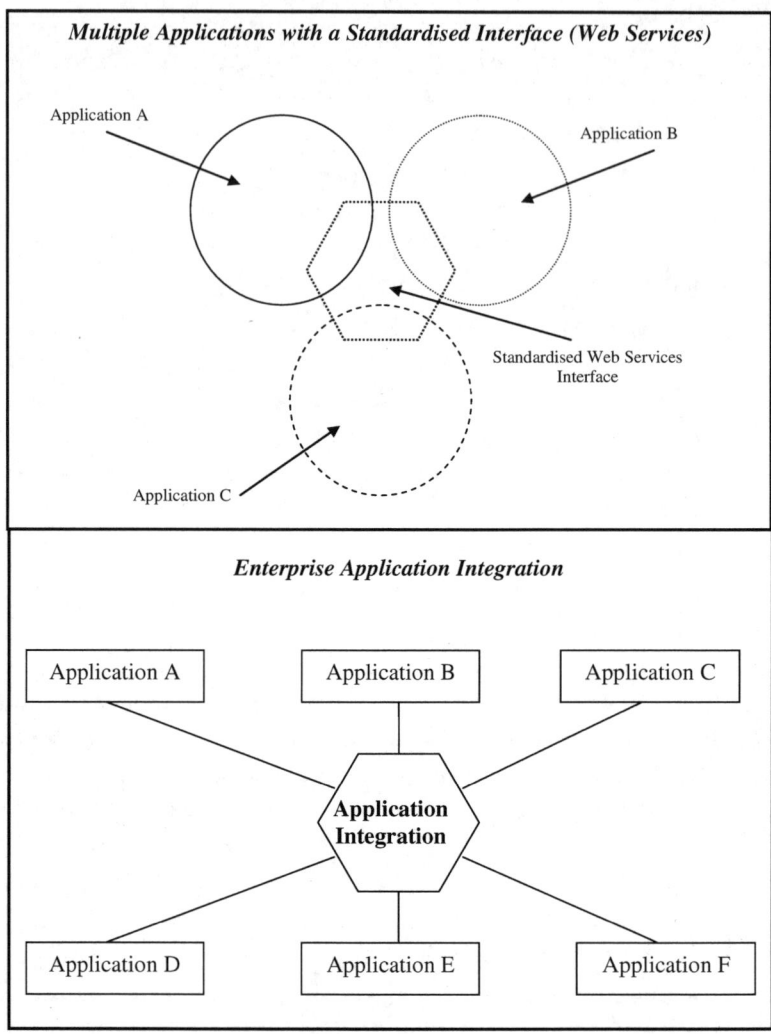

Figure 2.1 Enterprise Application Integration vs. Web Services

Services have been defined and invented to bridge the gap of such a paradigm (Cerami, 2002). Using the ubiquitous and low-cost Internet, Web Services can easily provide interoperable software functions over the Intranet and the Internet (Chen, 2003). From this viewpoint, Web Services could be seen to construct co-operative intra or inter-organisational systems that allow trading partners to conduct transactions through connections to separate computer applications. Broadly speaking, Web Services are a stack of emerging standards that describe a service-oriented, component-based application architecture (W3C, 2002). Conceptually, Web Services represent a model in which discrete tasks within e-business processes are distributed widely throughout a value net (Stencil, 2001). Therefore, Web Services are reified as being "loosely coupled" [4], reusable software components that semantically encapsulate discrete functionality and are distributed and programmatically accessible through standard Internet protocols (StencilGroup, 2001).

This is a contrast to the traditional EDI technology for application integration, which couples the components by dedicated networks and proprietary messaging protocols, as Web Services can be loosely coupled using open, text-based standards over the Internet, thus significantly reducing the costs of application integration (Hailstone and Perry, 2002; Lin et al., 2003). Web Services integrate disparate applications within an enterprise through EAI, even though it is also rapidly elaborating and possesses an unusual degree of plasticity for informational layering and inter-organisational linking that articulates collaborative e-business and e-commerce. In this sense, Web Services make enterprise information systems no longer a proprietary (Xu et al., 2003). According to Lin et al. (2003), Web Services technology provides a new computing model, which greatly eases application integration within and across enterprises, and is being increasingly adopted, especially in SMEs.

Since Web Services are still new and have yet to be proven in terms of reliability, scalability, and manageability (Chen and Themistocleous, 2004), it is therefore better to understand the characteristics of Web Services and the view of how Web Services ease application integration. Thus, there is a need to study Web Services benefits, so these will be identified in the next section. Similar to EAI and ERP technologies, whose benefits and barriers were classified, the identified Web Services benefits are classified and verified through case studies in the following section. (See Appendix C for EAI and ERP benefits and barriers classification).

2.2.5.1 Web Services Benefits

From a technical perspective, one of the important advantages of Web Services over previous distributed-computing technologies is that they employ open standards (Linthicum, 2004; Newcomer, 2002). As organisations consist of a high volume of disparate systems, they need to bridge them together in a flexible and efficient way. One of the problems with integrating heterogeneous systems was the complexity and

---

[4] The term "loosely coupled" here implies that Web Services are independent of any programming languages, platforms, and object models. There are other meanings such as focusing on exchanging-sharing data among partners and low degree of integration, etc..

associated costs that were claimed to be expensive (Miller, 2003). The adoption of open standards not only facilitates communication among disparate applications and platforms (i.e. keeps flexibility between systems), but it also lowers the barriers and the cost of application integration, as well as simplifying the integration itself (Cordeiro and Carvalho, 2002; Manes, 2003). Also, organisations are able to develop applications much faster. For instance, enterprises can easily integrate their disparate systems at both intra and inter-organisational levels (Gaynor et al., 2003).

Web Services use open standards like XML, WSDL, SOAP and UDDI that have been widely accepted (Linthicum, 2004). By employing these open standards, Web Services are able to offer many benefits to the organisations and developers. For instance, standards like XML can be formatted in a variety of different ways, and thus support different applications' programming languages and platforms. Therefore, they improve flexibility, reusability and interoperability (Deitel et al., 2003; Iyer et al., 2003). The use of XML can also simplify the integration with external data sources, as each application no longer needs to copy and maintain its external data sources. In this manner, organisations can request and obtain information in real time and transform it to a particular format that the organisations require (WebCollage, 2001). Thus, this might allow organisations to deliver individualised software and services while keeping the maintenance costs low (Newcomer, 2002).

Standards like WSDL enable organisations to reduce application development time and costs, and facilitate integration without having to rewrite existing applications (i.e. simplify integration with the legacy application) (Ratnasingam and Pavlou, 2002). The consistent interface and infrastructure reuse can also simplify integration with other services. Hence, it will enable tighter business relationships and more efficient business processes.

UDDI is another essential standard which simplifies the process of creating Business-To-Business (B2B) relationships and connects electronic systems to exchange data and services (Deitel et al., 2003). It also increases the collaboration among customers, services providers and intermediaries. Also, SOAP can be used to transfer data between any two systems that are connected to the Internet, regardless of programming languages, operating systems and hardware platforms. Thus, it provides platform and language independence (W3C, 2002). The benefits derived from these standards are summarised in Table 2.2.

Table 2.2 Open Standards and Web Services Benefits

Standard	Description	Benefits

XML	Widely accepted open standard for describing data and creating mark-up languages. Originally designed to meet challenges of large-scale electronic publishing, XML is also plays increasingly important role in exchange of a wide variety of data on Web and elsewhere (W3C, 2002). Any application that understands XML regardless of application's programming language or platform has ability to format XML in a variety of different ways (Deitel *et al.*, 2003). Thus, XML can improve Web functionality and interoperability.	By adopting XML, Web Services can be performed in any platform and in any language and application. Hence, improving flexibility, reusability and interoperability (Deitel *et al.*, 2003). XML can also simplify integration with external data sources as each application no longer needs to copy and maintain external data sources, so organisations can request and obtain information in real time and transform it to particular format organisations require (WebCollage, 2001).
WSDL	Document written in XML and describes a Web service. Specifies the location service and operations or methods that service exposes (Linthicum, 2004). Extensible to allow description of endpoints and their messages, regardless of message formats or network protocols e used to communicate.	Since most Web Services development tools generate WSDL documents automatically, not necessary for developers to understand the syntax of WSDL fully when building and deploying Web Services (Deitel *et al.*, 2003; Newcomer, 2002; W3C, 2002). By employing this standard, organisations are sharing same standards for data description and connection protocols, which enables them to reduce application development time and costs and facilitate integration without having to rewrite existing applications (Ratnasingam and Pavlou, 2002). Consistent interface and infrastructure reuse can also simplify integration with other services. This enables tighter business relationships and more efficient business processes. Thus, increasing customer satisfaction and giving organisations competitive advantages (Gaynor *et al.*, 2003; Manes, 2003).
SOAP	Lightweight protocol for exchange of information in decentralised, distributed environment (Iyer *et al.*, 2003). Provides method of communication between applications running on different operating systems with different technologies and programming languages (Newcomer, 2002; Ratnasingam and Pavlou, 2002; Yu and Chen, 2003). Potential for use in combination with variety of other protocols.	Since SOAP employs XML to communicate, can be used to transfer data between any two systems that are connected to Internet, regardless of programming languages, operating systems and hardware platforms (Deitel *et al.*, 2003; W3C, 2002). In doing so, Web Services are platform and language independences.
UDDI	Relatively new standard. Provides support for service providers to publish information about services they have created and lets service consumers or requesters search and bind to existing services (Lublinsky and Farrell, 2002).	Enables developers and businesses to publish and locate Web Services on a network. This enables businesses to quickly, easily and dynamically find and transact with one another (Yu and Chen, 2003). UDDI simplifies process of creating B2B relationships and connecting electronic systems to exchange data and services (Deitel *et al.*, 2003; Hailstone and Perry, 2002). Thus, increasing the collaboration among customers, services providers and intermediaries.

Apart from the benefits mentioned above, Hailstone and Perry (2002) conducted a study on Web Services where they assessed the experiences of seven IBM customers. They discovered some Web Services benefits such as: (a) increased productivity, (b) reduced time to market, (c) increased revenue, (d) higher Return On Investment (ROI) and (e) increased business efficiency and flexibility. They also reported that by deploying Web Services, these organisations have experienced significant cost savings in a short span of time (around 6 months) and are expecting an average reduction in costs of $39.7 million over three years.

2.2.5.2 Web Services Benefits Classification

The author classifies Web Services benefits and barriers using the model proposed by Shang and Seddon (2000b). This model was proposed to classify the benefits derived from the integration provided by the ERP systems. The same model was used by Themistocleous et al. (2001c) to categorise the benefits and barriers of EAI technology (see Appendix C). EAI is used to integrate IT infrastructures and automate business processes, and Web Services are used for similar purposes. Moreover, many IS benefit analyses and frameworks have been organised around Anthony's (1965) trinity of operational, managerial and strategic levels of management (Hicks, 1997; Mirani and Lederer, 1998; Porter and Millar, 1985; Willcocks, 1994). Based on Anthony's (1965) framework, Shang and Seddon (2000b) further proposed a framework which added two more dimensions (IT infrastructure and organisational) to analyse ERP systems. Furthermore, there are very strong precedents in the IS literature for attempting to classify the benefits of enterprise systems in terms of their operational, managerial and strategic dimensions (Shang and Seddon, 2002). Thus, the model proposed by Shang and Seddon (2000b) is used to categorise the benefits and barriers of Web Services, and their framework is presented in Table 2.3.

Table 2.3 Classification of ERP Benefits

Source: Shang and Seddon (2000b)

Dimensions	Sub Dimensions
Operational	• Cost reduction • Cycle time reduction • Productivity improvement • Quality improvement • Customer services improvement
Managerial	• Better resource management • Improved decision making and planning • Performance improvement
Strategic	• Support business growth • Support business alliance • Build business innovations • Build cost leadership • Generate product differentiation (including customisation) • Build external linkages (customers and suppliers)
IT Infrastructure	• Build business flexibility for current and future changes • Information Technology (IT) costs reduction • Increased IT infrastructure capability
Organisational	• Support organisational changes • Facilitate business learning • Empowerment • Build common visions

Web Services benefits found in the normative literature are classified according to the Shang and Seddon (2000b) model and are summarised in Table 2.4. In addition, the researcher analysed data derived from published case studies in an attempt to explore and better understand this area. In doing so, 35 case studies on Web Services were analysed and the data derived from 20 of them were finally used to validate the identified benefits; 15 cases were excluded on grounds of content and relevance (technical in nature). Although many of these 20 cases were published by practitioners, consultants and software companies, they were included in the sample, as only a limited number of relevant cases were reported in the normative literature. Table 2.5 summarises the case data on the benefits derived from the use of Web Services.

2.2.5.3   Web Services Barriers and Classification

Similar to many other technologies, Web Services have their own limitations. Many articles have indicated that security is currently cited as a major concern that holds back their adoption (Damiani et al., 2002; Linthicum, 2004; Rosenberg, 2003). Web Services allow direct access to a company's applications which can expose corporate networks to security threats (Rosenberg, 2003). The current security issues of Web Services are also lacking support for authentication, encryption, and access control at this stage, since the standards used in Web Services (SOAP, XML, WSDL, and UDDI) do not address authorisation matters such as access control and user-privilege rights (Linthicum, 2004; Yasin, 2001). Due to these security concerns, many enterprises are reluctant and hesitate to employ Web Services as they do not want to share their sensitive/confidential business data (e.g. financial, sales and customer information) over open networks (Manes, 2003).

Another concern over Web Services security is the maturity of standards (SOAP, WSDL and UDDI), since the security infrastructure which allows for the safe delegation of trust and identity are still under development (Rosenberg, 2003; Watch, 2002), for example, UDDI 3.0 standard is still under development. Most of these standards are new, and the overall technical standard and protocols have not yet been established. This will require further development before they can be finalised (Deitel et al., 2003). Yu and Chen (2003) are among those who claim that the structures of Web Services are not yet mature. Therefore Web Services can not replace other integration technologies, but instead provide an alternative approach for integrating applications. Another problem related to Web Services standards is the issue of royalty fees. Large software vendors like IBM and Microsoft, which always hold intellectual property rights on any protocols (SOAP, WSDL, and UDDI), could legally impose royalties on Internet traffic. If those protocols have not been made available on a royalty-free basis, then once they become part of the

Table 2.4. Classification of Web Services Benefits

Web Services Benefits	Cape Clear (2003)	Cordeiro and Carvalho (2002)	Curbera et al (2001)	Deitel et al (2003)	Fletcher and Waterhouse (2002)	Gaynor et al (2003)	Iyer et al (2003)	Hailstone and Perry (2002)	Linthicum (2004)	Manes (2003)	Miller (2003)	Milroy and Doyle (2002)	Murray (2003b)	Newcomer (2002)	Patankar (2003)	Radeka (2002)	Katnasingam and Roslehberg (2002)	Mateos (2003)	WebCollage (2001)	Ye and Chen (2002)
Operational																				
Reduce operational costs								✓												
Achieve customer satisfaction																			✓	
Minimise errors, delays and increase accuracy of data								✓												
Increase productivity through Web								✓					✓							
Managerial																				
Improve inventory control and quick access to information								✓												
Achieve higher ROI								✓					✓							
Increase revenue								✓											✓	
Reduce processing time and provide faster delivery of products or services								✓											✓	✓
Simplify transaction flow																				✓
Strategic																				
Increase business and management efficiency								✓								✓				
Increase competitive advantage			✓					✓											✓	✓
Increase collaboration among customers, services providers and intermediaries			✓		✓			✓										✓	✓	
Increase business opportunities				✓											✓					
IT Infrastructure																				
Offer solutions to problems of legacy systems	✓												✓			✓				✓
Minimise cost of ownership and development costs			✓		✓			✓								✓	✓			
Reduce development complexity, times and risks						✓					✓					✓				
Automate business processes								✓						✓	✓	✓				
Provide open standard			✓				✓							✓		✓				✓
Reduce integration cost																	✓	✓		
Reduce integration complexity and speed up application integration								✓		✓		✓								✓
Permit full-scale integration																				✓
Provide real-time service-oriented architecture (SOA)			✓																✓	
Provide multiple connect points for other systems to integrate with																				✓
Offer ease of integration with other pieces of software	✓			✓												✓				
Simplify the design development, maintenance and usage	✓		✓											✓						✓
Provide platform and language independence		✓		✓		✓	✓	✓	✓							✓			✓	✓
Achieve reusability and flexibility					✓		✓		✓						✓	✓		✓		
Provide stability using dynamic integrated interface to integrate systems																		✓	✓	✓
Achieve interoperability			✓	✓			✓	✓					✓				✓	✓		
Able to unite all major systems vendors (i.e. vendor neutral)								✓											✓	
Reduce time and cost to launch applications								✓												
Organisational																				
Increase flexibility		✓						✓												✓
Quick response to change and business needs								✓			✓									
Reduce time to market								✓												✓

Table 2.5 Summary of Case Companies and Web Services Benefits

Web Services Benefits	A Large Financial Company (Kirzner, 2001)	American Life Insurance Company (IBM, 2003c)	British Telecom (CapeClear, 2002a)	Daimler Chrysler (IBM, 2003a)	Entergy Corporation (Systinet, 2002a)	Epigraph, Inc (Microsoft, 2001)	Ford Motor Company (IBM, 2003b)	IBM Global Services IT (IBM, 2003b)	Interwoven (Systinet, 2002b)	J.P.Morgan Chase & Co. (IBM, 2003a)	Lee Crowder (Elite, 2002)	MoneyMate (CapeClear, 2002c)	Panasonic Security & Digital Imaging (Jurinsyc, 2003)	ProcessClaims (Microsoft, 2001)	Retail Decisions (ReD) (Systinet, 2002c)	Swiss Winterthur Insurance and Swiss Pension (Grupnan, 2003)	T-Motion (Hurwitz Group, 2002)	UNC Health Care (IBM, 2003a)	Win Vision Inc (CapeClear, 2002b)	Yamato Transport Group (IBM, 2003a)
Operational																				
Reduce operational costs		✓		✓	✓		✓							✓			✓			
Achieve customer satisfaction		✓			✓			✓										✓	✓	
Minimise errors, delays and increase accuracy of data				✓																
Increase productivity through the Web				✓																
Managerial																				
Improve inventory control				✓								✓	✓							
Quick access to information				✓								✓	✓							
Achieve higher ROI																				
Increase revenue															✓					
Reduce processing time		✓												✓		✓				✓
Simplify transaction flow																				
Strategic																				
Increase business and management efficiency				✓								✓	✓			✓				
Increase competitive advantage									✓				✓			✓				✓
Increase collaboration among customers, services providers and intermediaries				✓	✓			✓					✓	✓			✓			✓
Increase business opportunities		✓												✓						
IT Infrastructure																				
Offer solutions to problems of legacy systems			✓			✓	✓	✓		✓		✓	✓	✓	✓			✓		
Minimise cost of ownership and development costs		✓		✓		✓	✓	✓				✓	✓					✓		✓
Reduce development complexity, times and risks	✓	✓		✓	✓				✓		✓		✓	✓	✓			✓		✓
Automate business processes	✓			✓										✓	✓	✓				
Provide open standard	✓	✓	✓	✓		✓	✓		✓			✓		✓				✓		✓
Reduce integration cost				✓																
Reduce integration complexity and speed up application integration		✓							✓			✓	✓					✓	✓	
Permit full-scale integration												✓				✓				
Provide real-time service-oriented architecture (SOA)				✓								✓	✓							
Provide multiple connect points for other systems to integrate with	✓															✓				
Offer ease of integration with other pieces of software	✓					✓				✓	✓	✓	✓	✓				✓		
Simplify design development, maintenance and usage	✓	✓						✓	✓					✓				✓		
Provide platform and language independence				✓	✓				✓									✓	✓	✓
Achieve reusability and flexibility		✓		✓	✓	✓		✓	✓							✓				
Provide stability using dynamic integrated interface to integrate systems																				
Achieve interoperability			✓	✓				✓	✓							✓		✓	✓	
Able to unite all major systems vendors (i.e. vendor neutral)			✓										✓						✓	
Reduce time and cost to launch applications	✓			✓	✓	✓	✓	✓	✓	✓		✓	✓	✓	✓	✓	✓			✓
Organisational																				
Increase flexibility		✓		✓		✓										✓		✓		✓
Quick response to change and business needs		✓		✓	✓		✓	✓		✓		✓		✓						✓
Reduce time to market								✓						✓	✓	✓			✓	✓

core Internet infrastructure, this could guarantee the owners of the intellectual property rights, providing them with the legal right to place a tax on the Internet traffic that depends on those protocols (Berlind, 2002).

There is also a concern over whether the current network and Internet infrastructure are able to manage the quantity of SOAP message transmissions that Web Services interactions might generate (Deitel et al., 2003; Newcomer, 2002). As SOAP is an XML-based technology, SOAP messages must be parsed so that they can be processed. XML routing and parsing take time, which might slow down the data transmission, as well as increase traffic on networks, since SOAP is reliant on Internet communications (Neel, 2002). The lack of a standardised measurement procedure provided by the services providers has caused problems too (Rosenberg, 2003). Most service vendors today only provide organisations with minimum information regarding service quality. It is therefore difficult to evaluate whether Web Services meet the requirements of specific processes or applications (Deitel et al., 2003). Currently, there is also no formal system for billing, payment, or provisions for commercial Web services (Macehiter, 2002). Many providers are still experimenting with payment plants for Web Services at this stage. Web Services barriers found in the normative literature are classified based on Shang and Seddon's (2000b) model, and are summarised in Table 2.6.

Again, the researcher analysed 20 case studies on Web Services and use the data derived from them to validate the barriers identified, as shown in Table 2.7. It was found that the majority of the cases studied do not report any encountered barriers. The reasons for this might be that: (1) most of these case studies were written for commercial purposes, therefore they normally highlight the strengths and hide the weaknesses of the technology, (2) most of the case companies might not be aware of, or had not realised, the barriers of Web Services at this stage owing an insufficient knowledge of Web Services, and (3) the case study companies focus more on Web Services benefits instead of their barriers. Only three companies among the 20 pointed out that they had concerns over Web Services security and standards. This shows that there is lack of literature and real practices yet available on Web Services. Thus, the researcher proposes that further investigation regarding this area is needed.

Table 2.6 Classification of Web Services Barriers

Web Services Barriers	Aponovich (2002)	Damiani et al (2002)	Deitel et al (2003)	Hailstone and Perry (2002)	Krill (2003)	Linthicum (2004)	Lublinsky and Farrell (2002)	Miller (2003)	Newcomer (2002)	Ramasingam and Paviou (2002)	Rodgers (2003)	Rosenberg (2003)	Rosenberg and Mateos (2003)	Sullivan and Lamonica (2001)	Yu and Chen (2003)
Operational															
Face operational challenges													✓		
Managerial															
Face difficulty in managing relationships	✓														
Strategic															
Lack of business perspective													✓		
IT Infrastructure															
Lack of large-scale implementation examples and experiences available				✓			✓	✓					✓		✓
Lack of security protocols and standards		✓	✓		✓	✓	✓		✓						✓
Concern over security					✓				✓			✓	✓		✓
Lack of user-interface encapsulation						✓									
Concern over maturity of integration						✓									
Concern over transaction distribution															✓
Add complexity to business transaction						✓									
Lack of system reliability at any moment													✓		✓
Concern over whether old generation solutions are agile enough to react to changes			✓										✓		
Concern over maturity of Web Services payment methods														✓	
Inexperience in architecting Web services	✓		✓												
Lack of XML-based management protocol							✓								
Organisational															
Increase organisational complexity											✓				
Difficult to change internal organisational culture to embrace Web services	✓														

Table 2.7 Summary of Case Companies and Web Services Barriers

Web Services Barriers	Aponovich (2002)	Damiani et al (2002)	Deitel et al (2003)	Hailstone and Perry (2002)	Krill (2003)	Linthicum (2004)	Lublinsky and Farrell (2002)	Miller (2003)	Newcomer (2002)	Ratnasingam and Pavlou (2002)	Rodgers (2003)	Rosenberg (2003)	Rosenberg and Mateos (2003)	Sullivan and Lamonica (2001)	Yu and Chen (2003)
Operational															
Face operational challenges													✓		
Managerial															
Face difficulty in managing	✓														
Strategic															
Lack of business perspective													✓		
IT Infrastructure															
Lack of large-scale implementation examples and experiences available				✓			✓	✓					✓		✓
Lack of security protocols and		✓	✓		✓	✓	✓		✓						✓
Concern over security						✓				✓		✓	✓		✓
Lack of user-interface encapsulation						✓									
Concern over maturity of integration						✓									
Concern over transaction distribution															✓
Add complexity to business transaction						✓									
Lack of system reliability at any													✓		✓
Concern over whether old generation solutions are agile enough to react to changes			✓										✓		
Concern over maturity of Web Services payment methods														✓	
Inexperience in architecting Web services	✓		✓												
Lack of XML-based management protocol							✓								
Organisational															
Increase organisational complexity											✓				
Difficult to change internal organisational culture to embrace Web services	✓														

Having discussed the characteristics of the integration technologies, in the next section, the researcher evaluates their benefits and barriers to gain a better understanding of these technologies.

2.3 Evaluate Benefits and Barriers of Integration Technologies

Most organisations see integrative technologies as tools to help them increase efficiency, improve relationships with their customers, reduce costs and increase flexibility. However, each integration technology has its own strengths and weaknesses, and it is difficult to judge in what ways one is better than the others. Certain benefits/relative advantages have been consistently identified as critical adoptive factors for adopting integration technologies and for IT growth in small organisations (Cragg and Zinatelli, 1995; Kuan and Chau, 2001; Themistocleous, 2002). Apart from the benefits, integration technologies have their own limitations (Themistocleous and Chen, 2004), and some barriers have been reported by Chwelos et a.(2001), Ling (2001b), Iacovou et al.(1995), Themistocleous (2002), and Zinner (1999) as factors that influence the adoption of EDI and EAI. Thus, it is expected that barriers may influence an organisation's decision to adopt integration technologies. Therefore it is vital to analyse both the benefits and the barriers.

Hence, based on the literature, the researcher first identifies, summarises and compares these benefits and barriers. After that, the identified benefits and barriers are classified and evaluated. Based on the discussion on the integrative technologies and their characteristics from the previous section, the major benefits and barriers of EDI, EAI, ERP and Web Services have being identified and summarised in Table 2.8.

Taking the now identified benefits and barriers of the integration technologies the researcher classifies and evaluates them according to the Shang and Seddon (2000a) benefits classification model, as shown in Table 2.9   and 2.10 respectively. The ranking of the technologies follows a low (○), medium (◒), high (●) scale, similar to that used by Miles and Huberman (1994), which helps in easily understanding in what ways one integration technology is better than the others, and vice versa.

So far, the researcher has reviewed the literature on integrative technologies to provide a better understanding of them. It is found that all technologies mentioned in this section might be used to help organisations automate their business processes and information systems. Although each integrative technology provides some solution to integration problems, no single integrative technology addresses or solves all the integration problems (Ruh et al., 2000). Organisations adopt a new technology only if it provides significantly better benefits than existing ones (Rogers, 1995). It was found that new

Table 2.8 Summary of Benefits and Barriers for Integration Technologies

Integration Technology	Benefits	Barriers
EDI	• speed up of transactions and reduction of paperwork (Gaugler *et al.*, 1996) • minimise errors and delays • improve data accuracy (Clarke, 1998) • reduce operational costs (Gaugler *et al.*, 1996) • improve inventory control and provide quick access to information (Charlesworth *et al.*, 2002b) • provide strategic integration of EDI data and information processing (Zinner, 1999)	• value-added networks requires very high expenditures, making them too expensive (Viswanadham and Gaonkar, 2001) • time consumption of initial setup (Viswanadham and Gaonkar, 2001) • lack of flexibility on file formats, i.e. same file format is needed (Iacovou *et al.*, 1995) • high risk of data loss i.e. during the exchange, several types of data conversions involved (Doukidis *et al.*, 1998)
ERP	• provide solution to problems of legacy systems (Holland and Light, 1999) • reduce development risk (Kelly *et al.*, 1999) • increase global competitiveness (Holland *et al.*, 1999) • increase business efficiency (Markus and Tanis, 1999) • integrate all parts of organisation (Beretta, 2002)	• implementation complexity (Martin, 1998) • integration problems (Linthicum, 1999) • customisation problems (Glass and Vessey, 1999) • over-budget and late projects (Themistocleous and Irani, 2001) • organisational change and resistance to change (Sumner, 1999) • problems with business strategy and competitive advantage (Davenport, 1998)
EAI	• integrate business processes (Edwards and Newing, 2000) • achieve customer satisfaction (Pender, 2000) • reduce overall integration costs (Ring and Ward, 1999) • increase collaboration among trading partners (Kalakota and Robinson, 2001) • provide quicker responses to change and faster time for marketing (Morgenthal and La Forge, 2000) • reduced development risks (Themistocleous *et al.*, 2001a)	• market place confusion (Ring and Ward, 1999) • lack of technical skills (Markus *et al.*, 2000) • high level of investment (Zahavi, 1999) • choice and maturity of integration technologies (Edwards and Newing, 2000) • lack of technical standards (Themistocleous *et al.*, 2001c) • complexity and flexibility concerns (Charlesworth and Jones, 2003)
Middleware	• provide ability to invoke a function within one program (Ruh *et al.*, 2000) • use notion of messages to communicate between applications (Linthicum, 2004) • facilitate inter-application communication (Linthicum, 2004) • facilitate communication with database (Edwards and Newing, 2000) • facilitate communication between two or more applications (Linthicum, 1999)	• demand high-speed networks, high processing power and high level of detailed technical input (Edwards and Newing, 2000) • high maintenance costs and complexity (Linthicum, 1999) • Complex to replicate results (Edwards and Newing, 2000)
Web Services	• offer platform independence and achieved interoperability (Curbera *et al.*, 2001) • reduce time and cost of launching applications (Hailstone and Perry, 2002) • easier to integrate software with other pieces of software (Charlesworth *et al.*, 2002b) • achieve higher ROI (Hailstone and Perry, 2002) • reduce costs (Wong.S., 2001) • increase productivity (Milroy and Doyle, 2002) • achieve customer satisfaction (Rosenberg and Mateos, 2003) • increase business flexibility (Wong, 2002)	• lack of security protocols and standards (Banks, 2003; 2002) • lack of user-interface encapsulation mechanisms (Samtani and Sadhwani, 2002) • concern over transaction distribution management (Charlesworth *et al.*, 2002b) • lack of large-scale implementation examples available (Yu and Chen, 2003) • risk of changing standards and vendor lock-in (Aponovich, 2002)

Table 2.9 Evaluation of Barriers for Integration Technologies

Key : low (○), medium (◐), high (●)

Barriers	Integration Technologies		
	EAI	EDI	Web Services
Operational			
Face operational challenges	●	◐	●
High level of investment	●	◐	○
Time-consuming initial setup	●	◐	○
Managerial			
Face difficulty in managing relationships with others	◐	◐	●
High risk of data loss	○	◐	○
Over-budget and late projects	◐	◐	○
Lack of technical skills	◐	◐	○
Strategic			
Lack of business perspective	◐	○	●
Problems with business strategy and competitive advantage	○	◐	○
Market place confusion	●	○	◐
IT Infrastructure			
Lack of large-scale implementation examples and experiences available	◐	○	●
Lack of security protocols and standards	◐	○	●
Concern over security	◐	◐	●
Lack of user-interface encapsulation mechanisms	○	○	●
Concern over maturity of integration technologies	●	○	◐
Concern over transaction distribution management	○	○	●
Add complexity to business transaction protocol implementation	●	◐	●
Lack of system reliability at any moment	◐	○	●
Concern over old generation solutions agile enough to react to change	●	◐	●
Lack of XML-based management protocol	◐	○	●
Lack of flexibility for file formats	○	◐	○
Customisation problems	○	◐	○
Integration problems	○	●	○
Organisational			
Increase organisational complexity	●	◐	●
Organisational change and resistance to change	●	◐	●

Table 2.10 Evaluation of Benefits of Integration Technologies

Key : low (○), medium (◐), high (●)

Benefits	Integration Technologies		
	EAI	EDI	Web Services
Operational			
Reduce operational costs	●	○	●
Achieve customer satisfaction	●	◐	●
Minimise errors, delays and increase accuracy of data	●	◐	●
Increase productivity	●	○	●
Managerial			
Improve inventory controls and quick access to information	●	◐	●
Achieve higher ROI	◐	○	●
Increase revenue	●	◐	●
Reduce processing time and provide faster delivery of products or services	◐	◐	●
Simplify transaction flow	●	◐	●
Strategic			
Increase business and management efficiency	●	◐	●
Increase competitive advantage	●	◐	●
Increase collaboration among customers, services providers and intermediaries	●	◐	●
Increase business opportunities	●	◐	●
IT Infrastructure			
Offer solutions to problems of legacy systems	●	○	●
Minimise cost of ownership and development costs	◐	◐	●
Reduce development complexity, times and risks	◐	◐	●
Automate business processes	●	◐	●
Provide open standard	◐	○	●
Reduce integration costs	◐	◐	●
Reduce integration complexity and speed up application integration	◐	◐	●
Permit full-scale integration	●	◐	●
Provide real-time service-oriented architecture (SOA)	●	◐	●
Provide multiple connection points for other systems to integrate with	◐	○	●
Offer ease of integration with other pieces of software	●	◐	●
Simplify design development, maintenance and usage	●	◐	●
Provide platform and language independence	◐	○	●
Achieve reusability and flexibility	●	◐	●
Provide stability using dynamic integrated interface to integrate systems	●	◐	●
Achieve interoperability	●	◐	●
Able to unite all major systems vendors (i.e. vendor neutral)	◐	○	●
Reduce time and costs of launching applications	◐	◐	●
Organisational			
Increase flexibility	●	◐	●
Quick response to change and business needs	●	◐	●
Reduce time to market	●	◐	●

technology has to provide solutions for existing problems or open up new opportunities to motivate an organisation to take a proactive decision to adopt them with a trading partner. Hence, after reviewing the existing integration technologies, in the next sections, the researcher reviews the existing literature to investigate how integration technologies are being adopted by SMEs to automate their business processes.

2.4 Current Research on Integration Technologies Adoption in SMEs

Nowadays, homogeneous IS architectures are no longer practical options. Many organisations are changing their strategies from a single sourcing or a point-to-point integration strategy to an approach of building and evolving a standardised integration architecture that enables fast assembly and disassembly of business processes and corresponding business software components. Thus, this section investigates the current state of knowledge concerning the adoption of integration technologies by SMEs.

As mentioned in Chapter 1, the literature has shown that some SMEs adopt ERP and EDI to automate and integrate their business processes. These studies included those by Iacovou et al., (1995), Daniel (2003), Hughes et al. (2003), Kuan and Chau (2001), Waarts et al. (2002), Ravarini et al. (2000), and Tagliavini et al, (2002). Among these, the framework proposed by Iacovou et al. (1995) presented the most comprehensive research, by focusing on the adoption of integration technologies by small businesses (Kuan and Chau, 2001).

Iacovou et al. (1995) proposed an adoption framework to address the issue of the major factors that explain the EDI adoption behaviour of small organisations and the expected impact of the technology in the small business context, based on a multi-case study. These factors were: (1) perceived benefits of EDI, which are categorised into direct benefits and indirect benefits. Direct benefits are operational savings related to the internal efficiency of the organisation, whereas indirect benefits refers to the impact of EDI on the business processes and relationships (e.g. tactical and competitive advantages), (2) organisational readiness, which measures the level of the financial and technological resources of the company, and (3) external pressures, which refers to influences from the organisational environment. The two main sources of the latter include the competitive pressure and impositions by trading partners. Several other factors that inhibit EDI adoption in small organisations were also identified by Iacovou et al. (1995) as being: (1) costs, (2) complexity of the technology, (3) the need to change internal systems, (4) lack of technological skills, and (5) lack of system integration.

However, these factors were not included in their model, as they claimed that these factors have generally been identified through studies of large organisations, thus their applicability to small business is questionable. Based on Iacovou et al. (1995), Heck and Ribbers (1999) proposed a model which explains the adoption and impact of EDI in Dutch SMEs. They found that apart from the perceived benefits, organisational readiness, and external pressures, the availability of EDI standards appears to be an important factor that influences the adoption of EDI in SMEs.

The Iacovou et al. (1995) study investigated EDI adoption in small businesses by focusing on factors in the technological (perceived benefits), organisational (organisational readiness) and environmental (external pressure) contexts (Kuan and Chau, 2001). This is very similar to the general framework in innovation studies suggested by Tornatzky and Fleischer (1990), this in which there are three elements that influence the process by which innovations are adopted: (1) external environmental context, (2) technological context, and (3) organisational context. This framework has been empirically tested, and has been found useful in understanding the adoption of technological innovations. An example is the study by Chau and Tam (1997) on the adoption of open systems. This study integrated the work by Iacovou et al. (1995) and Tornatzky and Fleischer (1990) to examine small business EDI adoption in the three context. In a more recent study, Kuan and Chau (2001) also integrated Iacovou et al. (1995) and Tornatzky and Fleischer (1990) to examine the secondary characteristics (i.e. the perceived attributes of innovations) of EDI adoption in small business in the three contexts.

Chwelos et al. (2001) further validated the model proposed by Iacovou et al ,(1995) and used an empirical work to predict EDI adoption. They suggested that the factors identified by Iacovou et al. (1995) can be addressed in three major types of adoption perspectives: technological, organisational, and inter-organisational. By incorporating the factors proposed by Iacovou et al. (1995) with the other existing factors from the literature, Chwelos et al. (2001) reported those found from their studies, which included (1) competitive pressure, (2) dependency on trading partner, (3) enacted trading partner power, (4) industry pressure, (5) financial resources, (6) IT sophistication, and (7) trading partner readiness. Apart from EDI adoption by SMEs, Vidgen et al.(2004) explored the role of Web services in SMEs through the application of Venkatraman (1994) business transformation model, using case study strategy. The case identified the potential benefits for SMEs provided by Web Services technology and considered those factors that enabled successful Web Services adoption, which they suggested were (1) senior management support, (2) a knowledge of transfer mechanisms, and (3) employing a suitable technical architecture.

Many other factors that influence the adoption of IT in SMEs are also identified from the literature. Hughes et al. (2003) conducted a study to investigate the reasons underpinning the diverging adoption rates of different types of inter-organisational systems among SMEs. They found that, under the right conditions, SMEs could be successful innovators of new technology. These conditions include (1) low costs, (2) relevance of and flexibility to business needs, and (3) previous experience with technology, while high costs, lack of relevance and flexibility and lack of previous experience with technology are proven factors that restrict the adoption of traditional inter-organisational systems amongst SMEs. Based on the existing literature, Ling (2001a) examined and identified factors that were considered to be relevant to the adoption and diffusion of e-commerce, which are (1) organisation: firm size, top management support, organisational readiness, organisational structure and organisational culture, (2) innovation: perceived relative advantage, complexity, trainability, observability, and compatibility, (3) communication: information sources, communication channels, and communication amount, (4) industry: competitive pressures, pressures from trading partners, and critical mass, and (5) national: level of government support, level of national infrastructure, and cultural differences. Morrell and Ezingeard (2002) proposed a framework for the adoption of inter-organisational systems based on the objectives, drivers, inhibitors and enablers. They reported that the reasons for the lack of inter-organisation systems adoption amongst SMEs were (1) a culturally-rooted lack of vision and awareness, and (2) the realisation of benefits.

Based on the literature review in Section 2.4, most of the literature on SMEs adopting integration technologies has mainly focused on the adoption of EDI. The literature concerning the adoption of EAI or Web Services by SMEs has remained very limited. Although EAI and Web Services adoption models for larger organisations is available, currently there is still an absence of models explaining the adoption of EAI and Web Services by SMEs. This might be partly due to the fact that EAI and Web Services are only beginning to emerge, and adoption is still in the early stage, and partly due to the issue of whether it is accepted that EAI and Web Services implementation is necessary for SMEs (Hailstone and Perry, 2002). Thus, a better understanding of the ways in which SMEs adopt and implement integration technologies is necessary because previous research in the area is limited and a significant percentage is out of date, due to the rapidly changing economics of using IT, and the resulting increased adoption by smaller enterprises (Caldeira and Ward, 2003).

Based on the literature review in this section, the researcher has summarised the factors for EAI, EDI, ERP and Web Services adoption in SMEs, as shown in Table 2.11.

Table 2.11 Summary of Factors Influencing Decisions on Adoption of Integration Technologies in SMEs

Factors	EDI	ERP	Web Services
Availability of Standards	✓		
Business Complexity		✓	
Competitive Pressures	✓		
Control Procedure	✓		
Dependency on Partners/ Trading Partner Readiness/Pressure	✓		
Environmental Characteristics			
Evaluation Framework for Integration of Technology and Packages			
External Pressure	✓		
Extent of Organisational Change		✓	
IT Sophistication	✓		
Knowledge Transfer Mechanism			✓
Organisational Readiness	✓		
Perceived Financial Cost/ Financial Resources	✓		
Perceived Benefits (Direct and Indirect)	✓		
Perceived Technical Competence/ Technological Skills Readiness	✓		
Perceived Industry Pressure	✓		
Perceived Governmental Pressure	✓		
Prior EDI experience	✓		
Support/ Organisation Support	✓		
Senior Management Support			✓
Suitable Technical Architecture			✓

After this review of current research on the adoption of integration technologies by SMEs, the next section studies the theory/theories used to predict integration technology/IT adoption in SMEs, in order to locate the appropriate theory/theories that might be applied to study them.

2.5 Review of Theories Applied to Study Adoption of Integration Technologies by SMEs

Most of the initial studies on innovation have used two distinct perspectives for analysis: (1) adoption, and (2) diffusion (Premkumar et al., 1994). While studies using the former have evaluated the characteristics of an organisation or society that make it receptive to innovation and change, studies using the latter have attempted to understand why and how an innovation spreads, and what characteristics of the innovation lead to widespread acceptance. An innovation is any idea, practice, or material artifact perceived to be new by the relevant unit of adoption (Zaltman and Holberk, 1973). Damanpour (1991) also defined organisational innovation as the implementation of an internally generated or borrowed idea, whether pertaining to a product, device, system, process, policy, program, or service, that was new to the organisation at the time of adoption. According to Rogers (1995), the term 'technology' is often used as a synonym for innovation.

The study of innovation, adoption or acceptance, adaptations and usage of IT has a long and rich history in the management and organisation-oriented research traditions and have been empirically examined in wider contexts (Rogers, 1995). A number of theories and models have been adopted from diverse disciplines and have been modified, developed and validated by IS researchers to understand and predict technology adoption and usage. These include various theories such as Theory of Acceptance Model (TAM), Diffusion of Innovation Theory, Theory of Reasoned Action (TRA) and Theory of Planned Behaviour (TPB) (Ajzen, 1985; Attewell, 1992; Bharadwaj, 2000; Caldeira and Ward, 2003; Davis, 1989; Fishbein and Ajzen, 1975; Hu et al., 1999; Rogers, 1995). However, according to the literature, the work on the adoption of technological innovations rests alone in two major areas: (1) intention-based models such as the Technology Acceptance Model proposed by Davis (1989), and (2) innovation models such as Rogers' (1995) that focus on innovation characteristics and processes.

A review of the literature shows that many of the studies on the adoption of IT innovation e.g. EDI studies, have used the Rogers' (1995) diffusion of innovations theory to identify those attributes of the innovation that influence its adoption. Recent works along this line include Moore and Benbasat (1991), Attewell (1992), Rai and Howard (1993), and Premkumar and Potter (1995). The innovation adoption/diffusion literature examines the various factors that influence the adoption of innovation, the characteristics of the adopters, the process of adoption decision making, and the diffusion of innovation in the population. Rogers (1995) provided a number of generalisations regarding classical adoption/diffusion:

- Innovations have certain characteristics that adopters perceive as determining the rate of adoption. Some of the characteristics are their advantages, and their compatibility, complexity, trialability and observability.

- There are personal characteristics (e.g. level of education) for potential adopters that make them more innovative than others.

- The decision to adopt and use them unfolds in stages: the awareness stage of acquiring information about the innovation, the persuasion stage of being persuaded to adopt the innovation, the decision stage of deciding to adopt it, the implementation stage of implementing the innovation and using it, and finally, the confirmation stage of evaluating the actual outcomes with expectations. Different factors influence the adopters during each of the various stages.

- The behaviour of some individuals (champions or change agents) can accelerate the adoption of the innovation.

- The diffusion process usually starts out slowly, but 'takes off' rapidly after an initial period, before eventually leveling off.

There are a few studies concerning EDI adoption by SMEs that are based on Rogers' (1995) diffusion of innovation theory. Chau and Tam (1997) identified the key determinants of small business EDI adoption. Iacovou et al. (1995) study the EDI adoption in small business based on the attributes proposed by Rogers (1995). Other studies, such as Kendall et al.(2001), used a portion of Rogers' model of innovation diffusion as the framework, and treated e-commerce as a form of new innovation. They analysed those factors that affected the adoption of e-commerce by SMEs in Singapore.

In addition, the resource-based theory is often used to explain the adoption and use of information systems and technology in SMEs, since it emphasises an understanding of the internal capabilities that enable firms to secure competitive positions, and the importance of internal resources in a firm. This theory has been hailed as a promising approach to the study of firms (Barney, 1991; Caldeira and Ward, 2003). The theory focuses on the idea of costly-to-copy attributes of the firm as sources of business returns and the means to achieve superior performance and a competitive advantage (Barney, 1991; Bharadwaj, 2000; Conner, 1991; Conner and Prahalad, 1996). A firm can also be understood as a collection of resources: physical capital, human capital, and organisational (Barney, 1991). Resources that can not be easily purchased, that require an extended learning process, or are a result of a particular corporate culture, are more likely to be unique to the enterprise and, therefore, more difficult to imitate by competitors. There are a few studies that use the resource-based theory to explain the adoption of IS by SMEs. Thong (2001) developed a resource-based model of IS implementation for small businesses, based on the resource-based and diffusion of innovation theories. Caldeira and Ward (2003) used the resource-based theory to interpret the adoption and use of information systems and technology in manufacturing SMEs.

Despite most of the studies having used the diffusion of innovation theory proposed by Rogers (1995) to identify attributes of innovation that influence its adoption, many researchers have questioned the validity of its application for complex technological innovations at an organisation level (Attewell, 1992). This situation might become more complex when looking at the diffusion and adoption of innovation in SMEs, since they have very different characteristics from other organisations, as mentioned earlier. Thus, the researcher suggests that simply using the diffusion of innovation theory may not be able to provide a complete explanation for the adoption of integration technologies by SMEs. Other theories, such as resource-based theory, as mentioned above, might be expected to be used in conjunction with the diffusion of innovation theory to help explain the integrative technologies research for SMEs. Thus, in this thesis, both suggested theories have been applied to study the integration technologies adoption between SMEs and large organisations in this thesis.

After discussing the current research on the adoption of integration technologies by SMEs and its related issues, the next section will examine the research on the adoption of integration technologies by large organisations. It is observed that the studies related to the adoption of integration technologies by SMEs, which this research focuses on, has not been analysed as much as the adoption of integration technologies by large companies, especially in the areas of EAI and Web Services adoption.

2.6 Current Research on Integration Technologies Adoption in Large Organisations

The adoption of integration technologies is a problematic area of concern as the variables involved are fluid, transparent and difficult to determine (Currie et al., 2004). The essence of the analysis requires to a large extent on the intuitive experiences of the managers engaged within the business interface and in many instances are also associated with trust (Ratnasingam, 2004). Consequently, analysts are not concerned with the specifics of IS assessment metrics, detailed benefits measurement or mechanistic evaluation techniques, they are concerned only with successful outcomes (Currie et al., 2004). A neglected feature of any improved integration technologies performance is to ensure a context specific and appropriate technological infrastructure. DeLone & McLean (2003) note, in reviewing variables, no single measure is intrinsically better than another, so the choice of a success variable is often a function of the objective of the study, the organisational context, the aspect of the information system which is addressed by the study, the independent variables under investigation, the research method, and the level of analysis. DeLone & McLean's (2003) assertion clearly identifies the complexity of 'factor' selection and the impact of their relationship. These theoretical arguments are consistent with Tornatzky & Fleischer (1990) popularly known innovation process framework. Since they model innovation processes in general the implications of 'contingency' would suggest a way along which integration technologies innovation adoption studies can usefully be evaluated.

A review of the adoption literature in an organisational context indicates a considerable amount of research on the topic. These studies have focused on different aspects of EDI, EAI, ERP and Web Services adoption in large organisations. Banerjee and Golhar (1994) examined the positive and negative impacts of various factors on the EDI selection decision alone, to assess the impact of EDI on an organisation's employees. Hart and Saunders (1998) studied the role of power and trust in EDI adoption and use. The study also evaluated the differences between proactive and reactive firms, in terms of the extent of the adaptation, external connectivity with trading partners, and the integration of EDI information. They found that the specific factors that affected the adoption of EDI in large organisations were: (1) supplier dependence, (2) customer power, (3) volume of EDI use, (4) supplier commitment, (5) supplier trust, and (6) diversity of EDI use.

Moreover, Vega et al. (1997) define a model which examined the role of several factors related to the external environment and the organisational context in influencing the extent to which EDI is integrated, and whether more extensive integration impacts on organisational outcomes. These factors were (1) competitiveness, (2) uncertainty, (3) dependence, (4) communication needs, (5) technology and services, (6) organisational maturity, (7) IT maturity, (8) rationale for EDI, (9) implementation process, (10) top management support, and (11) perceived benefits. Premkumar and Ramamurth (1995) examined the role of inter-organisational factors on the decision mode for the adoption of EDI. These factors were (1) competitive pressure, (2) exercised power, (3) internal need, and (4) top management support.

Furthermore, Themistocleous (2002) studies the adoption of EAI in multinational organisations and identified several factors for EAI adoption, such as the benefits, barriers, costs, internal pressures, external pressures, IT sophistication, IT infrastructure, support, and the evaluation framework for the integration of the technology and packages.

In more recent studies, Wu and Sawy (2003) studied Web Services as a special case of IT industry innovation. They first reviewed two key issues at the innovation level of analysis: the type of innovation and innovation characteristics. They then developed a 3-layer nested-stage model as a road map for studying Web Services innovation. Zhang and Huang (2004) proposed a Web Services adoption model by applying the diffusion theory and security-related research to technology adoption. Chen (2003) developed a framework for analysing the driving forces for the adoption of Web Services, based on a literature review, a technical information analysis, and field and Web-based case studies.

In addition, Bradford and Florin (2003) discussed the adoption of ERP in a general organisational context. They found that the factors affecting the adoption of ERP by large organisations were (1) innovation characteristics, (2) organisational characteristics, and (3) environmental characteristics. Waarts et al. (2002) reported that the assumption that the factors explaining adoption decisions do not change over time. Their study challenges this assumption, and adds to the existing literature by investigating the dynamics of the factors influencing adoption.

The researcher has summarised the factors influencing the adoption of integration technologies discussed in this section, as shown in Table 2.12.

2.7 Conclusions

This chapter provided a detailed description and critical overview of the theoretical background of this thesis and identified research issues. Thus, this chapter discussed various integration technologies and reviewed the literature on integration technologies adoption by large organisations and SMEs. In doing so, this chapter

- Classified the benefits and barriers of Web Services.

- Evaluated the integrative technologies benefits and barriers.

- Identified various factors affecting the adoption of integration technologies by SMEs.

- Reviewed the theories applied to study the adoption of integration technologies by SMEs.

Table 2.12 Summary of Factors Influencing Decisions on Adoption of Integration Technologies in Large Organisations

Factors	EAI	EDI	ERP	Web Services
Adopter Characteristics			✓	
Availability of Standards		✓		✓
Barriers	✓			
Compatibility				✓
Complexity				✓
Competitive Pressures	✓	✓		
Communicability				✓
Customer Power		✓		
Customisability				✓
Ease of Use				✓
Dependency on Partners/ Trading Partner Readiness/Pressure	✓	✓		
Divisibility				✓
Environmental Characteristics			✓	
Evaluation Framework for Integration Technology and Packages	✓			
External Pressure	✓	✓		
External Environment Characteristics			✓	
Image				✓
IS Innovation Type				✓
IT Sophistication	✓	✓		✓
IT Infrastructure	✓			✓
Internal Environment Characteristics			✓	
Internal Pressure	✓			
Innovation Characteristics/ Perceived Innovation Characteristics			✓	
Organisational Characteristics			✓	
Perceived Financial Cost/ Financial Resources	✓	✓		✓
Perceived Benefits (Direct and Indirect)	✓	✓		✓
Perceived Technical Competence/ Technological Skills Readiness	✓	✓		✓
Relative Advantage				✓
Result Demonstrability				✓
Security/ Control Procedures		✓		✓
Support/ Organisation Support	✓	✓		✓
Stakeholders				✓
Supplier Trust		✓		
Supplier Commitment		✓		
Technical Factors	✓			✓
Triability				✓
Visibility				✓
Voluntariness				✓
Web Services Awareness Readiness				✓
Web Services Fit Readiness				✓

- Identified various factors affecting the adoption of integration technologies by large companies.

The researcher also determined several theoretical issues/gaps, summarised as follows:

- There is an absence of a theoretical model that explains the ways in which SMEs adopt integration technologies.

- Since EAI and Web Services are relatively new areas, only a few studies have been carried out. Thus, there are limited studies focusing on EAI or Web Services adoption by SMEs.

- The existing works point out that smaller organisations have been shown to have different technology adoption patterns than large ones (Chwelos *et al.*, 2001; Kuan and Chau, 2001; Raymond and Bergeron, 1996). However, it is unclear whether SMEs and large organisations take decisions for the adoption of integration technologies by focusing on the different factors.

These research issues derived from the literature review and presented in this chapter are taken into consideration and addressed in Chapter 3.

Chapter 3: Conceptual Model

Summary

The previous chapter has highlighted some issues for further investigation. The main research issues derived from Chapter 2 emphasised that: (1) the theoretical models that describe the adoption of integration technologies by SMEs are limited, especially in the areas of EAI and Web Services; (2) the existing works point out that smaller organisations have been shown to have different technology adoption patterns from large ones; however, it is unclear whether the differences between SMEs and large firms can affect their integration technologies adoption decisions; and (3) it is also unclear whether SMEs and large organisations focus on different factors when taking decisions for the adoption of integration technologies. Thus, to address these research issues, this chapter aims to conceptualise a model that can be used to explain the adoption of integration technologies based on a comparative analysis between SMEs and large organisations. The author uses the findings and literature reported from the previous chapter to further analyse the area under study. Additionally, a case study exploratory investigation by the researcher supports the comparative analysis between SMEs and large firms for their integration technologies adoption. This is done with a particular focus on the research aim of this thesis, as stated in Section 1.7. The proposed model attempts to contribute in the integration technologies adoption area, as it describes the dimensions that influence the different adoption factors in SMEs and large organisations, and critically analyses and classifies the different adoption factors in them (e.g. common factors, factors explicitly for SMEs, and factors explicitly for large organisations).

3.1 Introduction

Despite the advantages that IS integration can offer to organisations (as mentioned in Sections 2.2 and 2.3), little attention has been paid to the adoption of integration technologies by SMEs (Hughes et al., 2003; Tagliavini et al., 2002). Iacovou et al. (1995) reported that SMEs differ from large companies in many ways that affect the adoption of integration technologies. These differences include: (1) the lower levels of resources available for this (Iacovou et al., 1995; Kuan and Chau, 2001), (2) the substantially less sophisticated IS management (Kagan et al., 1990; Tagliavini et al., 2002), (3) the needs for integration and their characteristics, and (4) the quantity and quality of the available environmental information (Pearce et al., 1982). For these reasons, Kuan and Chau (2001), among others suggested that the general applicability of the studies in large organisations may be questionable if applied to small businesses. Thong (1999) also argued that because of the unique characteristics of small businesses, there is a need to examine whether those models for IS adoption developed for the large-business context can be equally applied to small businesses.

Although the adoption of integration technologies is recognised in the normative literature as being different between large and small companies, the literature on the adoption of integration technologies by SMEs remains limited (Kuan and Chau, 2001). Nevertheless, among the existing works, their focus mostly emphasises on either the adoption decision or the successful implementation factors (Chwelos et al., 2001; Kuan and Chau, 2001; Raymond and Bergeron, 1996). To the best of the researcher's knowledge, there are no studies on the reasons why SMEs and large companies take the decision to adopt integration technologies, which focus specifically on the different factors. Thus, this presents a research issue which needs further investigation.

Therefore, based on the issues identified in Chapter 2 that (1) theoretical models describing the adoption of integration technologies by SMEs are limited, especially in the areas of EAI and Web Services, and (2) existing works point out that smaller organisations have been shown to have different technology adoption patterns from large ones. However, it is unclear whether SMEs and large organisations take adoption decisions by focusing on different factors. This chapter attempts to address these issues by studying the factors affecting the adoption of integration technologies by comparatively analysing the adoption factors between SMEs and large companies. In addition, results from a case study exploratory investigation by the researcher in the form of a survey study (with 68 usable responses and 87% of the responding firms integration technologies users) are also used to assist the comparison. (See Appendix A for survey results).

Therefore, this chapter aims to identify the significant differences in the way that SMEs and large companies approach integration technologies, and to conceptualise a model that can be used to explain the factors that influence the different adoption factors between SMEs and large organisations. In doing so, the parameters are first identified that can be used to explain the adoption of integration technologies between SMEs and large firms, which are the nature of the organisations, company size, integration needs, adoption factors for SMEs and large organisations, and time. The next step is to investigate further whether the identified parameters can be used to explain the factors that influence the different adoption factors between SMEs and large organisations. Thus, a conceptual model is then introduced based on the analysis of the existing adoption factors reported in the literature. The proposed model can be used as a decision-making tool, and to support management when taking decisions regarding the adoption of integration technologies. Additionally, it can be used by researchers to analyse and understand the differences between SMEs and large organisations in their adoption of integration technologies.

The organisation of Chapter 3 is as follows. Section 2 will introduce the analysis of the research issues identified in Chapter 2 and will identify the parameters that can be used to explain the adoption of integration technologies between SMEs and large organisations. Section 3 will discuss the different adoption factors between SMEs and large organisations. Thereafter, the next section proposes and describes the conceptual model that explains the different factors between SMEs and large firms in relation to their adoption of integration technologies.

3.2 Research Issues Analysis

3.2.1 Nature of Organisations

Globalisation forces many enterprises to change the way they do business. To compete in global markets, SMEs need to develop new business strategies and deploy new technologies (e.g. Web Services and EAI). However, Storey (1994) argued that the size of small businesses creates a special condition, which can be referred to as resource poverty, that distinguishes them from their larger counterparts and requires some different management approaches. Thus, it is vital to identify the nature of SMEs to assess what makes them distinct from other types of organisation (e.g. large organisations), as the nature of SMEs might be a real obstacle to their adoption of integration technologies.

SMEs comprise a significant part of the economy and are characterised by high firm failure rates (Storey, 1994). Storey and Cressy (1995) reported that about 11% of small businesses fail to survive in any given year, a failure rate six times higher for smaller than for larger businesses. This is due to the fact that SMEs usually:

- Have little ability to influence market price by altering their output (Kirby, 2003).

- Have small market shares, so are unable to erect barriers to enter their industry (Deakins and Freel, 2003).

- Can not easily raise prices and tend to be heavily dependent on a small number of customers (Storey, 1994).

Small businesses cannot usually afford to pay for the kind of accounting and book-keeping services they need, nor can their new employees be adequately tested and trained in advance (Welsh and White, 1981). Small businesses are also under increasing pressure to employ IS to maintain their competitive positions. At the same time, there are more barriers to IS implementation in small businesses than there are for large businesses, due to the high capital investment and skilled manpower involved in implementing and operating IS (Thong, 2001). Welsh and White (1981) also pointed out that resource constraints (time, finance and expertise) in small businesses are based on the concept of resource-based theory. As mentioned in Section 2.4, resource-based theory is often used to explain the adoption and use of information systems and technology in SMEs. According to it, firms are characterised as being collectors of resources or capabilities. A firm's resources may include both tangible and intangible assets, including capabilities, organisational processes, information, and knowledge, that are all controlled by a firm to enable it to conceive and implement strategies that improve its efficiency and effectiveness (Barney, 1991). Resource-based theory emphasises an understanding of the internal capabilities that enable organisations to secure competitive positions, and the importance of internal resources in a company (Barney, 1991; Caldeira and Ward, 2003). In this research, resources-based theory is applied to explain the importance of the natural resources of a company, in terms of the integration of its technologies adoption decision (e.g. time, finance, and expertise constraints).

- **Time constraints** refer to the limited amount of time available for activities beyond the normal job responsibilities of individuals in small businesses.

- **Financial constraints** refer to the limited amount of finance available for activities beyond the normal operations of small businesses.

- **Expertise constraints** refer to the limited amount of expertise within small businesses to carry out activities beyond designated job responsibilities.

Based on these, Welsh and White (1981) reported that (1) SMEs have to control their cash flows carefully, as they do not have unlimited funds for their IS project, (2) SMEs tend to choose the cheapest system, which may be inadequate for their purposes, (3) SMEs usually underestimate the amount of time and effort required for adopting integration technologies, and (4) SMEs normally engage consultants and IT vendors to develop and support their information systems (Thong, 2001). For example, SMEs might prefer to outsource most of their activities, whereas large companies might prefer to outsource only those activities which are not directly related to their business strategies, or even to manage these activities totally on their own.

Resources such as time, finance, and expertise that are all necessary for planning, represent the most critical difficulties for small businesses (Cohn and Lindberg, 1972). For this reason, Kagan et al. (1990) and Tagliavini et al. (2002) claimed that SMEs usually have substantially less management over their sophisticated IS, and that this might affect the way that they approach integration technologies. In addition, according to Attewell's (1992) technology diffusion theory, it emphasises the role of external entities (e.g. consultants and IT vendors) as knowledge providers in lowering the knowledge barrier or knowledge deficiency on the part of potential IS adopters. Small businesses tend to delay in-house IS implementation as they have insufficient knowledge to implement IS successfully (Thong, 2001).

Additionally, according to the survey results reported in Appendix A, Section A.1, it suggests that the nature of SMEs might be an obstacle to their adoption of integration technologies. The reasons for this are (1) the results show that cost is still an obstacle to SMEs as they can not really afford to spend extra amount of money on R&D investment, (2) some SMEs still find it unnecessary to implement integration technologies as there are not that many employees within the organisation, and (3) most SMEs still lack of knowledge about integration technologies compared to large counterparts.

Thus, based on the discussion in this section, it appears that the nature of SMEs, in terms of external and internal resources (e.g. time, finance and expertise), impacts on the way that they approach integration technologies. To this end, the following research question is raised for further investigation.

RQ1: *Is the nature of SMEs a real obstacle to integration technologies adoption?*

3.2.2 Company Sizes

As mentioned in the literature, SMEs and large organisations manage their systems in different ways due to company size differences (DeLone, 1988; Iacovou et al., 1995; Kuan and Chau, 2001). Apart from organisational or strategic remarks, various literature emphasises size as one of the issues that is increasing the need for the co-ordination and control of organisational activities (Howard and Hine, 1997; Ling, 2001; Nilakanta and Scamell, 1990; Yasai-Ardekani and Haung, 1997). Tagliavini et al.(2002) proposed that company size is an important factor affecting ERP adoption. DeLone (1981) also suggested that computer usage characteristics are different in organisations of different sizes. Other research work, like IDC's (1999), suggests a direct relationship between the size of organisations and the percentage of those organisations in which ERP has been implemented. All these studies indicated that the size of the organisations have many different impacts on the ways that the organisations do business. For example, the same system might be managed by 200 employees from the IT department in large companies, but managed only by 20 or fewer employees in small companies.

Moreover, as reported in Chapter 1, SMEs can be categorised as micro sized companies if they have up to 20 employees, small-sized if they have up to 100 employees, and medium-sized if they have up to 500 employees. With more than 500 employees, companies can be seen as large organisations. Company size is important, as a company with 20 employees and a company with 500 employees have different ways of managing their IS. According to the survey results reported in Appendix A, Section A.2, it suggests that SMEs and large organisations manage their IS in different ways. For example, the results show that the majority of the integration technologies users in large organisations (around 71.4%) reported that the MIS department is in charge of the companies' information systems. As for SMEs, around 40% responds report that their information systems are managed by the MIS department, and around 60% of them claim that their IS are managed by managers or outsourced. The possible explanations are that firstly, the culture of a small enterprise is tied in with the needs, desires and abilities of its owner (Bridge et al., 1998). The owners of SMEs often like controlling their own destiny and doing things differently. Thus, most of the SMEs managers like to manage IS on their own. Secondly, according to Carter and Evan (2000), due to the lack of financial resources and expertise in IT, SMEs usually do not develop IS on their own. Instead, they rely more on standardised and off-the-shelf software packages, and normally seek external support for their IT problems, such as friends, vendors or consultants. As a result, many SMEs like to outsource their systems. Thus, the discussion here indicates that companies of different sizes manage their IS differently.

In accordance with the views discussed in this section, the researcher suggests that it is possible that companies of different sizes may follow different approaches for their adoption of integration technologies. Thus, a research question is proposed for further investigation:

> **RQ2:** *What is the relationship between integration technologies and their adoption in companies of different sizes?*

3.2.3 Need for Integration

Rogers (1995) suggests that organisations adopt a new technology only if it provides significantly better benefits than their existing ones. A new technology needs to provide solutions for existing problems or open up new opportunities to motivate an organisation to take a proactive decision to adopt it with a trading partner (Rogers, 1995). Although the organisational structure of larger organisations could be very different from SMEs, companies of any size show a critical need for the coordination and control of business activities (Tagliavini et al., 2002). Thus, it is important to understand organisations' motivations/needs for adopting a new technology.

According to Themistocleous (2002), the reasons that push large companies to turn to EAI include, among others: (1) Enterprise Resources Planning (ERP) systems limitations to systems integration, (2) technical reasons, (3) financial reasons, (4) managerial reasons, and (5) strategic reasons. However, the researcher found that not all of the motivations mentioned by Themistocleous (2002) are appropriate to explain SMEs' needs for integration. For instance, some small firms might not even have ERP systems. Thus, the motivation reported by Themistocleous (2002) that the ERP systems can not fully automate and integrate organisations might not be appropriate to explain SMEs' motivations to adopt integration technologies. Therefore, apart from the reasons reported by Themistocleous (2002), additional reasons that push SMEs to turn to integration technologies to support their IS have been identified by the researcher from the existing literature. These reasons are explained as follows:

External Pressures: External forces tend to have more impact on small businesses than on large businesses (Iacovou et al., 1995; Welsh and White, 1981). In many cases, a company may adopt a technology due to the influences exerted by its business partners and/or its competitors, having no relation to the technology and organisation itself. For example, pressures from business partners or competitors have been found to be an important factor in the adoption of integration technologies (Hart and Saunders, 1998; Kuan and Chau, 2001; Premkumar et al., 1994). Since SMEs are usually the weaker partners in inter-organisational relationships, small businesses are susceptible to impositions by their larger partners (Saunders and Hart, 1993). Therefore, SMEs are under pressure to adopt integration technologies if its business partners request or recommend it to do so.

Internal Pressures: Internal pressures include both the financial and technological resources of the firm. Financial resources are related to those available to pay for the integration technologies installation costs and for the implementation of any subsequent enhancements, as well as for ongoing expenses during usage. Technological resources refer to the level of sophistication of IT usage and IT management in an organisation. As mentioned before, SMEs need to control their cash flows carefully, as they do not have unlimited funds for their IS projects. Thus, smaller firms tend to choose the cheapest system which may be adequate for their purposes (Thong, 2001). Furthermore, Levy et al. (2001) report that large firms use IS/IT to add value rather than simply to reduce costs. SMEs' exploitation of IS tends to mimic the early use in large firms – cost reduction. However, SMEs may use IS to co-ordinate internal activities, to add value through collaboration, particularly with customers, and occasionally to innovate (Levy et al., 2001). In addition, Thong (2001) also reported that small businesses tend to have insufficient knowledge to implement IS successfully, thus SMEs might need to seek external expertise (e.g. IT vendors, etc.). These all indicate that SMEs' need for integration technologies might be based on their internal pressures. Since SMEs are normally lacking in internal resources, when compared to large companies, it was thus argued that SMEs might make different adoption decisions from their larger counterparts (Kuan and Chau, 2001).

Competition: The main reason SMEs adopt IT is to enhance their competitiveness (Iacovou et al., 1995; Pollard and Hayne, 1998). Therefore, SMEs may feel the pressure when they see more and more companies in the industry adopting the integration technologies to solve the technical difficulties caused by the incompatibility of systems, especially if it is their business partners, competitors or larger trading partners. Thus, SMEs will feel under pressure and the need to adapt to the IS integrated environment to remain competitive. According to various literature, like Iacovou et al. (1995), the most significant reason that pushes SMEs to adopt integration technology is to gain a competitive advantage.

Based on the discussion above, it suggest that firstly, due to SMEs' resource poverty, SMEs' motivations to turn to adopting integration technologies mostly come from external forces. This is different from large organisations, as their motivations mostly arise from their technical, financial, strategic and managerial needs (Themistocleous, 2002). Secondly, the different integration needs between SMEs and large organisations might be caused by their different business complexity (Tagliavini et al., 2002). The interpretation of business complexity here means whether the condition of being a complex organisation is related to its adoption of integration technologies. After years of different technological purchases, enterprises have ended up with disparate systems spread throughout different units. However, the number of systems to be managed (i.e. disparate systems) is different between SMEs and large companies. For example, SMEs may only have a few systems, whereas large organisations may have many. Therefore, some SMEs (with only 10 employees or fewer) may find it ineffective to adopt integration technologies, since there are not many disparate systems within the organisations. In this case, adopting integration technologies to support SMEs' IS integration will only increase their capital or maintenance costs and add complexity to their existing operations, unless there are some irresistible reasons. For example, an SME's trading partners might require them to do so, or pressure from the government may make them act. As for larger organisations, since they are relatively complex organisations compared to SMEs (e.g. with many disparate systems within the organisation), adopting integration technologies can help them solve their integration problems, increase effectiveness, and speed up transactions, etc..

Additionally, the survey results reported in Appendix A, Section A.3 show that the reasons that push SMEs and large firms to turn to integration technologies are different. The majority of large organisations reported that integration technologies can provide real-time data which can help them to eliminate: (1) systems heterogeneity, (2) data redundancy, and (3) low data quality. For example, multiple applications store data for the same entity (e.g. orders), but there is often an inability to combine data and take decisions, since there is (1) data incompatibility, (2) confusion regarding data latency, or (3) communication problems. As for SMEs, the majority stated that external pressure and competition are the main reasons pushing them to adopt integration technologies. There are only 2.6% and 7.7% of large organisations agreed on this. Thus, these clearly show that there is a high possibility that integration needs are different between SMEs and large organisations, and this can influence the ways the companies approach integration technologies.

Furthermore, the survey results also reveal that the newer the technologies are, the less likelihood SMEs will adopt it. For instance, the adoption rate for EAI and Web Services among SMEs is relatively low compared to large counterparts. This demonstrates that the more complex and expensive the integration technologies are, the less likelihood SMEs will adopt them. For large counterparts, they will use the integration technologies in a circumstance where the adoption of such technologies will give them competitive edge or solve a particular problem they are encountering.

Thus, the discussion in this section demonstrates that different sized companies might have different needs and ways of managing their adoption of integration technologies. Hence, the researcher suggests that SMEs' integration needs might be different from those of large companies, and this might affect their adoption decisions. Therefore, the following research question is formed:

> **RQ3:** *In what ways does SMEs' integration needs differ from large companies?*

3.2.4 Integration Technologies Adoption by SMEs and Large Organisations

Due to SMEs' inadequate resources, limited knowledge, lack of 'know-how' about IS, and several other constraints, some researchers have found that small businesses generally face greater risks in IS implementation and the use of IT than large businesses (Cragg and King, 1993; Cragg and Zinatelli, 1995; Iacovou et al., 1995). Thus, managers in SMEs have been characterised as having reservations about the adoption and use of IS (Chang and Powell, 1998; Thong, 2001). However, these reservations have not always obviated the benefits and successes such organisations can achieve from IS. In the early days, SMEs tended to use IS as tools to automate their standard administrative functions, e.g. accounting, budgeting and inventory control, etc.. Until recently, there has been growing literature addressing the issues of using IS for a competitive advantage amongst SMEs (Pollard and Hayne, 1998). According to Lin et al. (1993), the increasing interest in the strategic use of IS by SMEs is based on three factors: (1) the increased adoption of IS and its effective use by competitors, (2) a decrease in the cost of IS so that it is accessible to SMEs, and (3) the ability for IS to allow SMEs to mask their size from their external partners. For these reasons, the researcher suggests that some SMEs have turned to the adoption of integration technologies as a new strategy to improve their competitiveness (Chen et al., 2003).

The review of the literature has shown that only a few prior studies have focused on EDI and ERP in small businesses, as reported by Iacovou et al. (1995), Daniel (2003),

Hughes et al. (2003), Kuan and Chau (2001), Waarts et al. (2002), Ravarini et al. (2000) and Tagliavini et al. (2002). Among these studies on adoption, the model proposed by Iacovou et al. (1995) presents the most comprehensive research that focuses on the adoption of integration technologies (EDI) in small businesses (Kuan and Chau, 2001). Most of the literature on this subject that has been reviewed mainly focuses on the adoption of EDI and ERP, with studies related to EAI and Web Services adoption in SMEs proving to be largely lacking. This might be due to the fact that EAI and Web Services are only beginning to emerge and are in the early stages of adoption (Hailstone and Perry, 2002). Another reason might be that SMEs feel it unnecessary to adopt EAI or Web Services due to the extra costs and expertise required to implement these integrative technologies.

In contrast to studies on SMEs, EAI and Web Services adoption models and studies for larger organisations are available. Many studies have focused on different aspects of adopting EDI, EAI and Web Services in supporting IS integration in large organisations. To better understand the current state of the literature on the adoption of integration technologies in SMEs and large organisations, the researcher has summarised some of the current studies related to this in Tables 3.1 and 3.2. These papers were selected as they specifically focus on the adoption of the integration technologies, rather than their implementation or any other issues. Since the focus of the research is to investigate the adoption of integration technologies, these papers will thus justify the purpose of this research.

Table 3.1 Current Research on EDI Adoption

Factors	Description	SMEs	Large	References
• Perceived benefits • Organisational readiness • External pressure	Proposed adoption framework to address issue of major factors that explain EDI adoption behaviour of small organisations and expected impact of technology in the small business context.	✓		Iacovou et al. (1995)
• Perceived Industry Pressure • Perceived Governmental Pressure • Perceived Financial Cost • Perceived Technical Competence • Perceived direct benefits • Perceived indirect benefits	Technology-organisation-environment framework to propose perception-based small business EDI adoption model, tested against data collected from 575 small firms in Hong Kong.	✓		Kuan and Chau (2001)
• Customer and peer pressure • The desire for speedier and better communications	Positive and negative impacts of various factors on EDI selection decision along with the impact of EDI on organisation's employees.		✓	Banerjee and Golhar (1994)
• Supplier dependence • Customer power • Volume of EDI use • Supplier commitment • Supplier trust • Diversity of EDI use	Role of power and trust in EDI adoption and use. Also evaluated differences between proactive and reactive firms in terms of extent of adaptation, external connectivity with trading partners, and integration of EDI information.		✓	Hart and Saunders (1998)
• Organisational support • Implementation processes • Control procedures	Factors that account for EDI adoption in SMEs.	✓		Raymond and Bergeron (1996)
• Competitiveness • Uncertainty • Dependence • Communication needs • Technology and services • Organisational maturity • IT maturity • Rationale for EDI • Implementation process • Top management support • Perceived benefits	Model to examine role of several factors related to external environment and organisational context in influencing extent to which EDI is integrated, and whether more extensive integration has impact on organisational outcomes.		✓	Vega et al. (1997)
• Competitive pressure • Exercised power • Internal need • Top management support	Role of inter-organisational factors on decision mode for adoption of EDI.		✓	Premkumar and Ramamurth (1995)
• Governmental influence • Business partners' influence • Perceived direct benefits • Perceived indirect benefits • Prior EDI experience • Perceived support from vendor • Perceived costs	Study to identify key determinants of small business EDI adoption.	✓		Chau and Hui (2001)
• Perceived benefits • Organisational readiness • External pressure • Availability of EDI standards	Focus on adoption and impact of EDI in Dutch SMEs.	✓		Heck and Ribbers (1999)
• Competitive pressures • Industry pressures • Enacted trading partners' pressure • Dependency on partners • Financial resources • IT sophistication • Trading partners' readiness	Further validation of model proposed by Iacovou et al. (1995) and performed empirical work predicting EDI adoption. Suggested that factors identified by Iacovou et al. (1995) can be addressed in three major types of adoption perspectives: *technological*, *organisational*, and *inter-organisational*.		✓	Chwelos et al. (2001)

Table 3.2 Current Research on ERP, EAI and Web Services Adoption

	Factors	Description	SMEs	Large	References
ERP	• Innovation characteristics • Organisational characteristics • Environmental characteristics	Adoption of ERP in general organisational context.		✓	Bradford and Florin (2003)
	• Perceived innovation characteristics • Adopter characteristics • Internal environment characteristics • External environment characteristics	Challenges assumption that factors explaining adoption decisions do not change over time, and adds to the existing literature by investigating dynamics of factors influencing adoption.		✓	Waarts et al. (2002)
	• Business complexity factors • Extent of organisational change	Proposed conceptual framework for exploring use of ERP systems by SMEs.	✓		Tagliavini et al. (2002)
EAI	• Benefits • Barriers • Costs • Internal pressures • External pressures • IT sophistication • IT infrastructure • Support • Evaluation framework for integration technology and packages	Adoption of EAI in multinational organisations and identifies several factors for EAI adoption.		✓	Themisto-cleous (2002)
Web Services	• IS innovation type • Compatibility • Divisibility • Customisability • Cost • Complexity • Relative advantage • Communicability • Web Services awareness readiness • Web Services fit readiness • Technological skills readiness • Financial resource readiness	Web Services as a special case of IT industry innovation. Two key issues reviewed at the innovation level of analysis: type of innovation and innovation characteristics. Then 3-layer nested-stage model developed as a road map for studying Web Services innovation.		✓	Wu and Sawy (2003)
	• Relatively advantage • Compatibility • Image • Ease of use • Security • Trialability • Result demonstrability • Visibility • Voluntariness	Proposed Web Services adoption model by applying diffusion theory and security-related research in technology adoption.		✓	Zhang and Huang (2004)
	• Standards and stakeholders • Technical factors • Perceived benefits	Framework developed for analysing driving forces for adoption of Web Services based on literature review, technical information analysis, and field and Web-based case studies.		✓	Chen (2003)
	• Senior management support • Knowledge transfer mechanism • Suitable technical architecture	Role of Web services in SMEs through application of Venkatraman (1994) business transformation model via case studies.	✓		Vidgen et al. (2004)

To better understand the factors listed in Tables 3.1 and 3.2, the researcher further analyses them by re-organising them. This is shown in Table 3.3. Factors like Competitive Pressure, Dependency on Partners/ Trading Partners' Pressures, Trading

Partner Readiness, External Pressure, Perceived Financial Cost/ Financial Resources and Perceived Governmental Pressure, that particularly focus on SMEs, are highlighted.

Table 3.3 Summary of Factors that Influence Organisations' Integration Technologies Adoption Decision

FACTORS	EAI	EDI	ERP	Web Services
Adopter Characteristics			✓	
Availability of Standards		✓		✓
Barriers	✓			
Business Complexity			✓	
Competitive Pressures	✓	✓		
Customer Power		✓		
Dependency on Partners/ Trading Partners' Pressure	✓	✓		
Trading Partners' Readiness	✓	✓		
Environmental Characteristics			✓	
Evaluation Framework for Integration Technology and Packages	✓			
External Pressure	✓	✓		
Extent of Organisational Change			✓	
External Environment Characteristics			✓	
IS Innovation Type				✓
IT Sophistication	✓	✓		✓
IT Infrastructure	✓			✓
Internal Environment Characteristics			✓	
Internal Pressure	✓			
Innovation Characteristics/ Perceived Innovation Characteristics			✓	
Organisational Characteristics			✓	
Organisational Readiness		✓		
Perceived Financial Cost/ Financial Resources	✓	✓		✓
Perceived Benefits (Direct and Indirect benefits)	✓	✓		✓
Perceived Technical Competence/ Technological Skills Readiness	✓	✓		✓
Perceived Industry Pressure	✓	✓		
Perceived Governmental Pressure		✓		
Prior EDI experience		✓		
Security		✓		✓
Support/ Organisational Support	✓	✓		✓
Stakeholders				✓
Supplier Trust		✓		
Supplier Commitment		✓		
Technical Factors	✓			✓
The desire for faster and better communication		✓		

Tables 3.1, 3.2 and 3.3 show that similar factors are sometimes used to explain the adoption of different integration technologies (i.e. common factors). For example, IT sophistication, perceived benefits, technical competence, support, and financial resources (i.e. cost) factors were applied to explain EAI, EDI and Web Services adoption in many studies. Therefore, these factors can be considered as the most important for explaining the adoption of integration technologies. In other words, these are common factors, since many studies have mentioned them in their research models.

Secondly, only a few factors were used to explain the adoption of integration technologies by both SMEs and large organisations. For instance, factors like perceived benefits, perceived financial costs and external pressures were used to explain adoption by SMEs as well as large organisations. However, among the research papers as mentioned in Tables 3.1 and 3.2, there was only one which referred to research concerning the EAI and Web Services adoption in SMEs. This indicates that (1) there is a lack of literature on EAI and Web Services adoption in SMEs, and (2) most of the factors identified from the normative literature can not be equally applied to both SMEs and large companies to interpret their decision whether to adopt integration technologies, because having one piece of evidence is not enough to represent every example.

Thirdly, similar factors were highlighted in many research papers to explain the adoption of integration technologies by SMEs. For example, competitive pressures, dependency on partners, external pressure, perceived financial cost, prior EDI experience and perceived governmental pressure were used in many studies to explain the adoption of integration technologies by SMEs. This indicates that these factors are the main/important factors for the adoption by SMEs. However, these factors can also be used to explain the adoption decision by large organisations, even though it may not be necessarily a good one. For example, perceived governmental pressure might not be a factor that assists the studying of adoption decisions in large organisations, as this factor is particularly used to explain the adoption decision by SMEs. The reason is that SMEs often find it hard to adopt integration technologies without any kind of support (e.g. not only support from vendors and consultants, but also from the government and their suppliers, etc) due to their natural resource constraints, e.g. a lack of 'know-how' and resources. Moreover, as mentioned in Section 3.2.3, SMEs might be forced to adopt integration technologies as their business partners or governments require them to do so (Chen et al., 2003). This situation might not be appropriate for their larger counterparts, as they are usually the stronger partners in inter-organisational relationships, when compared to the SMEs (Saunders and Hart, 1993; Storey, 1994). Another explanation is that most of the research papers that focused on the adoption of integration technologies in large companies did not include perceived governmental pressure as a factor that might explain or influence their adoption decision. (See Tables 3.1, 3.2 and 3.3).

Besides, according to the survey results reported in Appendix A, Section A.5, suggest that SMEs and large organisations face different problems when integrating their information systems. The majority of SMEs reported that they have encountered many technical problems due to their lack of technical skills. As for large firms, the majority (around 33.3%) reported that they have encountered many strategic problems. For example, 25% of SMEs claimed that dependency on partners is the factor that influences their adoption decisions, but there were only 7.7% of large firms which reported this.

In accordance with the above considerations, the researcher proposes that there is a high possibility that SMEs and large companies take their decision for the adoption of integration technologies by mostly focusing on different factors (as shown in Tables 3.1, 3.2 and 3.3). This will be illustrated in more detail in Sections 3.3 and 3.4. This assumption matches with the literature, where it is reported that the adoption of integration technologies is different for both large and small companies (Iacovou et al., 1995; Kuan and Chau, 2001). Thus, the following research question is raised for further investigation:

> **RQ4:** *Do SMEs and large companies consider different factors when taking decisions for the adoption of integration technologies?*

3.2.5   Time

As reported in the literature that most of the factors that focused on the adoption of integration technologies by SMEs are mostly from the external forces, e.g. governmental support, external pressures, pressure from trading partners, etc..   This indicates that in many situations, SMEs are forced to adopt integration technologies as their partners require them to (Iacovou et al., 1995; Kuan and Chau, 2001). Thus, to remain competitive, SMEs have no choice but to adopt integration technologies. For these reasons, when referring to the adoption life cycles, some literature suggests that SMEs tend to be late adopters (late majority/laggards) in the adoption of new technology/innovation, rather than early adopters (Iacovou et al., 1995; Kuan and Chau, 2001; Ling, 2001).

Laggards can be summarised as those who adopt a technology only when they have no choice. In fact, many laggards do not explicitly adopt technologies at all, but rather acquire them accidentally when a particular technology is a component of a packaged solution (Rogers, 1995). Laggards' innovation-decision process is relatively lengthy, with adoption and use lagging far behind the awareness-knowledge of a new idea. Resistance to new technologies on the part of laggards may be entirely rational from the laggards' viewpoint, as their resources are limited, and they must be certain that a new idea will not fail before they adopt it. Kirby (2003) and Storey (1994) are among those others who claim that SMEs can not afford to fail due to their limited resources. Therefore, most SMEs might be categorised as laggards.

The adopters in the late majority group not only like to be certain that the new technology works, they also like to wait until it has been widely adopted and standardised. They do not consider that the technology offers them any competitive advantage, even though they recognise that they can not live without it once their partners or competitors have adopted it. The pressure of peers is necessary to motivate adoption. In accordance with this point, as mentioned before, sometimes SMEs are forced to adopt integration technologies as their partners require them to (i.e. external pressure). Thus, SMEs can also be categorised in the late majority group. There might be an exceptional case where SMEs might be considered as innovators, such as when SMEs are hi-technology firms. Hi-technology SMEs might use more advanced or sophisticated information technologies for their production or IS management than those SMEs from other sectors. Thus, SMEs from hi-technology firms might be able to develop their own systems. However, there is no evidence at this stage to prove whether SMEs from hi-technology firms can be considered as innovators, and thus this point needs to be further investigated.

Nevertheless, most large companies tend to be in the early adopters/early majority group, with some of them even being classified as innovators. Early adopters are more interested in the business and competitive advantages that a new technology brings about rather the technology itself, but they are still risk-takers, since they are willing to adopt a new technology before it has been proven or widely accepted. Those in the early majority group are the pragmatists (Rogers, 1995). They do not intend to take the risk of adopting a technology too early, even though they also recognise that waiting too long can put them at a substantial disadvantage. They want to make sure the technology works for others before they invest (Kaye, 2003). (See Figure 3.1).

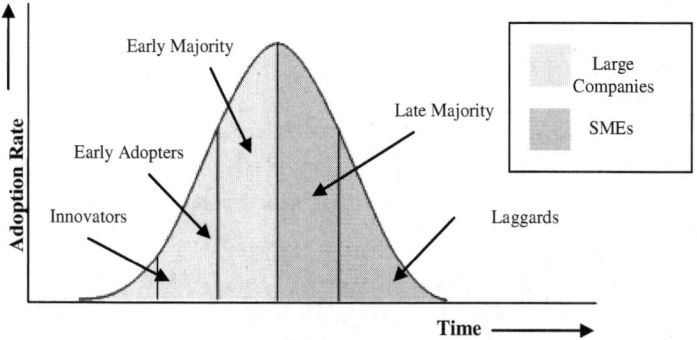

Figure 3.1 Adoption Life Cycles
Sources: Rogers (1995)

The survey results in Appendix A, Section A.4 show that the timing of adoption is different between SMEs and large firms. For example, the majority of large organisations indicate that they have adopted integration technologies for more than 10 years, whereas there are only around 15% of SMEs. Most SMEs lie in between 5 to 10 years. This shows that SMEs tend to be later adopters compared to their large counterparts. In addition, the survey results also reveal that the early adoption of integration technologies can give organisations some minor competitive advantages. However, many of the respondents claimed that it is hard to judge whether adopting integration technologies can actually help them to gain competitive advantage, but they are sure that not having implemented any of these integration technologies will gradually become a problem for them.

Thus, based on the above discussion, it suggests that time plays an important role in terms of integration technologies adoption, as late adopters may find that they have a competitive disadvantage (Kaye, 2003). Kaye (2003) suggested that by extending the middle of the early-adopter phase into the start of the late-majority phase, this period may offer a competitive advantage to the adoption of integration technologies. However, at some time early in the late majority phase, having implemented integration technologies ceases to offer any competitive advantage, and not having implemented anything begins to be a problem. To this end, the following research question is raised:

> **RQ5:** *Can early adoption of integration technologies by the organisations gain competitive advantages?*

3.2.6   Parameters for Adoption of Integration Technologies

Based on the discussion and identified research questions in Sections 3.2.1, 3.2.2, 3.2.3 and 3.2.4, the researcher identified the potential parameters that can be used to explain the adoption of integration technologies by SMEs and large companies. These adoption parameters are company size, time, nature, integration needs, adoption factors for large companies and adoption factors for SMEs, which are then illustrated in a cube diagram in Figure 3.2, which shows the dimensions for the integration technologies adoption between SMEs and large organisations.

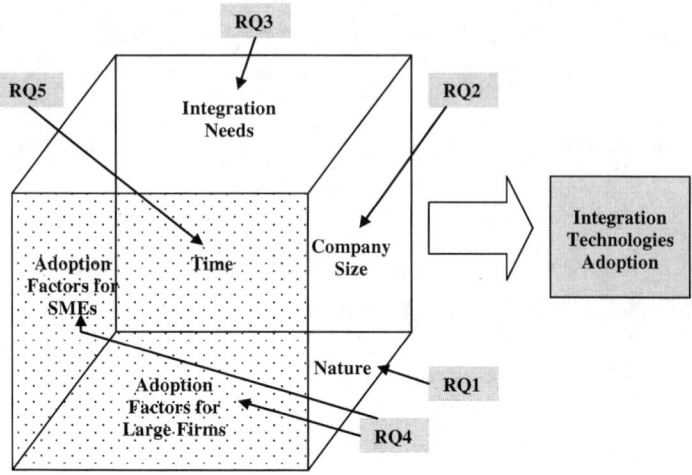

Figure 3.2 Dimensions for Adoption of Integration Technologies between SMEs and Large Organisations

3.3 Investigating Integration Technologies Adoption Factors for SMEs and Large Companies

As mentioned in Section 3.2.3, there is a possibility that SMEs and large organisations take decisions for the adoption of integration technologies by focusing on different factors. Therefore this section further analyses this area in more detail. If this is proved to be true, the next stage is to find out whether the identified parameters (nature resources of the firms, their integration needs, company size and time) influence the different adoption factors among SMEs and large organisations.

The factors identified in Tables 3.1 and 3.2 are summarised and categorised into SMEs and large organisations to determine whether SMEs and large organisations take decisions for the adoption of integration technologies by focusing on different factors, as shown in Table 3.4. The common factors highlighted in the table are those used by most researchers to explain the adoption of integration technologies by both SMEs and large companies. The factors that are often applied to explain the adoption of integration technologies by SMEs are in bold, so as to distinguish them from the factors of their larger counterparts.

Table 3.4. Factors Influencing Integration Technologies Adoption Decision in SMEs and Large Organisaitons

Factors	SMEs	Large Orgs
Adopter Characteristics		✓
Availability of Standards/EDI Standards	✓	✓
Barriers		✓
Business Complexity Factors	✓	
Compatibility		✓
Competitive Pressures/Competitiveness	✓	✓
Complexity		✓
Control Procedures	✓	
Customer Power		✓
Customisability		✓
Dependency on Partners/ Trading Partners Readiness/pressure, Influence	✓	✓
Dependency		✓
Diversity of EDI use		✓
Divisibility		✓
Ease of Use		✓
Environmental Characteristics		✓
Evaluation Framework for Integration of Technology and Packages		✓
Exercised Power		✓
External Pressure	✓	✓
External Environment Characteristics		✓
Extent of Organisational Change	✓	
Image		✓
IS Innovation Type		✓
IT Maturity		✓
IT Sophistication	✓	✓
IT Infrastructure		✓
Internal Pressure/Internal Needs		✓
Internal Environment Characteristics		✓
Innovation Characteristics/ Perceived Innovation Characteristics		✓
Implementation Processes	✓	✓
Knowledge Transfer Mechanism	✓	
Uncertainty		✓
Organisational Maturity		✓
Organisational Readiness	✓	
Organisational Characteristics		✓
Perceived Financial Cost/ Financial Resources/Financial Resource Readiness	✓	✓
Perceived Benefits (Direct and Indirect)	✓	✓
Perceived Technical Competence/ Technological Skills Readiness	✓	✓
Perceived Industry Pressure	✓	
Perceived Governmental Pressure/Government Influence	✓	
Prior EDI experience	✓	
Rationale for EDI		✓
Relative Advantage		✓
Result Demonstrability		✓
Security		✓
Senior Management Support	✓	
Support/ Organisation Support/Top Management Support/Vendor Support	✓	✓
Stakeholders		✓
Supplier Trust		✓
Supplier Commitment		✓
Suitable Technical Architecture	✓	
Technical Factors		✓
Technology and Services		✓
Desire for Faster and Better Communication/Communication Needs		✓
Triability		✓
Visibility		✓
Volume of EDI use		✓
Vouluntariness		✓
Web Services fit readiness		✓

From Table 3.4, it can be seen:

(1) To explain the adoption of integration technologies by both SMEs and large companies, researchers often use factors such as Availability of Standards/EDI Standards, Competitive pressures/Competitiveness, Dependency on partners/Trading partners readiness/ Trading partner pressure/ Trading partner influence, External pressure, IT sophistication, Implementation processes, Perceived financial cost/ Financial resources/Financial resource readiness, Perceived benefits (Direct and Indirect benefits), Perceived technical competence/ Technological skills readiness, and Support/ Organisation support/Top management support/Vendor support. Therefore, these factors are considered as the common factors for the adoption of integration technologies. In other words, these factors should be used in the research model as the starting point to illustrate the adoption of integration technologies in both SMEs and large companies.

(2) Factors like Knowledge transfer mechanisms, Perceived industry pressure, Perceived governmental pressure/influence, Prior EDI experience, Suitable technical architecture, Business complexity factors, Control procedures, and Extent of organisational change have particular focus in SMEs' adoption of integration technologies. These factors are mostly from the external pressures/forces. The reason is that unlike large firms, SMEs' natural resources are relatively weak, as discussed in the previous sections. Therefore, the external support (expertise) and forces are an important motivation to push them to adopt integration technologies (Attewell, 1992; Thong, 2001). Hence, the appropriateness of applying the factors mentioned here to explain the adoption of integration technologies in large organisations may be questionable.

(3) Apart from the factors mentioned in the previous paragraph (2), other factors listed in Table 3.4 are often used to explain the adoption of integration technologies in large organisations. The factors for large organisations cover a wider range of areas and answers to their decisions to adopt integration technologies. For example, technical factors like complexity, compatibility, etc., and organisational factors such as organisational characteristics and organisational maturity, etc.. Hence, this shows the difference between SMEs and large organisations in their adoption of integration technologies.

The discussion in this section suggests that the research findings regarding large businesses should not be generalised to include small organisations, due to their different technology adoption patterns (DeLone, 1988; Ein-Dor and Segev, 1978; Iacovou et al.,

1995; Kuan and Chau, 2001). Raymond (1985) also reported that small organisations have long been found to be different from large organisations in the IS context, as they are not a simple scaled-down model of large organisations. Thus, it is clear that SMEs and large organisations take decisions for the adoption of integration technologies by mostly focusing on different factors.

3.4 Investigating Factors for Different Adoption Factors Considered by SMEs and Large Companies

Since SMEs and large organisations take decisions for the adoption of integration technologies by focusing on the different factors as these were discussed in Section 3.3, in continuing this analysis, this section will examine the extent to which the four adoption parameters identified in Section 3.1, namely integration needs, nature resources of the firms, company size and time, influence the different adoption factors between SMEs and large organisations. A summary of the influential parameters is given in Figure 3.3.

NATURE	TIME
Factors influenced by natural characteristics and resources of organisations, e.g. internal and external resources.	Factors influenced by timing of adoption.
COMPANY SIZE	INTEGRATION NEED
Factors influenced by size of company.	Factors influenced by organisations' need for integration.

Figure 3.3 Summary of Influential Parameters

To analyse the relationship between the influential parameters and the different adoption factors between SMEs and large firms, the researcher has firstly classified the different adoption factors in Table 3.5, based on the influential parameters defined in Figure 3.3, excluding from the table the common factors.

Nature resources of firms. Small businesses face greater risks in IS implementation and the use of IT than large businesses do because of their inadequate resources, limited knowledge, lack of 'know-how' about IS, and several other constraints (e.g. human resources, financial, marketing, structural and managerial, as discussed in Chapter 1).

Table 3.5 Classification of SME and Large Company Adoption Factors

Influential Parameters	Adoption Factors	
	SMEs	**Large Organisations**
Nature Resources of firm	• Organisational readiness • Senior management support • Knowledge transfer mechanism	• Adopter characteristics • Organisation characteristics • External environment characteristics • Internal characteristics • Environmental characteristics
Integration Needs	• Perceived industry pressure • Perceived government pressure	• Barriers • Compatibility • Complexity • Customer power • Customisability • Dependency • Diversity of EDI use • Divisibility • Ease of use • Evaluation framework for integration technology and packages • Exercised power • Innovation characteristics • IS innovation type • IT infrastructure • Internal pressure • Internal needs • Rationale for EDI • Relative advantage • Security • Stakeholders • Supplier trust • Supplier commitment • Technical factors • Technology and services • Desire for faster and better communication • Communication needs • Triability • Visibility • Volume of EDI use • Voluntariness • Result demonstrability
Time	• Prior EDI experience • Suitable technical architecture • Extent of organisational change	• Image • IT maturity • Uncertainty • Organisational maturity • Web Services fit readiness
Company Size	• Business complexity factors • Control procedures	

(Cragg and King, 1993; Cragg and Zinatelli, 1995; Iacovou *et al.*, 1995). For these reasons, SMEs and large firms are focusing on different adoption factors. Table 3.5 shows that the adoption factors for SMEs are more focused on the external forces and internal resources availability like perceived governmental influence, senior management support, organisational readiness and knowledge transfer mechanism. All these factors are related to the natural characteristics of organisations. Thus, these factors indicate that the nature of organisations influence the different adoption factors between SMEs and large firms, as depicted in Figure 3.4.

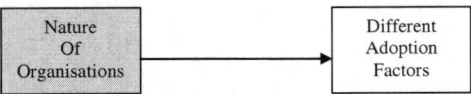

Figure 3.4 Nature Resources of Organisations Influence on Different Adoption Factors between SMEs and Large Organisations

Integration needs. As mentioned in Section 3.2.1, SMEs integration needs normally come from external forces. This can be explained by looking at the adoption factors for SMEs found in Table 3.4, such as the perceived industry pressure and perceived governmental pressure, as these factors are focused on external forces. Moreover, looking at the adoption factors for large organisations, they are focused on different aspects of why large firms adopt integration technologies, such as technical issues (e.g. complexity, etc.), internal needs to improve their services, etc.. Table 3.5 shows that the factors for SMEs emphasised the external forces, whereas the large organisations are more focused on their internal needs to solve their problems or to improve their services (e.g. internal needs, communication needs etc.). The discussion here indicates that integration needs influence the different adoption factors between SMEs and large organisations, as indicated in Figure 3.5.

Figure 3.5 Integration Needs Influence on Different Adoption Factors between SMEs and Large Organisations

Time. As discussed in Section 3.2.4, SMEs are often categorised in the laggards/late majority groups, as they often adopt technology when they have no choice or after they are certain that the new technology will assist them. Thus, they often wait until the new technologies have been widely adopted and standardised or until they are sure of having suitable technical architecture, support or knowledge to manage the new technologies (Thong *et al.*, 1996). This explains why factors such as prior EDI experiences and suitable technical architecture (Table 3.5) are often used by researchers to explain the adoption of integration technologies by SMEs, and why there is as yet a lack of literature on the adoption of Web Services and EAI by SMEs (see Table 3.3). On the other hand, large organisations are often categorised as early adopters, as they are more willing to adopt a new technology before it has been proven or widely accepted. This explains why most of the existing literature focuses on the adoption of Web Services and EAI by large organisations (see Table 3.3). Moreover, according to the adoption factors for large organisations in Table 3.4, although Web Services and EAI are in the early stage of adoption, large organisations still take the initiative to adopt them (i.e. risk-takers). This explains why factors like IT maturity, uncertainty, Web Services fit readiness, organisational maturity, and image are used to explain the adoption decisions for large organisations. Based on the discussion here, the timing of when to adopt integration technologies seems to be an important factor that influences the different adoption factors among SMEs and large organisations, as depicted in Figure 3.6.

Figure 3.6 Timing Influence on Different Adoption Factors between SMEs and Large Organisations

Company size. Table 3.5 shows that companies of different sizes approach integration technologies adoption differently as, they take decisions focusing on different factors (as there are factors explicit to SMEs and large organisations). For example, SMEs usually lack resources compared to larger counterparts (Storey, 1994). Thus, SMEs might be more focused on their resources and abilities to adopt integration technologies, e.g. factors like senior management support. This is depicted in Figure 3.7.

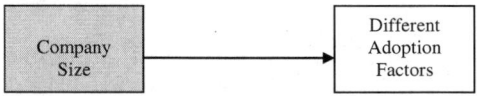

Figure 3.7 Company Size Influence on Different Adoption Factors between SMEs and Large Organisations

In Section 3.2, some parameters were identified from the existing literature to explain the adoption of integration technologies between SMEs and large organisations. These parameters were then further analysed in Section 3.3 to study whether adoption decisions mostly focus on different factors between SMEs and large organisations. In doing so, the literature suggests that this is the case. Based on this analysis, the adoption factors were then classified into three categories, namely (1) adoption factors explicit to SMEs, (2) adoption factors explicit to large organisations, and (3) common factors. Based on the discussion and analysis in this section and Section 3.2 (i.e. combining the first stage (parameters identification) with the second stage (different adoption factors)), the researcher has introduced a conceptual model that can be used to explain the adoption of integration technologies. This is shown in Figure 3.8.

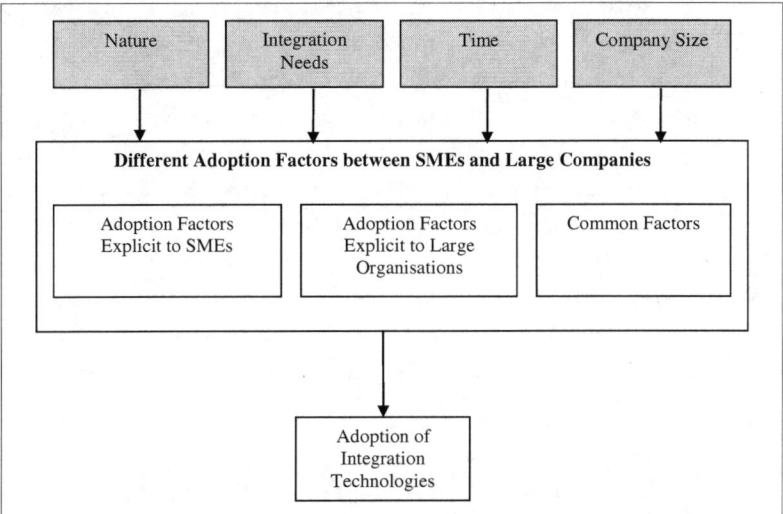

Figure 3.8 Conceptual Model for Adoption of Integration Technologies Based on Comparative Analysis between SMEs and Large Organisations

The proposed research model makes a novel contribution at two levels. Firstly, at the conceptual level, the model incorporates factors identified in previous studies as influencing adoption of integration technologies the organisations. This is extended by comparatively analysis resulting in identification of parameters that can be used to explain the integration technologies adoption and the classification of factors between SMEs and large organisations. Based on the identified parameters and the factors classification, a novel conceptual model is developed for the adoption of integration technologies. Secondly, the concepts of the proposed model can be used as a frame of reference for the adoption of integration technologies between SMEs and large organisations. A new aspect of the proposed model is that it introduces parameters that explain the different adoption factors focused on. Thus, the conceptual model clarifies the issue reported by Kuan and Chau (2001) and others like Thong (1999) that the general applicability of the findings for large organisations may be questionable if applied to SMEs. Thus, the conceptual model: (1) addresses the research questions derived from the literature regarding the adoption of integration technologies between SMEs and large organisations, and (2) supports understanding and decision-making.

3.5 Conclusions

This chapter studied the factors that affect the adoption decision for integration technologies, based on a comparative analysis between SMEs and large companies. In Chapter 2, it was made evident that it was unclear whether companies of different sizes take the decision for the adoption of integration technologies by focusing on different factors. It was also shown that the general applicability of the integration technologies adoption studies for large organisations may be questionable if applied to SMEs. Given the importance of widespread adoption for the success of integration technologies, there is clearly a need to understand more about which factors are important when an SME makes a decision to adopt integration technologies, and why these adoption factors are different from large organisations. Thus, to address these issues, this chapter critically analysed the normative literature regarding the adoption of integration technologies in SMEs and large organisations.

In Section 3.2, the researcher attempted to analyse the research issues for the adoption of integration technologies identified from the normative literature. In doing so, a number of research questions arose which are summarised as:

- In what ways does SMEs' integration needs differ from large companies'?

- Is the nature of SMEs a real obstacle to the adoption of integration technologies?

- What is the relationship between integration technologies and their adoption in companies of different sizes?

- Can early adoption of integration technologies by organisations gain competitive advantages?

- Do SMEs and large companies consider different factors when taking decisions for adoption of integration technologies?

- If the adoption factors for SMEs and large organisations are thought to be different, to what extent do: (1) integration needs, (2) nature of organisations, (3) company size and (4) time, influence the different adoption factors?

Based on the research questions, the author found that the differences between SMEs and large companies for their integration technologies adoption are influenced by the following parameters: nature resource availability, time, integration needs, company size, adoption factors for SMEs and adoption factors for large organisations (see Figure 3.2). Based on this, the adoption factors for SMEs and large organisations were further analysed to find out whether they focus on different factors when taking adoption decisions. The adoption factors for SMEs and large organisations were then classified into three categories: common factors, factors explicit to SMEs and factors explicit to large organisations. Thus, a novel conceptual model was introduced (see Figure 3.8). The model takes into consideration parameters identified in normative literature as factors influencing the integration technologies' adoption between SMEs and large organisations. The model also takes into account the different adoption factors that SMEs and large organisations focus on when taking adoption decisions. The proposed conceptual model is novel since it includes: (1) a number of parameters that explain the different integration technologies adoption factors between SMEs and large organisations, and (2) a classification of adoption factors between SMEs and large organisations. The proposed model thus meets the aim of this thesis reported in Chapter 1 Section1.7.

The conceptual model proposed in this chapter was designed as a way to illustrate how the research questions (i.e. gaps) in the literature can be bridged as a guide for the empirical work in the next chapters. In the next chapters, the proposed conceptual model will be used as a basis for the empirical study of the issue under investigation, starting with the next chapter (Chapter 4), where there will be a presentation of the methodological approach used in this research.

Chapter 4: Research Methodology

Summary

In the light of the knowledge gained and issues raised in the preceding literature review, and the introduction of the conceptual model in Chapter 3, this chapter describes the research methodology of the work presented in this thesis. This description is within the context of research methods commonly used in the area of IS. It begins with a review on positivism, interpretivism, critical and post-positivism epistemological stances. This review results in the justification of interpretivism as an appropriate research stance to be adopted by this thesis. Thereafter, the author justifies why qualitative research is used in this research and explains why a case study research strategy is employed. Then, the author presents an empirical research methodology, which acts as a framework for conducting the empirical enquiry. Finally, data collection method and data analysis tools are chosen, and the reasons are explained.

4.1 Introduction

The purpose of this chapter is to elaborate on the methodology followed towards meeting the objectives of the present study within the context of research methods commonly used in the area of IS. Information Systems are a multidisciplinary field, and the selection of an appropriate research method for their study is not an obvious one. According to Galliers (1992), the study of information systems is a complex topic, multidisciplinary and very much a social, rather than a wholly technical subject. Thus the researcher in the field has to choose among a variety of research methods, approaches and techniques to develop an appropriate research framework.

This chapter illustrates the research methods used in this thesis for the examination of issues related to the adoption of integration technologies by SMEs, taking into consideration the differences between SMEs and large counterparts as they have been presented in Chapters 2 and 3. The interpretive research approach has been selected as the most appropriate for the development of the thesis research framework. Interpretive research is used increasingly as an approach that can help the understanding to complex phenomena related to the use of information systems (Walsham, 1995a). Such issues can be strategic planning, competitive advantage, organisational learning, information systems' role, and the alignment of the IS function in the organisation with other organisational strategies (Brancheau and Wetherbe, 1990).

This chapter discusses first the appropriate research approach which forms the basis of this research. In addition, it examines the selected research methodology, and makes a detailed presentation of the specific methodological approach followed.

4.2 Selection of Appropriate Research Approach

According to Land (1992), information systems are essentially social systems of which information technology is but one aspect. Land (1992) supports that it is a multi-disciplinary endeavour, as contributions to its study come from the natural sciences, mathematics and engineering, behavioural sciences and linguistics. For this reason, he reports that there is no single framework which encompasses all the domains of knowledge needed for the study of information systems (Galliers, 1992). As Galliers (1991) and Walsham (1995b) among others argue, it is unlikely that there is a universal

IS research approach. Thus, selecting an appropriate research approach when studying IS is one of the most difficult decisions for a researcher.

In addition, Orlikowski and Baroudi (1991) claim that as IS is not rooted in a single theoretical perspective, there is therefore a wide range of philosophical consequently research approaches and strategies which researchers can choose from. For these reasons, the selection of the appropriate approach is a major task during the research design process. In accordance with that, awareness of the researcher about the whole range of research paradigms, approaches and strategies may facilitate informed choice and lessen the persistent bias towards one or another approach.

In the following section, the research methods and paradigms that have been selected during the development of the research framework of this thesis are presented, as well as the justification for the selection of the specific research approaches.

4.2.1 Underlying Research Assumptions

All research (whether quantitative or qualitative) is based on some underlying assumptions about what constitutes valid research and which research methods are appropriate. Several philosophical approaches are available for IS research including: (1) positivism, (2) interpretivism, (3) critical, and (4) post-positivism (Chau, 1986; Orlikowski and Baroudi, 1991). While these research epistemologies are philosophically distinct, in the practice of social research these distinctions are not always so clear-cut (Myers, 1997). There is considerable disagreement as to whether these research paradigms or underlying epistemologies are necessarily opposed, and there is further debate about whether they can be accommodated within one study (Myers, 1997).

Evidence from IS literature suggests that the positivist approach has been the dominant epistemology in IS research (Galliers, 1992; Miles and Huberman, 1994; Walsham, 1995a; Yin, 1994). Orlikowski and Baroudi (1991) found that almost all IS articles published in leading IS journals during the previous decade continued to report the results of surveys and experiments. Positivists generally assume that reality is objectively given and can be described by measurable properties, which are independent of the observer and his or her instruments. Positivist studies generally attempt to test theory, in an attempt to increase the predictive understanding of phenomena. In line with this, Orlikowski and Baroudi (1991) classify IS research as positivist if there is evidence of formal propositions, quantifiable measures of variables, hypothesis testing, and the drawing of inferences about a phenomenon from the sample to a stated population.

According to Galliers (1992), IS research can be classified as interpretive if it is assumed that our knowledge of reality is gained only through social constructions such as language, consciousness, shared meanings, documents, tools, and other artifacts. Interpretive studies generally attempt to understand phenomena through the meanings that people assign to them, and interpretive methods of research in IS are "aimed at producing an understanding of the context of the information systems, and the process whereby the information system influences and is influenced by the context" (Walsham, 1993).

Information systems research can be classified as critical if the main task is seen as being one of a social critique, whereby the restrictive and alienating conditions of the status quo are brought to light (Hirschheim and Klein, 1994). Critical researchers assume that social reality is historically constituted, and that it is produced and reproduced by people. Although people can consciously act to change their social and economic circumstance, critical researchers recognise that their ability to do so is constrained by various forms of social, cultural and political domination (Myers, 1997).

It is also important to mention here the post-positivist approach that is positioned between positivism and critical theory in the literature, as it has been introduced as a need to change direction from positivism and to transcend its limitations (Lincoln and Guba, 2000). According to Galliers (1992) and Winefield (1991) post-positivism challenges the tradition that knowledge is actually apodictic, asserting instead that knowledge claims are simply those accepted by the community. From a methodological stance, an interesting part of post-positivist thought is its belief in what might be termed "methodological pluralism" – the assertion that there is no one correct method of science, but many methods (Galliers, 1992; Morgan, 1980; Polkinghorne, 1983).

4.2.2   Selecting Interpretive Research Approach

The diversity of research paradigms posed complex challenges for the selection of the appropriate approach for this research. The author argues that for the purpose of this thesis, the interpretive approach has been selected as the underlying research assumption of this research. The reasons for that choice are twofold. Firstly, the literature review and analysis presented in Chapters 2 and 3 indicate that there are many political, cultural, managerial, social and technical issues related to the adoption of integration technologies. These factors appear to be multiple, complex and interrelated. The study of integration technologies adoption in SMEs can not therefore be easily separated from its organisational, technical and cultural context. Thus, there is a need for a research approach that will allow the researcher to understand the process of adopting integration technologies as well as all these factors that influence adopting integration technologies in both SMEs and large companies.

Secondly, as Shaw (1999) reports, small firm research involves the study of human action and behaviour, it is essentially concerned with the nature of reality in the social world. In line with this, Gill and Johnson (1991) claim that researchers need to adopt an approach that allows them to "get close" to participants, penetrate their internal logic, and interpret their subjective understanding of reality. Moreover, as the social world can not be reduced to isolated variables, such as space and mass, it must be observed in its totality. According to the literature, findings produced by positivist approaches are generalisable only to the extent that the conditions under which data are collected exist in the social world (Borch and Arthur, 1995; Brown and Butler, 1995). Therefore, to study the adoption of integration technologies by SMEs, there is a need for a research approach that allows small firms to be viewed in their entirety and permits researchers to get close to participants, penetrate their realities, and interpret their perceptions (Brown and Butler, 1995). Hence, an interpretive research approach has been selected.

Having discussed the reasons for selecting the interpretive research approach, the theoretical foundations of this approach are described in the next section to identify their implications for the research design.

4.2.3 Theoretical Foundations of Interpretive Research

According to Gubrium and Holstein (2000), interpretive theory has diverse conceptual bases. These range from Schutz (1967) development of social phenomenology to the empirical concerns derived from ethnomethodological research programmes developed by Garfinkel's (1967) early studies, and the studies of talk and interaction. Since then, the theory has been extensively used in a number of disciplines such as psychology, sociology, anthropology, feminist studies and history (Schwandt, 2000).

According to Walsham (1995a), interpretive research is continuously gaining ground in the IS field as a methodological approach that can support IS research. Klein and Myers (1999), in their effort to set some principles for conducting interpretive field studies in information systems, have selected hermeneutics and phenomenology as the philosophical basis for their analysis. Indeed phenomenology and hermeneutics are two philosophical strands that are embedded in interpretive thinking (Schwandt, 2000;

Walsham, 1993). The following section presents the concepts of the two strands that are relevant to this research approach, and will be practically used in the analysis of the research results.

One important notion for this research is that of the hermeneutic circle. According to Schwandt (2000), the hermeneutic circle is based on the following view. To understand the part, the inquirer must grasp the whole (i.e. the complex of intentions, beliefs, and desires of the text, institutional context, practice, form of life, language games, and so on), and vice versa. The notion of the hermeneutic circle has been analysed by a number of researchers to guide interpretive researchers to realise the evolutionary nature of the interpretive process (Bernstein, 1983; Gadamer, 1989; Geertz, 1979). As Geertz (1979) argues, the process of understanding is a continuous dialectical talking between the most local detail and the most global structure in such a way as to bring both into view simultaneously. In line with this, the research covered in this thesis was undertaken for a long period of time and, as will be shown in Chapters 5 and 6 the interpretation of the field studies are made at a detailed as well as at a more general level.

The second hermeneutic notion relevant to this research is based on the idea that socio-historically inherited bias or prejudice is not regarded as a characteristic or attribute that an interpreter must strive to get rid of, or manage to come to a clear understanding of it (Schwandt, 2000). More specifically, according to Gadamer (1989), traditions shape what people are and how people understand the world, and the attempt to step outside the process of traditions would be like trying to step outside our own skins. In other words, understanding requires the engagement of one's biases. In this thesis, the personal view of the author is expressed during the interpretation in an effort to explore the author's expertise for analysing the results.

In the next section, the nature of the qualitative research approach is described in order to justify its relevance to this research.

4.3 Justifying Use of Qualitative Research

The simplest way to define qualitative research is to describe it as a type of research which involves interpreting non-numerical data (Miles and Huberman, 1994). Van (1983) defines qualitative methods in a more appropriate way as "an array of interpretive techniques which seek to describe, decode, translate and otherwise come to terms with the meaning, not the frequency of certain more or less naturally occurring phenomena in the social world" (p. 9). Denzin and Lincoln (1994) also propose that qualitative research is multi-method in focus, involving an interpretive, naturalistic approach to its subject matter. These definitions here imply that qualitative researchers study things in their natural environment, and they understand events in terms of meanings.

According to the literature, the term 'interpretive' research is frequently used interchangeably with 'qualitative' research (Galliers, 1992; Schwandt, 2000; Walsham, 1995a). Hakim (1987) also reports that qualitative research tends to be used most heavily in disciplines where the emphasis is on description and explanation (such as psychology, sociology and social anthropology), rather than on prediction (as in economics). However, some researchers such as Denzin and Lincoln (1994) support qualitative research as cross-cutting disciplines, fields and subject matter. There are a number of concepts, traditions and assumptions related to qualitative research. These include traditions such as positivism, post-positivism, and many perspectives and methods connected to cultural and interpretive studies. Myers (1997) also supports that qualitative research may or may not be interpretive, depending upon the underlying philosophical assumptions of the research, and suggests that qualitative research can be positivist, interpretive, or critical.

In order to gain a clearer understanding of qualitative research, it is necessary to compare its basic purpose and focus to those of quantitative research. The differences mainly result from the positivist perspective of quantitative research (the belief that the world can be measured, understood, and generalised about) versus the non-positivist perspective of qualitative research (the belief that the world cannot be generalised about). (See Table 4.1 for a further description).

Table 4.1 Differences between Qualitative and Quantitative Research

Sources: Galliers (1992); Schwandt (2000); Walsham (1995a); Denzin and Lincoln (1994)

Characteristic	Quantitative Research	Qualitative Research
Approach	Deductive	Inductive
Purpose	Theory testing, prediction, establishing facts, hypothesis testing	Describing multiple realities, developing deep understanding, capturing everyday life
Research Focus	Isolates variables, uses large samples, is often anonymous to participants, uses tests and formal instruments	Examines full context, interacts with participants, collects data face-to-face from participants
Research Plan	Developed before study is initiated, structured, formal proposal	Begins with an initial idea that evolves as researcher learns more about participants and setting, flexible, tentative proposal
Data Analysis	Mainly statistical, quantitative	Mainly interpretive, descriptive

The qualitative research approach is selected in this research since a main assumption of this approach is that qualitative researchers study things in their natural settings, attempting to understand phenomena in terms of the meanings that people bring to them (Denzin and Lincoln, 1994). The qualitative paradigm recommends that researchers observe human behaviour and action as it occurs in "mundane" everyday life (Schutz, 1967). The research presented in this thesis focuses on the factors that influence the decisions of SMEs and large organisations when adopting integration technologies. As small firm, large organisations and IS research involves the study of human action and behaviour, it is essentially concerned with the nature of reality in the social world (Shaw, 1999). Therefore, the principle of scientific methods, e.g. quantitative methods applied to the study of people is questioned, hence a qualitative approach is suggested. Additionally, Marshall and Rossman (1999) describe the types of research for which qualitative research would be appropriate:

- Research that examines in depth complexities and processes.

- Research on little-known phenomena or innovative systems.

- Research that seeks to explore where and why policy and local knowledge and practice are at odds.

- Research on informal and unstructured linkages and processes in organisations.

- Research on real, as opposed to stated, organisational goals.

- Research that can not be carried out experimentally for practical or ethical reasons.

- Research for which relevant variables have yet to be identified.

This research also can be categorised as one of those that study in-depth the complexities of the integration technologies' adoption process, examining a new phenomenon while the linkages among the organisations involved in the process are highly unstructured. In other words, rich empirical data is required to provide more understanding regarding the integration adoption process. The need for rich empirical data indicates that the use of qualitative research methods is appropriate, since they allow examining in-depth processes. Additionally, it is useful to notice that the qualitative research approach has been used in a number of studies presented in Chapter 2 related to integration technologies adoption, for example Themistocleous (2002) and Iacovou *et al.* (1995).

In addition, Putney and Green (1999) support that the qualitative research approach provides many benefits, such as: (1) qualitative approaches have provided ways of transcribing and analysing the discursive construction of everyday events, of examining the consequential nature of learning within and across events, and of exploring the historical nature of life within a social group or local setting; (2) qualitative research has also provided insights into the knowledge needed by members of a group to participate in socially and academically appropriate ways; (3) qualitative research provides information about why and how miscommunication among actors occurs, particularly when such actors are members of different groups; and (4) qualitative approaches and the theories guiding them have also made us aware of different voices and the need to consider whose voice will be represented.

However, the qualitative research approach presents a number of drawbacks, which should be taken into consideration when adopting it. Disadvantages include the fact that qualitative data have certain, rather problematic characteristics, which set them apart from quantitative data (Miles and Huberman, 1994). Qualitative data are usually predominantly textual, with a richness that can be lost when aggregation or summarisation occurs. The data can be fairly unstructured and unbounded, as they concern people' behaviour and attempting to understand their perception of a particular situation. It is often longitudinal, to a greater or lesser extent, as the observations may continue for an extended period of time. Interviews maybe repeated at intervals of a few days, weeks or months. However, Lee (1991) identified the disadvantages of qualitative analysis as a lack of controllability, deductibility, repeatability, and generalisability.

Smithson and Cornford (1996) found that there are more drawbacks to qualitative research. As the research uses a small number of cases (perhaps only one case), it is difficult to generalise this to a wider range of situations. Secondly, since the data are rich and complex, it means that they are open to a number of interpretations, so that researcher bias is a constant danger. Thirdly, researchers involved in dynamic cases where the situation is changing frequently, face inherent problems in trying to make controlled observations, controlled deductions (e.g. using mathematical and statistical methods), and predictions. This causes problems for the validity and verifiability of the research.

Bearing these points in mind, and due to the epistemological stance being followed in this thesis, qualitative research was selected to be most suitable for this research. The reasons for selecting this approach are based on the following assumptions:

- The first of these is what academic researchers refer to as the ontological issue. This means how people view their world, what they see as reality (i.e. their natural settings). The researcher thus attempts to understand a phenomenon (e.g. integration technologies adoption in SMEs) in terms of the meanings that people bring to it (Denzin and Lincoln, 1994).

- A qualitative approach will allow the research on little-known phenomena like integration adoption in SMEs, and in-depth examination of adoption processes and its complexities. This will also allow the researcher to seek to explore where and why policy and local knowledge and practice are at odds. In addition, the research described in Chapters 1, 2, and 3 is not appropriate to be carried out experimentally, as it is neither a technical nor a programming development research.

- As explained in Chapters 2 and 3, integration technologies (e.g. Web Services and EAI) are a state of the art technology with limited literature and research. Thus, qualitative research will support the researcher in studying integration technologies in their natural settings, and learning from practice. This will allow an understanding of the nature and the complexity of the integration technologies adoption process in SMEs and large organisations.

- Many proponents of the qualitative paradigm suggest radical approaches to generalisation (Hill and McGowan, 1999). The key issue here though is how one is to generalise from one or two non-randomly selected cases. The issue regarding generalisation is overcome by using Walsham's (1995b) comments in that interpretivist case studies offer four types of generalisations, thereby overcoming this particular issue. The bias that is considered to be a danger in using the qualitative research approach can be overcome by data triangulation.

Based on the research assumptions and approaches presented to this point, the adoption of qualitative research for this study seemed a useful approach to the acquisition of a better understanding of the phenomena under investigation. In the next section, the qualitative research process will be discussed.

4.4 Selecting Research Strategy

Having justified the use of interpretivism as an epistemological stance, and of the qualitative research approach and its process, this section focuses on selecting an appropriate research strategy. Galliers (1992) reports that research strategy is the means of going about one's research, taking on a particular style, and utilising different research methods to collect data. Therefore, to decide on a strategy that would dictate the way in which data are collected and analysed, different research strategies must be reviewed. Their characteristics should be identified, and a research strategy should be justified in light of these study characteristics.

4.4.1   Selecting and Justifying Use of Case Study Strategy

Klein and Myers (1999) report that case study research is accepted as a valid research strategy within the IS research community. Case study represents a way to systematise observation, and aims for in-depth understanding of the context of a phenomenon (Cavaye, 1996). The strategy is versatile and open to a lot of variation, and it can be carried out taking a positivist or an interpretivist stance (Stake, 2000). Benbasat et al.(1987) and Yin (1994), among others, suggest that a case study is an intensive examination of a phenomenon in its natural setting, employing multiple methods of data to gather information from one or more entities (e.g. people, groups or organisations). Data are collected by interviews, observation, questionnaires, and written materials. The main characteristics of case studies, as summarised by Benbasat et al. (1987) are:

- Phenomenon is examined in a natural setting.

- Data are collected by multiple means.

- One or few entities are examined.

- The complexity of the unit is studied intensively.

- Case studies are more suitable for the exploration, classification and hypothesis development stages of the knowledge building process; the investigator should have a receptive attitude towards exploration.

- No experimental controls or manipulation are involved.

- The investigator may not specify the set of independent and dependent variables in advance.

- The results derived depend heavily on the integrative powers of the investigator.

- Changes in site selection and data collection methods could take place as the investigator develops new hypotheses.

- Case research is useful in the study of 'why' and 'how' questions, because these deal with operational links to be traced over time rather than with frequency or incidence.

- The focus is on contemporary events.

Bonoma (1983) reported that a case methodology is clearly useful when a natural setting or a focus on contemporary events is needed. Similarly, research phenomena not supported by a strong theoretical base may be fruitfully pursued through case research. A rich natural setting can be fertile ground for generating theories. The selection of case study strategy has been based on the fact that case studies attempt to examine contemporary phenomena in real-life contexts, which is the case for this research.

Moreover, both Yin (1994) and Bonoma (1983) discuss the usefulness of the case approach in various phases of research. Yin (1994) suggests that there are different types of case study, such as exploratory, descriptive and explanation, depending on whether they are used to answer what, how and why research questions, respectively. Based on this terminology, the case study followed in this thesis can be classified as exploratory. The reasons for this are:

- The research focuses more on questions of the *what* type (e.g. what are the factors which influence the adoption of integration technologies in SMEs and large organisations?).

- A case study exploratory investigation was performed in parallel to the literature review process. The data found from this exploratory study were then used to refine the identified research questions and support their identification of research question.

Exploratory case studies like the one presented in this thesis are useful for theory building, as they are valuable in developing and refining concepts for further study. Roethlisbeger (1977) suggests that case study research is particularly appropriate for certain types of problems, such as those in which research and theory are at their early formative stages. As stated in Chapters 2 and 3, there is limited literature regarding the adoption of integration technologies by SMEs. In addition, EAI and Web Services are emerging technologies and new areas with limited literature. Based on the above discussion, the use of a qualitative case study strategy is considered appropriate for studying the phenomena of integration technologies adoption in SMEs and large organisations.

4.4.1.1 Single and Multiple Case Studies

Yin (1994) claims that a primary distinction in designing case studies is between single and multiple case designs. This means the need for a decision, prior to any data collection, on whether a single case study or multiple cases are going to be used to address the research questions. Central to case research design is the decision to include one or several cases in the project. Most research efforts require multiple cases, but single cases are useful in specific instances. Yin (1994) suggests single case study is appropriate if:

- It is a *revelatory* case, i.e., it is a situation previously inaccessible to scientific investigation.

- It represents a *critical case* for testing a well-formulated theory.

- It is an *extreme* or *unique* case.

Bonoma (1983) claims that single case study projects are most useful at the outset of theory generation and late in theory testing, which is not the case for this research. As Benbasat et al. (1987) and Bonoma (1983) suggest, a single case used for exploration may be followed by a multiple case study. Therefore, in the light of the characteristics of this research, a single case study will not be appropriate.

Multiple case studies enable the researcher to relate differences in context to constants in process and outcome (Cavaye, 1996). According to Miles and Huberman (1994), multiple case studies can enhance generalisability and deep understanding and explanation. Benbasat *et al.* (1987) also suggest that multiple case designs are desirable when the intent of the research is description, theory building, or theory testing, which is the case for the research proposed in this thesis. Multiple-case designs allow for cross-case analysis and the extension of theory. Additionally, multiple cases yield more general research results. Admittedly, multiple cases will not provide the 'richness' of data that a single case study can do. Multiple cases are often considered more compelling, and the overall study is therefore regarded as being more 'robust' (Herriott and Firestone, 1983). This is because multiple case study strategy allows the investigation of a number of viewpoints coming from different sources, and thus a more systematic and constructive use of integration technologies adoption analysis, which forms an essential theoretical basis for this research. Thus, based on the discussion here, multiple cases are proved more appropriate for the proposed research.

Yin (1994) suggests the logic underlying the use of multiple case studies are (1) predicts similar results (a literal replication), or (2) predicts contrasting results, but for predictable reasons (a theoretical replication). The number of case studies conducted will depend on how much is known about the phenomenon, and how information can be uncovered for conducting additional cases (Dyer *et al.*, 1991). Yin (1994) suggests that the ability to conduct 6 or 10 case studies, arranged effectively within a multiple case design, is analogous to the ability to conduct 6 to 10 experiments on related topics. A few cases (2 or 3) would be literal replications, whereas a few other cases (4 to 6) might be designed to pursue two different patterns of theoretical replications. If all the cases turn out as predicted, these 6 to 10 cases, in the aggregate, would have provided compelling support for the initial set of propositions. If the cases are in some way contradictory, the initial propositions must be revised and retested with another set of cases. In the context of the research presented in this thesis, a multiple case study strategy was adopted to investigate 15 integration technologies adoption activities within a project (can be seen as one case study) and 3 follow-up case studies.

4.4.2 Alternative Approaches

The previous sections justified the adoption of an interpretive, qualitative research approach with the use of the case study strategy for this study. This section considers alternative research approaches that can be used to further strengthen the data collection and analysis process for this research.

One alternative concerns the use of quantitative rather than qualitative research methods. For example, the differences between SMEs and large organisations in their integration technologies adoption could be investigated by a questionnaire addressed to SMEs' and larger organisations' managers to acquire their needs and intention for adoption. Such investigation would be a useful as a first step for understanding the integration technologies adoption process to support the research questions identificated in Chapter 3. Rossman (1991) suggests three broad reasons for linking qualitative and quantitative data: (1) to enable confirmation or corroboration of each other through triangulation, (2) to elaborate or develop analysis, providing richer detail, and (3) to initiate new lines of thinking through attention to surprises or paradoxes, 'turning ideas around', providing fresh insight.

Moreover, according to Siber (1973), quantitative data can help with the qualitative side of a study during design by finding a representative sample and locating deviant cases. It can help during data collection by supplying background data, getting overlooked information, and helping avoid 'elite bias'. During analysis, quantitative data can help by showing the generality of specific observations, correcting the 'holistic fallacy' (monolithic judgments about a case), and verifying or casting new light on qualitative findings. Thus, given the objective of this research to identify and understand the factors affecting the integration technologies adoption in SMEs and large organisations, a qualitative research approach is more appropriate to use. However, a quantitative approach is also used as an additional research technique (pilot study) to support the research questions identification and refinement.

The next section presents the techniques used for the collection and the analysis of the empirical material.

4.5 Empirical Research Methodology

The core of a good qualitative research design is the use of a set of procedures that are open-ended and rigorous, at the same time as they do justice to the complexity of the social setting under investigation (Flick, 1998). Janesick (2000) uses the choreography metaphor to describe the qualitative research design and proposes that a qualitative research methodology may follow three stages: (1) warming-up and preparation, (2) stretching exercises, and (3) cooling-down. Similarly, Themistocleous (2002) has developed an empirical research methodology, which is also based on three stages, namely: (1) research design, (2) data collection, and (3) data analysis. Based on these research designs, the researcher describes her research design which is shown in Figure 4.2.

4.5.1   Research Design

At the first stage of "warm-up/research design", the researcher decides the subject, the research questions, and the research strategy. In other words, the researcher first studies the background material to develop an understanding of the research area under investigation. From the literature review, several research issues will be identified for a more focused review. This leads to a specific research area and identifies a research need. Thereafter, a conceptual model is developed to represent the intended empirical research, and the aspects of the model will be investigated through empirical studies. The results of this process in this research are included in Chapters 1, 2, 3 and 4.

The second stage of "stretch exercising/case study data collection" involves some background work and the actual execution of the fieldwork. This stage is mainly reflected in Chapters 3, 4 and 5 of this thesis. In addition, a survey study is introduced

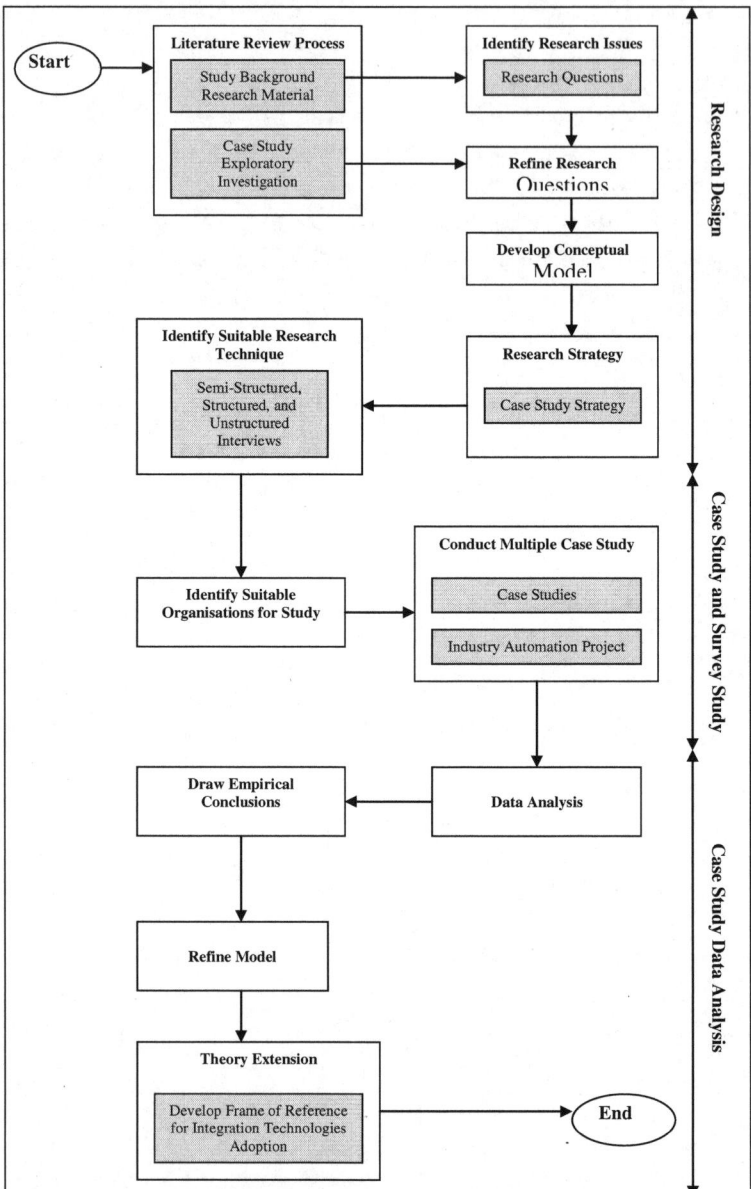

Figure 4.2. Research Methodology

here to support the case study. Finally, during "cooling-down/case study data analysis", the researcher has to decide when to 'ease out' of the research setting and start analysing and presenting the findings. The results of this stage are most obvious in Chapters 6 and 7. These stages are not necessarily sequential, as the researcher has to start analysing the empirical material before the end of the study to be flexible enough to revise the approach as needed. The research methodology for this research is described in Section 4.6.

4.5.2   Data Collection

Multiple data collection methods are typically employed in case research studies. Ideally, evidence from two or more sources will converge to support the research findings. Yin (1994) identifies several sources of evidence that can be used in case based research. These sources include: (a) documentation; (b) archival records; (c) interviews; (d) observation and, (e) physical artifacts. Table 4.2 depicts the strengths and weaknesses of the main sources of evidence in case based research and provides examples of their use in this thesis.

4.5.2.1 Interviews

One of the most important sources of case study information is the interview (Yin, 1994). Interviews are considered to be the main tool of the qualitative researcher for data collection (Denzin and Lincoln, 1998), and one of the frequently used data collection tools, also used for this research. Indeed, interviews are the primary data source for interpretive case studies. According to Walsham (1995b), interview is the method by which the researcher can best access the interpretations that participants have regarding the actions and events under investigation. An added benefit is that it allows the researcher to step back and examine the interpretations of fellow participants in some detail. This is an advantage that other methods may not allow.

There are various forms and types of interviews. According to Denzin and Lincoln (1998), there are three major types: (1) structured; (2) semi-structured, and (3) unstructured. Interviews can also be undertaken in various forms, like personal interviews, face-to-face group interviewing, telephone surveys, etc.. The duration of an interview is also not specific, as it could last as a five-minute conversation on the telephone, or it could take place over lengthy, multiple sessions (Frey and Fontana, 1991).

Table 4.2 Data Collection Methods – Strengths, Weaknesses and Use in this Study

Source of Evidence	Strengths	Weaknesses	Use of Sources in this Study
Documentation	• Stable - can be reviewed repeatedly • Unobtrusive - not created as a result of the case study • Exact - contains exact names, references and details of an event • Broad coverage - long span of time, many events and many settings	• Retrievability - can be low • Biased selectivity, if collection is incomplete • Reporting bias - effects (unknown) of bias of researcher • Access - may be deliberately blocked	• Reports from organisations before and after adoption activity • White papers • Reference material downloaded from Internet • Advertising material • Newspaper articles • Deliverables of Industry Automation Project in Taiwan on eBusiness interconnectivity
Archival Records	• {same as above for documentation} • Precise and quantitative	• {same as above for documentation} • Accessibility - for privacy reasons	• Organisational records
Interviews	• Targeted - focuses directly on case study topic • Insightful - provides perceived causal inferences	• Bias due to poorly constructed questions • Response bias • Inaccuracies due to poor recall • Reflexivity - interviewee gives what interviewer wants to hear	• Semi-structured interviews with organisers and participants • Unstructured interviews • Structured interviews
Direct Observation	• Reality - covers events in real time • Contextual - covers context of event	• Time-consuming • Selectivity unless broad coverage • Reflexivity - event may proceed differently because it is being observed • Cost-hours needed by human observers	• Formal and informal meetings with interviewees for gaining further insights
Participant Observation	• {same as above for direct observations} • Insightful into interpersonal behaviour and motives	• {same as above for direct observations} • Bias due to investigator's manipulation of events	• Simple participant • Presentation of research findings and discussions
Physical Artefacts	• Insightful into cultural features • Insightful into technical operations	• Selectivity • Availability	• Hardware and software and equipment used for adoption activities

In the context of this research, interviews constituted the main data source in the cases. The very important source of evidence of this study has been the mixture of structured, unstructured and semi-structured in-depth interviews with the parties involved in the activities under investigation. Structured interviews entail more structured questions, alone the lines of a formal survey. In this research, the structured interviews were based on the interview agenda and survey questionnaire presented in Appendix D and E. Using the interview agenda, the interviewees replied to specific questions regarding integration technologies adoption. The interview agenda focuses on collecting data from the following areas:

- **General Background:** This section attempts to collect general information regarding the organisation under study. Such data include (1) number of employees in organisation, (2) key business of organisation, (3) number of subsidiaries, (4) nature of organisation (e.g. SME or large organisation), (5) turnover, (6) number of customers, (7) market area, (8) company configuration, and (9) competitive strategy of company.

- **Business Information in SMEs:** The main purpose of this section is to collect data (1) related to the influential factors for integration technologies adoption in SMEs (e.g. benefits, barriers, external pressures, etc), and (2) related to integration technologies adoption decisions in SMEs.

- **Business Information in Large Organisations:** The last section of interview agenda aims at collecting data (1) related to the influential factors for integration technologies adoption in large companies, and (2) related to integration technologies adoption decisions in large organisations.

A survey questionnaire was designed as part of a case study and produced quantitative data as part of the case study evidence. It acted as a pilot study to support the research questions analysis presented in Chapter 3. The main purpose of the questionnaire was to explore the differences between SMEs and large organisations regarding their integration technologies adoption. Additionally, the survey was used to prove the appropriateness for selecting qualitative research for this research. (See Appendix D).

Semi-structured interviews took place, using of a semi-structured interview agenda (see Appendix E). This is a focused interview, in which respondents are interviewed for a short time, e.g. an hour. In such cases, the interviews still remain open-ended and take on a conversational manner. The interview process started by the interviewer to say 'Hello', and has introduction of the study at the beginning. The researcher tried to set the tone for the rest of the interview, and with a relaxed atmosphere in which the interviewees feels free to start the conservation under the unfamiliar situation between interviewee, and interviewers. After the open-up, the researcher asked interviewee's agreement to set up the recording equipment, and start the interview. During the process of interviewing, the researcher had monitored the progress and kept a discreet eye on the interviewee, and time. As reported by Scheurich J. (1997) and Delamont S. (1992), a good researcher needs to wind things up within the allotted time, and have covered most of the key issues during the time. If the interviewer can do this job well, the interview process can achieve the aim during the progress of the interview itself. Therefore, during the interview process, the researcher: (1) identified the main points stated and expressed by the interviewee, (2) looked for the logic of what was being said by the interviewee, (3) tried to find out the inconsistencies in the position being outlined by the respondent, (4) picked up the clues when the interviewee's answers just intended to pleased the interviewer; or when the respondents cannot be allowed to say the negative news to the researcher, (5) gave a suitable eye contact throughout the interview, and made a note of non-verbal communication. This process can help the interviewer interpret more things beyond the interview talk.

Unstructured interviews were also used, which dealt with discussions that the researcher had with interviewees, but without using a structured or semi-structured type of interview. The main purpose of such an interview was to corroborate certain facts that the researcher already thought had been established. In addition, using this type of interview helped to clarify some issues derived from structured interviews. In the majority of cases, structured or semi-structured interviews took place in the interviewees' office. Unstructured interviews have an open-ended nature, in which the author asks key respondents about the facts of a matter as well as their opinions about events (Yin, 1994). Using unstructured interviews, some important data regarding the case studies were collected (e.g. inside information regarding resistance to change, politics issues, business complexity, etc.).

Additionally, the collection of the data took place over a period of two and a half years. The author first interviewed the members of the case companies in 2001 using structured and semi-structured interviews (the project had just begun). After that, the interviews took place again with the same case companies in 2002, using semi-structured interviews. In 2004, the author revisited some of the case companies again (the project is now complete and mature). The adoption activities that took place in a different period of time, but were organised by the same parties, gave the researcher the possibility to discuss the same issues with the same people in a different time context. Consequently, the results of the study go well beyond a snapshot of a specific activity in a given time frame, but take into consideration events that took place over a long period of time, as well as views about the past and future of the activities under investigation (see Figure 4.3). In addition, the focus of the first case study is the Industry Automation Project (i.e. project perspective), not the case companies (i.e. organisation perspective).

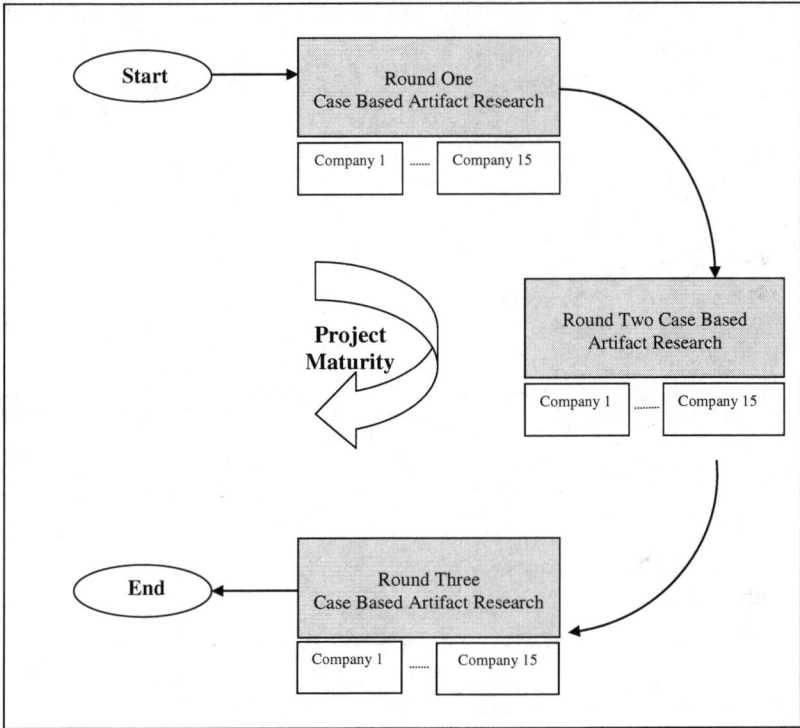

Figure 4.3 Case-Based Artifact Research

In all the case studies, interviewees selected for structured interviews were mainly (1) project manager, (2) MIS department manager, (3) a consultant (internal or external), all of whom have been directly involved in the Industry Automation Project organised and supported by the government. Such stakeholders had an important role during the decision-making process for integration technologies adoption and Industry Automation plan, as well as during the implementation. Therefore, it was considered important to select a cross-section of roles in the Industry Automation project to obtain the views of stakeholders at different levels in the organisations. This supports better understanding of the phenomenon of integration technologies adoption.

When researcher conducts an interview, she/he places a very important role with a good communication skill to create a phenomenon on listening, recoding, and decoding of what interviewees say Mishler E.G. (1986). Therefore, in all the case studies (the project plus the four additional case studies), the interviews were tape-recorded and transcripts prepared as soon as possible after each individual interview. Tape recording supported the researcher in collecting accurate data and interpreting them without time pressures. However, in the cases where interviewees' presence was impossible, telephone interviews were conducted, and filled-in questionnaires from the participants were sent to the researcher by e-mail and surface post. Apart from the structured interviews, during the research there were opportunities to obtain views of other users, managers, developers and government committee members through informal meetings and unstructured interviews.

4.5.3   Analysis of Data

The analysis of the data was taking place during, as well as after the collection of the interviews. The analysis of the data has been based on the conceptual model developed in Chapter 3 (Figure 3.7). Empirical data derived from case studies were triangulated (see Section 4.5.4), and then analysed to draw empirical conclusions. During this study, data analysis involved examining the meaning of people's words and actions. Similar to other studies like Themistocleous (2002) and Papazafeiropoulou (2002), the research findings of this study are inductively derived from empirical data. Empirical evidence was then used to draw conclusions, and resulted in the formulation of a frame of reference for integration technologies adoption in SMEs and large organisations.

4.5.4   Data Triangulation

Another important issue that concerns interpretive researchers is the validity and reliability of the research findings. The term that is usually related to those issues is that of triangulation as a means of validating the results. Janesick (2000) cites four types of triangulation, namely data, investigator, theoretical and methodological triangulation, originally suggested by Denzin (1978), adding a fifth called interdisciplinary triangulation.

Data triangulation means the use of variety of data sources in a study. The second type of triangulation is investigator triangulation, which is the use of several different researchers or evaluators. Theoretical triangulation refers to the use of multiple theoretical perspectives to interpret a single set of data. Methodological triangulation means the use of multiple methods to study a single problem. Finally, interdisciplinary triangulation is related to the investigation of issues related to more that one discipline.

In the context of this research, four types of triangulation are used: (1) data, (2) investigator, (3) theory, (4) methodological, and (5) interdisciplinary. Firstly, data triangulation, as various data sources such as documents, interviews and questionnaires are used. Secondly, the combination of resource-based theory and theoretical diffusion theories to explain the adoption of integration technologies by SMEs leads to theoretical triangulation. Thirdly, the use of multiple data collection methods presented in Section 4.4.2 is methodological triangulation. Finally, the last type of triangulation used by this research is interdisciplinary triangulation, as it falls in different domains such as information systems, technology, management, culture, and small and large organisations.

4.6 Case Study Protocol

According to Yin (1994), the protocol is a major way of increasing the reliability of case study research and is intended to guide the author/researcher in carrying out the data collection from a single-case study (even if the single case is one of several in a multiple-case study). The protocol is important for the following reasons: (1) it keeps the researcher targeted on the subject of the case study, and (2) preparing the protocol forces the researcher to anticipate several problems, including the way that the case study reports are to be completed. In other words, a case study protocol can act as a tool that would operationalise the research, acting as an action plan, and setting rules and regulations by which data would be gathered. Yin (1994) suggests that case studies may have questions at five levels, as presented in Table 4.3. He also added that a case study protocol should have the following sections: (1) overview of the case study project, (2) field procedure, (3) case study questions, and (4) guide for the case study report. Based on the case study protocol sections suggested by Yin (1994), the sub-sections describe the case study protocol outline for this research.

Table 4.3 Questioning Levels in a Multiple Case Enquiry Source (Yin (1994))

Question Level 1	Research Question	Section Reference
Level 1	Questions asked of specific interviewees	4.5.2.1/Appendix E
Level 2	Questions asked of an individual case study	4.6.1 / 4.6.2 / 4.6.3
Level 3	Questions asked across multiple case enquires	4.6.3
Level 4	Questions asked of entire study	1.7 / 7.1
Level 5	Questions about the recommendations and conclusions beyond the scope of the study	7.4

4.6.1   Case Study Overview

Case study overview covers the background information about this thesis, the substantive issues being investigated, and the relevant readings about the issue. In the case of this thesis, the researcher needs to collect data that are required to investigate the adoption of integration technologies by SMEs (e.g. the factors affecting the adoption decision). Thus, the issues needing to be addressed are as follows:

• To identify the integration technologies decision-making process used by the case study organisations.

• To identify those human and organisational factors associated with the adoption of integration technologies, and identify their suitability for inclusion in a conceptual model for integration technologies adoption in SMEs.

• To identify the differences between SMEs and large companies in terms of integration technologies adoption, and identify their suitability for inclusion in the framework proposed in Chapter 3.

• To identify the portfolio of benefits and barriers considered during the introduction of integration technologies.

4.6.2   Fieldwork Research Procedures

As reported in the previous section (Section 4.4.1), case studies are studies of events within a real-life context. This raises an important issue for which properly designed field procedures are essential, since the researcher will be collecting data from people and organisations in their everyday situations, not within the controlled confines of a laboratory, the sanctity of a library, or the structured limitations of a rigid questionnaire Yin, R. K. (1994). Therefore, in a case study, the researcher must learn to integrate real-world events with the needs of the data collection plan. In this sense, the researcher does not have the control over the data collection environment as others might have in using other research strategies. For interviewing key persons, the researcher must cater to the interviewee's schedule and availability, not his/her own. The nature of the interview is much more open-ended, and an interviewee may not necessarily cooperate fully in answering questions. Therefore, the author needs to take into consideration these constraints. Thus, there is a need to have explicit and well-planned field procedures to cope with such events. This section of the protocol presents those procedures that will be employed during the multi-case study investigation. These procedures include the following:

- Gaining access to key organisations or interviewees

- Having sufficient resources while in the field

- Developing a procedure for calling for assistance and guidance

- Making a clear schedule of the data collection activities that are expected to be completed within specified periods of time

- Providing for unanticipated events, including changes in the availability of interviewees, as well as changes in the mood and motivation of the case study investigator

4.6.3   Research Questions

The heart of the protocol is a set of substantive questions reflecting the researcher's actual line of inquiry. These questions are posted to the interviewers (the author), not to an interviewee. The protocol questions, in essence, are the reminders regarding the information that needs to be collected and why. In some instances, the specific questions also may serve as prompts in asking questions during a case study interview. However, the main purpose of the questions is to keep the researcher on track as data collection proceeds. Before starting a particular interview, a case study interviewer (the author) can quickly review the major questions that the interview should address. For this reason, Table 4.4 presents the questions which were developed to support the interview.

4.6.4 Output of Case Study

This section deals with the consideration for the outline, format, or audience of the case study report after the data have been collected. In this thesis, the output of the empirical

Table 4.4 Questions Addressed by Empirical Inquiry

Question Number	Question
1	To what extent do SMEs' integration needs differ from large companies?
2	How come the nature of SMEs be a real obstacle to integration technologies adoption?
3	What is the relationship between integration technologies and their adoption in companies of different size?
4	How can early adoption of integration technologies by the organisations gain competitive advantages?
5	Do SMEs and large companies consider the same factors when taking decisions for the adoption of integration technologies?
6	If the adoption factors for SMEs and large counterparts are thought to be different, to what extent do the integration needs, the nature of the firms, and time influence the different adoption factors?

inquiry and the empirical data analysis are presented in Chapter 5. Due to the large amounts of data which will be gathered during case studies, it is thus useful to consider the format of the research output before collecting data. This is done by creating an interview agenda which addresses issues associated with the factors affecting the adoption of integration technologies by SMEs and large organisations. This approach contributed to the quality of the research output, as it focused on the development of an effective interview agenda for the investigation of those factors.

4.7 Conclusions

This chapter focused on the importance of methodology design employed within this research. The chapter presented the ontological and epistemological assumptions of the interpretive research methodology which forms the basis of this research. It was argued that interpretivism is gaining ground in IS research, and can prove a useful approach which can provide valuable insights in the study of integration technologies adoption phenomena. The use of a qualitative research approach within the case strategy was presented, giving a detailed description of the way this strategy was designed and carried out for this research. Particular emphasis was given to the techniques for the collection of the empirical material, such as interviews and unofficial meetings with the organisations, which were supported by a variety of relevant resources. The chapter also discussed the issue of generalisation from interpretive case studies. Finally, the case study protocol was used as a tool that would operationalise the research, acting as an action plan, and setting rules and regulations by which data were gathered. Based on this protocol, the researcher will use case study perspectives to allow others to relate their experience to the outcome of this research. Thus, the work presented in this thesis will provide a broader understanding of the phenomena of integration technologies adoption. In the next chapter, a detailed description of the empirical context of this research is presented.

Chapter 5: Empirical Context – Case Studies and Preliminary Research Findings

Summary

This chapter presents and analyses empirical data used to test the proposed model for the adoption of integration technologies in SMEs and large organisations. The case studies reported in this chapter act as the basis, i.e. preliminary research, to test the conceptual model proposed in Chapter 3 Figure 3.8 for the adoption of integration technologies in SMEs and large organisations. In doing so, this chapter offers an empirical analysis of different case study perspectives that describe human and organisation behaviour and perceptions during the adoption of integration technologies. Therefore, rather than generalising the outcome of these case studies, it is proposed to examine each case by describing respective approaches to the adoption of integration technologies. The first case study is the Industry Automation Project since the project aim was to push 15 case companies' suppliers to adopt integration technologies to support their supply chains. This project thus well justifies the purpose of this research. The second, third, fourth and fifth case studies are reported in this chapter, too, to further examine the issues related to the conceptual model. This chapter thus serves as a preliminary study to investigate the adoption of integration technologies in SMEs and large organisations, especially in the area of the different adoption factors focused on when taking decisions.

5.1 Introduction

According to Klein and Myers (1999), one of the main principles of interpretive case study research is that of contextualisation. This states that it is important for the interpretive researcher to reflect on the social and historical background of the research setting in order to depict the situation under investigation which emerges. This chapter serves this purpose and gives a detailed description of the empirical context of this research. Consequently, one project, which defined the framework of this research, namely the Industry Automation Programme, is described to depict the context of this study. Additionally, there is some background information about the organisations involved in the case studies and their experience in integration technologies adoption. The settings of the case studies are also presented in detail, focusing on the rationale behind the selection of the specific sites, based on how they could contribute to the overall study. The case studies conducted in parallel with the Industry Automation Programme are then first analysed. Thereafter, four additional case studies were carried out in a large organisation and two SMEs (adopter and non-adopter). The Industry Automation Programme case study and the four additional case studies served as a preliminary study to investigate the adoption of integration technologies in SMEs and large organisations. The aim of this chapter is to examine the adoption parameters identified in Chapter 3 (Figure 3.2), and the conceptual model proposed in Chapter 3 (Figure 3.8), regarding the different factors focused on when taking adoption decisions.

This chapter is structured as follows. In the next section, the Industry Automation Programme is briefly described. The way this research was conducted alongside this project and the reasons for the selection of the specific cases are also explained. Section 5.3 gives details of the practicalities involved in the implementation of the case studies and the principles of interpretive case research on which the collection and analysis of the empirical material were based. The analysis of the case study to examine the parameters identified in Chapter 3 (Figure 3.2), and the conceptual model proposed and shown in Figure 3.8 will be presented in Sections 5.4 and 5.5. In Sections 5.6, 5.7, 5.8, and 5.9, the second, third, fourth and fifth case studies will be reported and analysed.

5.2 Background of Research: Industry Automation Programme

The Industrial Automation project was executed in Taiwan by the Ministry of Economic Affairs, Technology Department. The government started a 2-year project to expedite the e-process of the information industry in 1999. The Industrial Automation Programme aimed at helping information industries construct a basic infrastructure of supply chains. The main goals of this programme were to establish Business-to-Business e-commerce operation capability in the IT industry to enhance the Taiwan IT industry's core competence, and to push forward 2,500 SMEs in the IT industry to establish operation capability. Meanwhile, to overcome the problems while promoting e-commerce in the IT industry, and serve as the reference for promotion in other industries. Helping the predominant company to set up the international open standard and technology, providing on-line training and education course for its suppliers, and encouraging IT service companies to provide the general solution and Application Service Provider (ASP) service for Taiwan SMEs are also important goals.

On one hand, the programme was for those international buyers whose annual purchasing of information products was over 1.5 billion US dollars. Those companies then associated with domestic information and electronic service industries to form the supply systems. After that, IBM, HP, and Compaq passed the committee's review and set up three e-supply chains of the procurement stage. On the other hand, it was for those domestic information industries with annual revenues over 10 billion dollars. They entered into an alliance with domestic information component suppliers to form other systems. There were 15 Taiwanese local companies which were approved to join this project.

The findings of this study were used as a basis (i.e. preliminary research) to investigate the adoption of integration technologies in SMEs and large organisations since there are both large companies (e.g. focal companies) as well as SMEs (e.g. suppliers) involved, and integration technologies were used to integrate their supply chains. Additional information was obtained from four more case studies (one large organisation and three SMEs – adopter and non-adopters) , which act as second stage case studies, and this will be reported in Sections 5.6, 5.7, 5.8 and 5.9. Figure 5.1 shows the structure of the case studies undertaken in this research.

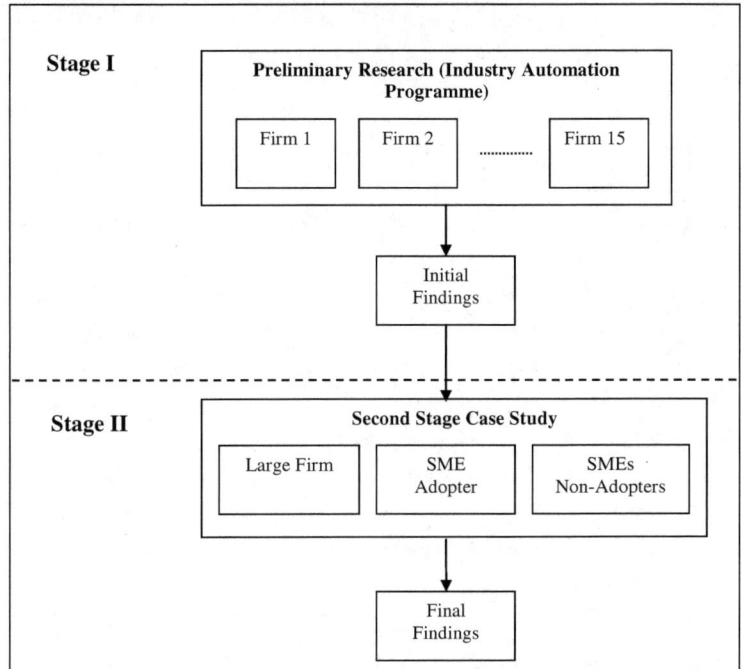

Figure 5.1 Two Stages Case Study Structure of Research

The decision to design this research around two stages of case study is based on the conceptual models presented in Chapter 3 Figures 3.2 and 3.8, where the intention is to examine the parameters affecting the integration technologies adoption in SMEs and large organisations along with the different factors are focused on when taking adoption decisions. For that purpose, the first stage serves as the initial investigation, as the large number of companies under investigation helped the identification of parameters and examination processes (since there are 15 large case-companies and a number of SMEs suppliers involved in the first case study project). In second stage case studies, a more in-depth analysis of the issues under investigation is performed to further examine and analyse the adoption factors, which involved four case studies. According to Yin (1994), having more than two cases could strengthen the findings.

The next sections comprise a detailed description of the Industrial Automation Programme, which constitutes the empirical framework of the first part of case study of this research.

5.3 Case Study One - Industrial Automation Programme

The Industry Automation Programme is executed in Taiwan by the Ministry of Economic Affairs, Technology Department, and started on 3rd June 1999. The main goals of this programme are to establish B2B e-commerce operation capability in the IT industry to enhance Taiwan IT industry's core competence and to push forward 2,500 SMEs in IT industry to establish operation capability; meanwhile, to overcome the problems while promoting e-commerce in the IT industry and serve as the reference for promotion in other industries. This e-commerce grant programme of the IT industry is divided into two categories as A-Plan and B-Plan, where A-Plan is for the International Procurement Office (IPO) of foreign companies, and its annual procurement amount should be over 1.5 billion USD[5]. The company proposed its e-commerce plan with its supply chain companies and other famous Taiwan IT service companies. The emphasis of the programme is to enhance the B2B e-commerce operation capability between Taiwan main IT product suppliers and international buyers. Besides, helping domestic companies to set up international open standard, and training and educating local suppliers are also important goals. Three companies, IBM, HP, and COMPAQ, have been approved for the A-Plan (Yuan, 2000).

B-Plan which the case study is focused on is however for domestic predominant companies of the supply chain, which is manufacturing IT products or key components and its annual revenue should be over 10 billion N.T Dollars. Besides, it should have over 100 suppliers of components, and forms the complete supply chain. The emphasis of B-Plan is to help construct the B2B e-commerce operation capability between the predominant company and its own suppliers. Moreover, helping the company to set up the international open standard and technology, providing an on-line training and education course for its suppliers, and encouraging IT service companies to provide the general solution and Application Service Provider (ASP) service for Taiwan SMEs are also important goals. The grant policy lays special responsibility on the predominant company for the cost of application set-up and upgrade for developing the e-commerce system between suppliers. There are 15 Taiwanese local companies that have been approved for the B-Plan (Yuan, 2000). At last, 15 systems came into existence, together with more than 1,800 suppliers to set up e-supply chains of procurement. The system connections between the case companies and their suppliers are shown in Figure 5.2.

---

[5] 30 N.T. Dollars = 1 U.S. Dollar

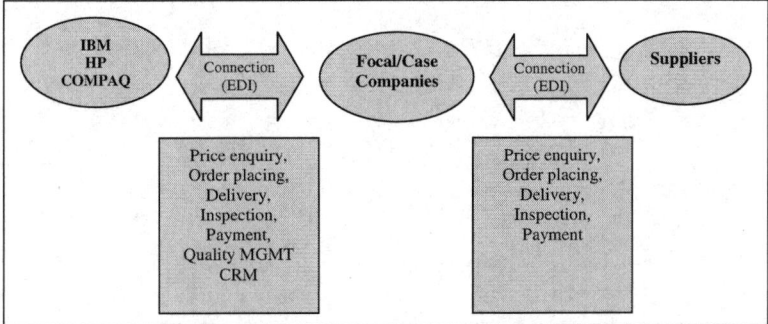

Figure 5.2 Content of Industry Automation Programme

The interconnection between the buyers, customers and suppliers are based on EDI over Internet technology. EDI is one of the integration technologies as defined in Chapter 2 Section 2.2.3. EDI over Internet technology is used for the following reasons:

- Internet software and online marketplace (eMarkets) have provided a platform for collaboration beyond what was achievable in the past. The Internet provides inexpensive connection, an open and scalable architecture, and common software and communication standards to support interoperability between the islands of information residing throughout the supply chain.

- EDI is essentially the foundation of eCommerce. EDI was developed in the 1970s by large corporations to facilitate the computer-to-computer exchange of standard business documents between trading partners. These documents (purchase orders, confirmations, shipping notices and invoices) are typically transmitted over private, secure networks known as VANs. Although EDI helps reduce transaction costs, it typically requires human intervention to process the documents, and often requires manual data re-entry. EDI does not support the purchase decision process, and the expensive VAN costs have excluded smaller companies from participating (see Section 2.2.3). Table 5.1 shows the disadvantages of EDI against the advantages of e-commerce-based EDI.

Table 5.1 EDI Disadvantages vs. EDI over Internet Advantages

Source: Case Companies from Industry Automation Programme

EDI Disadvantages	e-Commerce Based EDI Advantages
• Not suited for many buyers and suppliers • Does not support real-time interactions between trading partners (i.e. order status) • Primarily used for selected direct goods (high dollar volume with few suppliers) • Requires same proprietary software on both ends	• Automates both sides – buyer and supplier • Internet platform enables open marketplaces or trading communities • Automates approval process • Eliminates paperwork • Enforces purchasing policies • Reduces need for point-to-point integration • Inexpensive Web browser user interface

Usually, before enterprises implement the business-to-business integration (i.e. inter-organisational integration), they need firstly to integrate their internal information systems. This is called the Enterprise Application Integration, i.e. EAI (Linthicum, 2001), (see Section 2.2.4 for more details on EAI). EAI can be classified into 3 categories as reported by Themistocleous (2002): (1) intra-organisational application integration, e.g. ERP systems, (2) hybrid application integration, e.g. business to consumer, and (3) inter-organisational application integration, e.g. supply chain. Since inter-organisational application integration is the focus for the Industry Automation project, it is expected that most of the case companies have adopted EAI technology as well. This is investigated in more detail later. Since EDI and EAI are the integration technologies and both suppliers (SMEs) and focal companies (large organisations) were involved in the project, the Industry Automation project thus well justifies the aim of this research reported in Section 1.7. Therefore, the Industry Automation project is used in this thesis to investigate the adoption of integration technologies by SMEs and large organisations.

5.3.1   Background to Case Companies' Integration Problems and Motivations to Integration Technologies Adoption

Diversifying into complex products has increased case companies' communication requirements. These requirements are already complex. For example, case companies need to work with more than 500 suppliers and dozens of customers, but must now also cope with an increasing pace of change that has seen product life cycles shortened considerably. It is therefore now essential for case companies to be able to understand the status of their suppliers and the impact of that status on their own manufacturing processes, so customers can be assured they will receive products in a timely manner.

Efficiency and visibility decide the competitiveness of a supply chain system. The survival game is competing by supply chain systems instead of individual companies. Which supply chain system has better integration capability, the more chips it owns to win the game (Chen et al., 2004).

5.3.1.1 Poor EDI-ERP Integration

Case companies ought to address their communications issues through the use of EDI systems for the various suppliers of, for example, motherboard components, etc.. This solution did not, however, deliver substantial benefits, as few suppliers had IT infrastructure of sufficient complexity to operate EDI. Nor did the EDI system selected by case companies interface well to the ERP systems operating their manufacturing systems, or those used by some of their suppliers. This lack of integration hampered the hoped-for transparency that would facilitate the enhanced levels of customer service required. This lack of integration forced case companies to communicate with some suppliers manually, by fax or telephone. Manual communication was even required for those suppliers operating their own ERP systems, a situation deemed unacceptable in a quest to reach the standards required by customers. Thus, case companies and their suppliers and customers are seeking for open, standards-based communication. This was how the Industry Automation Programme started.

The case companies therefore decided they must put in place systems that would allow electronic procurement to as many suppliers as possible, while also providing links to customers and partners. Hence, they decided that their traditional EDI procurement mechanisms must be replaced by a B2B e-commerce mechanism, and its replacement must be standards-based, as only by adopting standardised data interchange mechanisms would they be able to meet the future needs of any possible type of supply chain integration. To address these issues, the case companies worked with their suppliers to ensure they adopt the RosettaNet[6] standards to describe electronic transactions and implement this standard in their ERP systems.

---

[6] RosettaNet which has been used in this "A, B Plan" programme is an XML-based standard built for the use in the IT industry. RosettaNet is a "global business consortium" creating the electronic commerce framework to align processes in the IT supply chain. Founded in 1998, RosettaNet is an independent, self-funded, non-profit consortium dedicated to the development and deployment of standard electronic commerce interfaces to align the processes between IT supply chain partners on a global basis.

5.3.1.2 Advantages of Web-Based Procurement

In the 1990s, the adoption of Internet Protocols (IP) became more prominent in the business-to-business e-commerce market, and has greatly expanded the ability to exchange information electronically among trading partners. As a result, EDI is now a subset of the more pervasive e-commerce market, an industry that has grown to include electronic catalogues, Web storefronts, information portals, digital markets, and more.

- **Sell-Side.** Initially, this period of e-commerce is centred on the websites of suppliers. Companies like Amazon and Cisco post product catalogues on their websites so customers can browse, search and order online (both B2B and B2C). Some companies use this strategy to support existing distribution channels, while others use it to initiate a direct sales model. Whether you believe intermediaries (i.e. channel partners) will continue to add value, or that manufacturers will do more direct selling, this phase of e-commerce has certainly allowed new business models to emerge, such as configure-to-order and direct-shipment.

- **Buy-Side.** Recently, companies like Commerce One have pioneered a new phase of e-commerce – Web-based procurement. These applications automate the buying process, including product evaluation and selection, internal purchasing reviews, routing and approval, and some post-sales support. Web-based procurement is engaging large and small companies, primarily for non-production goods (e.g. office supplies and computers). The main advantages of automating the procurement process are outlined in Table 5.2.

Table 5.2 Advantages of Web-Based Procurement

Advantages of Web-Based Procurement
• Reduces administrative and supplier costs
• Stems "maverick buying"
• Lowers inventories
• Tracks buying activities
• Consolidates orders
• Reduces lead times
• Saves internal process time

5.3.1.3 Competition

Industries in Taiwan have gained benefits of acquiring technology for decades. Through this continuing acquiring and adaptation process, the thrust of industrial development in the past decade has created a closely knit and very competitive industry verticalisation, especially in hi-tech manufacturing and semiconductor industries, which represent very interdependent industry webs, with many buyers and many suppliers right in Taiwan, and with increasing international business-to-business relationship. While acquiring technology is not a panacea for all, the reality is, for major manufacturers with active market development outside of Taiwan or those who have very close business relationship with partners overseas, the demand for acquired technology is higher, and sometimes becomes an indispensable part of business infrastructure. While the domestically available technology and services have made an enormous stride in its quality and market acceptance, and play a dominating role in the overall economy in Taiwan, acquired technology, technological products and services will continue to play an important role in supporting the fast growth of key industries in Taiwan.

In the realm of business IS, the acquired technology ranges from high-performance business servers and networking (the 'e-infrastructure') to enterprise solutions such as in ERP, Customer Relationship Management (CRM), manufacturing execution system, product development management, supply chain execution, supply chain management, and business-to-business/business-to-customer eMarketplace applications and models.

The rapid growth of the Internet as a medium through which businesses can communicate, streamline business processes, and transact more efficiently, has elevated the level of global competition. Escalating market dynamics like time-to-market pressures, high customisation demands, and increased dependence on outsourcing have elevated business-to-business collaboration to core competency status. Companies must not only find more efficient ways to share information internally, they must also find ways to collaborate with their business partners, suppliers and customers. Therefore, in this new Internet economy, it is not about Company A vs. Company B, it is about supply chain A vs. supply chain B.

5.3.2   Identification of Types of Connections

Referring to the Industry Automation Programme, the adoption of EDI (without any labour involved) to support supply chains was not a practical way for SMEs. Instead, they employed many other types of interconnections based on the EDI technology and RosettaNet standards. In total, 7 types of interconnection were identified by the researcher including 3 main types, A, B and C, and their subtypes. The types of connection between the suppliers and the core manufacturers classified by the researcher into three main types: Type A (Application to Application, i.e. AP-to-AP), Type B (e-commerce (EC) Turnkey), and Type C (Browser). Those main types were further classified into subtypes which are A, A+, A-, B, B+, C and C+, depending on their level of automation.

Type A - AP to AP: This type of process is to integrate the systems using a standard language – RosettaNet standard. Similar to Web Services standard, RosettaNet standard is an Extensible Mark-up Language (XML)-based standard built for use in the IT industry (RNT, 2001). A standard is necessary so that data and e-Commerce (EC) and other transactional processes operate well across the Web. The XML standard should ease the development of Web pages for EC and other activities that rely on pre-formatted data (Abreu, 2001). XML is the universal format for structured documents and data on the Web (W3C, 2002). XML schema allows Web developers to use a common method for identifying Web data. It also allows developers to transfer more easily formatted data, such as prices, dates and numbers, which are all key to EC, as well as video and audio. Unlike the existing standard, HTML (Hypertext Markup Language), which rigidly defines how Web page elements are displayed with predefined data tags, XML can be used to define what data the elements contain. Developers can write XML tags for specific purposes, allowing Web pages to function like database records (Abreu, 2001).

AP-to-AP connection integration testing can be categorised into three layers: the first is whether the enterprises have established PIP (Partner Interface Process), i.e. the public process between enterprises. PIP™ is to define business processes between supply-chain partners, providing the models and documents for the implementation of standards. PIP includes two enterprise processes: Private Process, and Public Process. Private Process means the enterprise internal business process whereas Public Process means the process between enterprises. The second layer is the enterprises which have not only established PIP, but can also proceed to receiving messages, and the messages are readable. The third layer is the process automation (MOEATD, 2001). For example, once the supplier receives an order called 3A4, this can be translated automatically into a sales order. Type A can be further categorised into three sub-types, A+, A- and A, according to their degrees of automation. The main difference between them is based on whether there are people involved between the EC platform and Enterprise Resource Planning (ERP) when accepting an order.

These connection types further categorised into A+, A and A-, according to their degree of automation. The normal EDI connection is type A+ which has no labour involved, and all the processes are performed automatically. However, in real practice, none of the case companies or their suppliers has adopted this type of connection. This shows that the adoption of EDI by SMEs to support their supply chains is not what we expected as the EDI to EDI (i.e. system to system) connection; instead, they have different ways of using EDI to interconnect with their customers. These types of interconnections used by SMEs have been identified in this research, and are defined as types B and C.

Type B - EC Turnkey: The suppliers install Turnkey software. The core manufacturer (i.e. buyers) can then push its purchase order to the suppliers' Turnkey system. Once the suppliers' server has received the purchase order, two actions will be taken. First, the sales department will be informed about this order, simultaneously it will manually perform the auto check function in the ERP system to check the database and process the order. The invoice will then be generated by the system, but the system will not reply to the manufacturer automatically. Turnkey's output is converted or transferred manually to the supplier's back office system, and the core manufacturer will inform the supplier about the purchase order by e-mail. The important point for type B connection is that the 'Push' method is used. This method does not consider the internal customer's needs. Rather, after processing a batch of units, a given workstation will push the batch to the next workstation, whether they are needed or not. The supplier's operating interface is unitary, and many buyers' orders can be manipulated in this single interface. For type B+, this has provided an information format which can convert or transfer the information into the ERP format in the back office system. However, the data transfer is still manipulated manually. The main difference between type B and its subtypes is whether there is a need to re-type the information into the back office system.

Type C - Browser: The core manufacturers set up a one-to-one supplier Web page. All the process information about the sales orders, delivery information and invoices, etc. can be looked up through browser. This type of connection is normally used when there is a small amount of orders. The manufacturers need to log on to the Internet to check the order information approximately once a day. In addition, the Purchasing Order (PO) information can be downloaded from the browser and saved in Excel or other formats for verification purposes or workflow process. Table 5.3 is a summary of the different types of connection.

5.3.3   Adoption of EAI by Case Companies to Integrate Supply Chains

EAI is used to integrate various systems in an enterprise to link data pieces to form valuable information which can be used to promote information visibility and support decision-making. The information can be managed from product design phase, manufacturing shop floors, supply/demand planning, to logistics execution. All transactions are recorded in the ERP system of an enterprise. Compaq's BusinessBus and

Table 5.3 Summary of Different Types of EDI Connection

Type	Differences between Types		Sub-Type	Differences between Sub-Types
A	Suppliers use 'PUSH method to handle PO.	Connect to back office system using Rosettanet's PIP.	A+	No Labour involved.
			A	Labour involved before confirmation
			A-	Labour involved between EC and ERP
B			B+	Information format provided which can convert or transfer information into ERP format in back office system, but data transfer still manipulated manually.
			B	Information cannot be converted or transferred automatically into back office system, needs to be re-typed into system.
C	Suppliers use 'PULL' method to handle PO. The pull method is driven by the customer. The customer workstation will pull units from its supplier workstation. This, in turn, will authorise production of the next batch at the supplier workstation.		C+	PO information can be downloaded from browser and saved in Excel or in other formats for verification purposes or workflow process.
			C	Manufacturers can check order information through browser.

TIBCO suites are the most popular EAI solutions used in local companies (see Figure 5.3). The case companies reported:

> "The main purpose of adopting EAI is to fulfil Process Automation. In order to be successful in the competition, firstly the enterprises need to integrate their internal resources. Further, the enterprises can then speed up their communication with their partners or customers via Business to Business integration (B2Bi). As by joining Business-to-Business Integration and EAI together is the way to success. The adoption of e-business applications is not enough to allow us to achieve our targets". "The reason for this is that the rapidly changing business environment requires organisations to support flexible and manageable IT infrastructures to gain competitive advantages".

It is for above-mentioned reason that the case companies have adopted B2Bi together with EAI. The case companies' B2Bi and EAI jointed Architecture are shown in Figure 5.4.

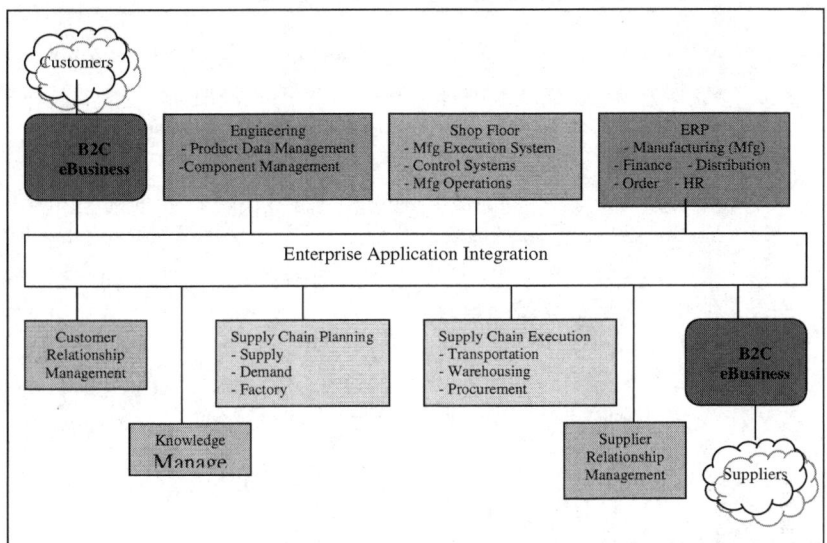

Figure 5.3 EAI Infrastructure Used by Project Companies to Integrate Systems

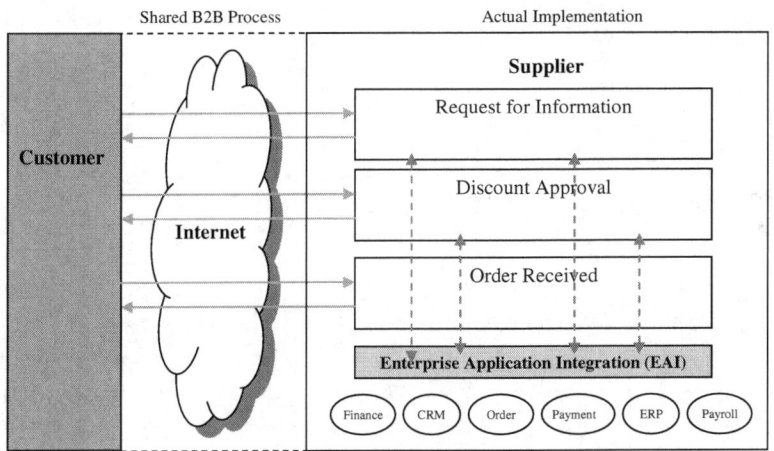

Figure 5.4 Case Companies' B2Bi and EAI Architecture

5.3.4   Industry Automation Programme Results

As a result, there were a total of 3948 suppliers forced to follow the main manufacturers to adopt the e-commerce management style and the majority of them have adopted the type C connection (3375 suppliers) to connect with their main manufacturers (see Figure 5.5). The case companies found that the accuracy of electronic transactions through its supply chain has reduced the amount of stock the company returns to suppliers. With inventory levels lower, the case companies are now more agile and able to respond to new technologies by using the latest most up-to-date components in their products, instead of having to consume inventory they have already acquired but cannot return. Electronic transactions are also consuming less human resource to key or re-key manually into the companies' systems. Additionally, adapting to the e-supply chain has also created a 15000 million US Dollars procurement (i.e. order opportunity) from the important international buyers each year.

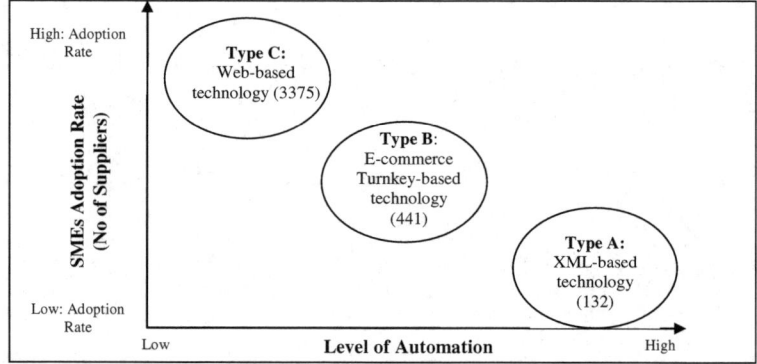

Figure 5.5 SMEs Adoption Rate and Level of Automation

Figure 5.5 shows that Web-based technology is the most popular technology for inter-organisational connection among SMEs (i.e. suppliers). This indicates that most of these SMEs are still not able to achieve a high degree of automation so far, i.e. fully automated systems without involving any labour. The reasons are: (1) suppliers are small-sized enterprises, their technology ability and application level of B2B e-commerce are limited, and the volume of business is smaller (or the product variety of the company is little), (2) most of the raw material productions from the suppliers are not key-production, (3) most of the suppliers produce standard products so they have goods in stock, and (4) the benefit of using this type of connection is conspicuous, and it does not affect the beneficial results of case companies' computerisation. For those suppliers which were able to fully automate their business processes (i.e. able to adopt Type A connection), most of them are larger in size compared to other SMEs suppliers.

5.3.4.1 Benefits of Adopting Integration Technologies to Support Supply Chain

Empirical data derived from the Industry Automation Programme were validated through Key Performance Indicator (KPI) analysis to examine the performance of integrating case companies' supply chains. This section is therefore to analyse and to evaluate the performance, and the effect of using KPI analysis (EuroControl, 2001). A KPI is a Key Performance Indicator that is linked to a business goal. In general, every KPI will have a target value that may change over time. The actual value of the KPI is compared to the target value to determine how much progress has been made towards achieving the business goal (RIS, 2002). KPI data can be entered manually, extracted directly from the attached real-time databases, or the result of complex calculations implemented using the Recalculated module.

The KPIs here on which the overall performance is judged are the volume of purchase, types and numbers of connection, speed, and capital cost. The summary of the KPI analysis is shown in Table 5.4.

According to the figures given by the case companies involved in the Industry Automation Programme, in the purchasing process from the manufacturers to their customers, the average speed in percentage has improved by 15.7% from before using e-purchasing 82.9%, to now 95.9%. For the suppliers to the B-Plan manufacturers, the process speed has improved by 24.2% from the average of 73.25% before, to 92% now. However, the response time for purchasing order has improved by 68.49% from the average of 4.38 days before to 1.38 days now, and the process cycle for purchasing has improved by 58.2%, from the average of 12.13 days before to 5.07 days now. The period of stock stored in the warehouse has shortened by 35.4%, from the average of 31.86 days before to the average 20.57 days now. The stock capital cost has dropped by 31.29%, from the average of 33.4 hundred million N.T. dollars before to 22.95 hundred million N.T. dollars now. The unused raw material stock has decreased 77.41%, from the average of 15.27% to 3.45% now.

Table 5.4 Summary of KPI Analysis

KPIs	Average value before B-purchasing Adoption	Average value before B-purchasing Adoption	Calculation	Improved Ratio (%)
Process from receiving orders to delivering goods (Purchasing Process)				
From B-Plan manufacturers to customers (%)	82.9	95.9	1-(95.9/82.9)*100%	15.7
From suppliers to B-Plan manufacturers (%)	73.25	92	1-(92/73.25)*100%	24.2
Order Handling Process				
Response time for purchasing order (Days)	4.38	1.38	1-(1.38/4.38)*100%	68.49
Process cycle for purchasing (Days)	12.13	5.07	1-(5.07/12.13)*100%	58.2
Stock Capital Cost				
Period stock stored in warehouse (Days)	31.86	20.57	1-(20.57/31.86) *100%	35.4
Stock capital cost (hundred million N.T.)	33.4	22.95	1-(22.95/33.4) *100%	31.29
Unused raw material stock (%)	15.27	3.45	1-(15.27/2.45) *100%	77.41
Purchasing Capital Cost				
Labour used for purchasing process (Days)	9.86	5.86	1-(5.86/9.86) *100%	40.6
Required time for whole purchasing process (Days)	7	3	1-(3/7) *100%	57.1
Purchasing arrangement and handling times (Days)	15.99	6.92	1-(6.92/15.99) *100%	56.7

The labour used for purchasing process has decreased by 40.6%, from the average of 9.86 days per month before to 5.86 days per month now. The required time for the whole purchasing process has shortened by 57.1%, from the average of 7 days before to 3 days now. The purchasing arrangement and handling times have dropped by 56.7%, from the average of 15.99 days before to 6.92 days now.

Based on the discussion above, the benefits of integrating supply chain have been identified by the researcher. According to Themistocleous and Irani (2001), they have identified some benefits upon the implementation of Application Integration. Chen et al.(2003) also have reported some benefits of using integration technologies in SMEs. However, the benefits of integrating supply chain have not been widely investigated. The adoption of integration technologies to support the supply chain management can be seen either as a way to provide efficiency savings, or as a strategic response either driven by necessity or due to competitive pressure. Therefore, the researcher has identified many benefits upon the implementation of supply chain integration by the case companies involved in the Industry Automation Programme. To help enterprises and researchers better understand these benefits, the identified benefits are summarised and classified in Figure 5.6. In the diagram, the benefits are split into two layers. The first layer indicates the main benefits, and the second layer shows the benefits derived from the main ones (i.e. consequences). For example, adopting supply chain integration can help organisations to standardise production, which can result in improved quality control, improved efficiency, and shortened production time.

5.3.5 Industry Automation Programme in Thesis

This research had be carried out in parallel with the Industry Automation project, and tried to investigate further the issues related to integration technologies adoption, which were also addressed by the project. It is important to note that although the Programme constitutes a basis for this research, its findings are not used as de facto and issues related to the e-supply chain are not investigated in this research. The researcher is interested in the issues related to their EDI, EAI and integration technologies adoption. Additionally, as demonstrated in the next chapter, views coming from SMEs (suppliers) and large organisations (focal companies) participating in the project are often criticised. During the operation of the project, its members had the obligation to perform and report about their e-supply chain integration activities. At the same time, they were asked by the researcher to provide further information about their activities in integration technologies adoption in the light of the theoretical findings and research questions described in Chapter 2 and 3. The aim was the in-depth investigation of the integration technologies adoption conceptual model (Chapter 3, Figures 3.2 and 3.8) addressing different factors in SMEs and large organisations in relation to their integration technologies adoption.

As a result, the Industry Automation Programme case study (includes 15 case companies and several of their SMEs suppliers) was conducted in a period of two and a half years, in order to give empirical evidence for an interpretive analysis of the integration technologies adoption process. It was mentioned in Chapter 4 that where the physical presence of the researcher was not possible, telephone interviews with the organisers were conducted, and completed questionnaires from the participants were sent later to the researcher by e-mail and surface post. In Section 5.4, a detailed presentation is given of the case study on 15 companies.

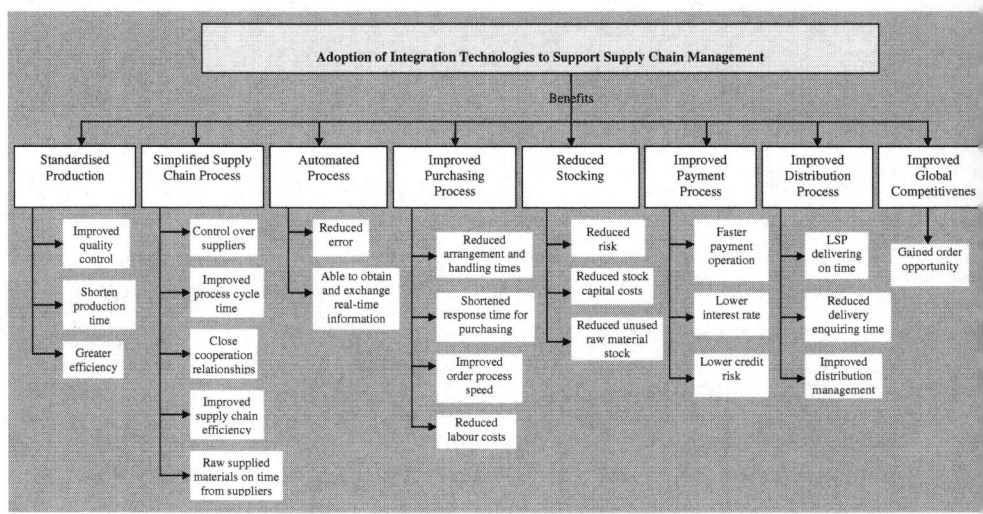

Figure 5.6 Classifications of Supply Chain Integration Benefits

5.4 Case Studies Description

In the previous section, the Industry Automation Programme was presented as the empirical background of this research. It was made obvious that the relevant of the companies to the objectives of this research made them appropriate frameworks for this study. This section includes a detailed description of the way these case studies were conducted within an interpretive and qualitative research approach.

5.4.1 Conducting Interpretive Case Studies Research

As discussed in Chapter 4 case study research is accepted as a valid research strategy within the IS research community. Nevertheless, although a set of methodological principles for case studies of a positivist nature has been formulated by a number of researchers, this is not the case with interpretive case studies (Benbasat et al., 1987; Lee, 1991; Yin, 1994). Klein and Myers (1999) detected this knowledge gap in IS research, and set some principles for interpretive field research, based on the philosophy of hermeneutics. They support that although the definition of a pre-determined set of criteria might violate the emergent nature of interpretive research, the use of some basic standards for conducting and evaluating interpretive research is important and useful. Table 5.5 presents a summary of the seven principles defined by Klein and Myers (1999) as they have been applied for this research.

The application of the principles described above has been made obvious throughout the presentation of this research. In the next section, details concerning the rationale behind the selection of the sites and details about the activities and the organisations under investigation are given.

5.4.2 Site Selection

As mentioned earlier, the unit of analysis during the first stage case study research was the integration technologies adoption conducted during the Industry Automation Programme. The selection of the sites for this interpretive case study research was based on theoretical as well as practical considerations.

At a theoretical level, according to (Benbasat and Zmud (1999), the site selection should be based on the nature of the topic under investigation. For example, research on organisation level phenomena would require site selection based on the characteristics of the firm. For this research, the interpretation of the integration technologies adoption as it

Table 5.5 Summary of Principles for Interpretive Field Research and Application in this Research

Source: Klein and Myers (1999)

Summary of Principles for Interpretive Research	Application of Principles in this Research
1. Fundamental principle of the hermeneutic circle This principle suggests that all human understanding is achieved by iterating between considering inter-dependent meaning of parts and the whole that they form. This principle of human understanding is fundamental to all other principles.	Application of this case study research. Longitudinal manner made application of hermeneutic circle possible. For example, examination of SMEs and large organisations behaviour and activities in different chronological points was useful process for understanding of factor related to timing for integration technologies adoption.
2. Principle of contextualisation Requires critical reflection of social and historical background of research setting, so that intended audience can see how current situation under investigation emerged.	Research background presented in detail in order to offer holistic picture of research context.
3. Principle of interaction between researchers and subjects Requires critical reflection on how research materials (or data) were socially constructed through interaction between researchers and participants.	Researcher's role for this study clearly described as involved researcher. This can lead to rich insight of research context.
4. Principle of abstraction and generalisation Requires relating idiographic details revealed by data interpretation through application of Principles 1 and 2 to theoretical, general concepts that describe nature of human understanding and social action.	Principles of abstraction and generalisation obvious for this research through conceptual model devised (Figures 3.2 and 3.8). Discussion of the findings is made in relation to conceptual model leading to theoretical contribution of research.
5. Principle of dialogical reasoning Requires sensitivity to possible contradictions between theoretical preconceptions guiding research design and actual findings (story which data tell) with subsequent cycles of revision.	Use of this principle is obvious in presentation of final findings, where initial conceptual model based on current research is amended using research results.
6. Principle of multiple interpretations Requires sensitivity to possible differences in interpretations among participants as are typically expressed in multiple narratives or stories of same sequence of events under study. Similar to multiple witness accounts, even if all tell it as they saw it.	In conjunction with the hermeneutic cycle, fundamental for this research. Considerations of multiple interpretations from widest range of SMEs and large organisations have been main focus of this research.
7. Principle of suspicion Requires sensitivity to possible biases and systematic distortions in narratives collected from participants.	Seriously taken into account by this research, as importance of issues under investigation can make SMEs and large organisations put forward views they wish to present to other organisations using researcher as intermediary. Collection of multiple perspectives triangulation has been used to ease effect of this phenomenon on research results.

has been described in Chapter 3 made imperative the selection of a multi-organisational empirical context. At a practical level, the ultimate goal was the investigation of organisations with different viewpoints about integration technologies adoption between SMEs and large organisations, and the examination of factors affecting their adoption.

5.4.3   Organisations Involved in First Stage of Research

The organisations involved in the Industry Automation Programme were interviewed as well as some of their suppliers (mainly SMEs), as shown in Table 5.6. These participants agreed to provide further information about their integration technologies adoption.

Two or three employees from each organisation were typically the interviewees for this research. They were contacted during and after the implementation of integration technologies to support their supply chains activities, while a number of unofficial discussions concerning the issues under investigation took place during the life span of the study. Table 5.7 presents the profile of the interviewees and the number of interviews conducted. In Appendix F, there is a detailed description of each organisation participating in the case study.

Moreover, each case company was also asked to specify what kind of integration technologies they had adopted or were planning to adopt, apart from EDI and ERP. This is reported in Table 5.8. Note that EDI here means EDI over Internet technology instead of the traditional EDI (Van-based) technology.

In the next sections, the analysis is presented of the empirical material from the Industry Automation Programme, which focuses on the parameters affecting the integration technologies adoption in SMEs and large organisations.

Table 5.6 Case Study Companies

Name of Company	Main Product	No. of employees	Turnover (US$)	Capital (US$)	Type of Organisa- tion
ACER Inc	• Note Book Computer	5600	7 billions	0.712 billions	Large Firm
ADI Corporation	• Monitor	1500	-	0.15 billions	Large Firm
Arima Computer Corp	• Note Book Computer	1400	0.57 billions	0.35 billions	Large Firm
ASUSTeK Computer Inc	• Mother Board	58000	7.7 billions	0.91 billions	Large Firm
Chia-Soon Electronics	• Automatic crimping machines	70	-	0.30 millions	SME
Compal Electronics Inc	• Note Book Computer	10000	4.71 billions	1.04 billions	Large Firm
Compeq Manufacturing. Co. Ltd	• PCB	8351	38 millions	0.28 billions	Large Firm
Delta Electronic	• Power Supply	30000	3.01 billions	0.41 billions	Large Firm
First International Computer Inc	• PC	10000	3.3 billions	0.34 billions	Large Firm
Inventec Corporation	• Note Book Computer	25800	3.88 billions	0.64 billions	Large Firm
Micon Technology Corp.	• CRT • LCD monitor • LCD TV	20	-	1.7 millions	SME
MicroStar Inc. (MSI)	• Mother Board	1700	1.7 billions	0.12 billions	Large Firm
MiTAC International Corporation	• PC	22000	10 billions	63 millions	Large Firm
Prohubs International Crop	• Electronic components • Mobile communications • Personal digital equipment • Household electronics	40	-	6.33 millions	SME
PRIMAX Electronics Ltd	• Scanner	5300	1.24 billions	0.11 billions	Large Firm
SAMPO Technology Corporation	• Monitor	5500	4.65 billions	0.4 billions	Large Firm
Sen-Kung Technologies Ltd	• PCB Board • LCD monitor board	60	-	1.51millions	SME
TATUNG Co	• PC	35000	4.32 billions	1.27 billions	Large Firm
Tex-Chu Trading Co. Ltd	• IC components • EMI gasket • Conductive fabric tape	40	-	0.60 millions	SME
Twinhead International Corporation	• Note Book Computer	1200	8.4 billions	85 millions	Large Firm
Yodi Technology Ltd	• Wire Harness • Computer application wire • Photoelectron application • Household electronic application wire • Customised design wire products	35	-	0.93 millions	SME

Table 5.7 Profile of Interviewees in Industry Automation Programme

Organisation	Position of Interviewees in Organisation	Number of Interviews
ACER Inc	• Manager from the MIS department • Project manager • Deputy director	3
ADI Corporation	• Manager from the MIS department • Project manager	2
Arima Computer Corp	• Manager from the MIS department • Project manager	2
ASUSTeK Computer Inc	• Manager from the MIS department • Project manager	3
Compal Electronics Inc	• Manager from the MIS department • Project manager	2
Compeq Manufacturing. Co. Ltd	• Manager from the MIS department • Project manager	3
Delta Electronic	• Manager from the MIS department	2
First International Computer Inc	• Manager from the MIS department • Project manager • Deputy director	3
Inventec Corporation	• Manager from the MIS department • Project manager	2
MicroStar Inc. (MSI)	• Manager from the MIS department • Project manager	2
MiTAC International Corporation	• Manager from the MIS department • Project manager	2
PRIMAX Electronics Ltd	• Manager from the MIS department • Project manager	2
SAMPO Technology Corporation	• Manager from the MIS department • Project manager	2
TATUNG Co	• Manager from the MIS department • Project manager	2
Twinhead International Corporation	• Manager from the MIS department • Project manager • Deputy director	3
SMEs (Suppliers)	• Managers • Technical personnel	6

Table 5.8 Integration Technologies Adopted by Case Study Companies

Key: Adopted (✓), Not adopted (X), Planning to adopt (P)

Name of the Company	EAI	EDI	ERP	Web Services
ACER Inc	✓	✓	✓	✓
ADI Corporation	✓	✓	✓	P
Arima Computer Corp	✓	✓	✓	✓
ASUSTeK Computer Inc	✓	✓	✓	✓
Chia-Soon Electronics	✓	✓	✓	✓
Compal Electronics Inc	✓	✓	✓	✓
Compeq Manufacturing. Co. Ltd	✓	✓	✓	✓
Delta Electronic	✓	✓	✓	✓
First International Computer Inc	✓	✓	✓	✓
Inventec Corporation	✓	✓	✓	✓
Micon Technology Corp.	✓	✓	✓	X
MicroStar Inc. (MSI)	✓	✓	✓	✓
MiTAC International Corporation	✓	✓	✓	✓
Prohubs International Crop	✓	✓	✓	X
PRIMAX Electronics Ltd	✓	✓	✓	✓
SAMPO Technology Corporation	✓	✓	✓	✓
Sen-Kung Technologies Ltd	X	✓	✓	X
TATUNG Co	✓	✓	✓	✓
Tex-Chu Trading Co. Ltd	X	✓	✓	X
Twinhead International Corporation	X	✓	✓	✓
Yodi Technology Ltd	X	✓	✓	X

5.5 Case Studies Analysis

The case study conducted in the first stage case study of this research (Industry Automation Programme and survey investigation) will be analysed in this section. The focus here is on the examination of factors affecting the integration technologies adoption based on a comparative analysis between SMEs and large organisations. The analysis of the cases is accordingly made around 2 clusters corresponding to the conceptual model described in Chapter 3 (Figure 3.8). In the first cluster, parameters affecting the integration technologies adoption in SMEs and large organisations are examined. In the second cluster, the identified parameters are further analysed to examine whether they are appropriate to use to explain the different adoption factors between SMEs and large organisations. The sources used for the analysis of the case study were:

- Description of the integration technologies adoption as part of the Industry Automation Programme deliverables

- Interviews with the SMEs participating in the Industry Automation Programme (where possible)

- Interview with the case companies participating in the Industry Automation Programme

- Informal conversations with organisers and their suppliers involved in the Industry Automation Programme

In the next section, the approach followed by the researcher for the analysis of the empirical material will be described.

5.5.1   Analysing Adoption of Integration Technologies between SMEs and Large Organisations

According to the parameters introduced in Chapter 3 Section 3.2, nature, integration needs, company size, adoption factors for large organisations, adoption for SMEs and time are the parameters for the adoption of integration technologies in SMEs and large organisations. These parameters were based on the research questions found from the existing literature for the adoption of integration technologies. Thus, the analysis strategy followed here relies on the theoretical propositions (e.g. research questions) that led to the case study (Yin, 1994). To examine whether the identified parameters are appropriate to explain the different factors that SMEs and large organisations focus on when taking adoption decisions, the researcher tests and analyses the identified parameters with the empirical material in the following sections.

5.5.1.1 Nature of Organisations

As mentioned in Section 5.3.3, most SMEs are not able to achieve a high level of automation when adopting EDI technology. One of the reasons reported in Section 5.3.3 was that SMEs' technology ability and application level of B2B e-commerce are limited. This shows a low level of adoption in organisations. To further verify this viewpoint, the author interviewed some of the SMEs (i.e. suppliers) involved in the Programme. When asked about their adoption of integration technologies (reasons for adopting or not adopting), they expressed opinions such as:

> *"Unlike large organisations, we do not have many employees or systems that need to be managed, therefore I am not sure whether EAI technology is necessary for us. In this case, cost is a very important issue for us; I think it can be quite expensive to adopt EAI".*

"Adopting standardised data interchange mechanisms with our customers is more useful than integrating the internal systems; as I mentioned before, we do not have many information systems like large companies". "Joining the Industrial Automation Programme does give us some benefits, as we can gain some knowledge on supply chain integration from the case companies".

"We have pressures from our customers (i.e. the case companies). This is why we are trying to adopt standardised data interchange mechanisms with our customers and try to increase efficiency of the procurement process".

When the organisers (large organisations) were asked about their adoption of integration technologies and what integration technologies they have actually adopted and why, they expressed opinions such as:

"We have adopted EDI, ERP, EAI and Web Services, as not having those technologies will become a problem. However, adopting these technologies does not guarantee to increase our competitiveness".

"We are seeking ways to improve our services and improve efficiency so as to provide the best services to our customers. Therefore, we see that adopting integration technologies is a way to improve our efficiency and to solve the integration problem we have encountered".

"Most of our enterprise applications were built to address a specific business need. As enterprises have grown, the need to share information across departments, divisions, and globally throughout the enterprise has become critical. Thus, we are turning to integration solutions to provide a method for interconnecting these distributed and often proprietary silos of information systems".

Based on the findings here, the researcher suggests that the characteristics of SMEs and large organisations are different, and this difference can affect their integration technologies adoption decision-making.

5.5.1.2 Integration Needs

According to the description addressed in Sections 5.3.1 and Section 5.5.1.1 above, it suggests that the reasons for why large organisations (i.e. case companies) adopting integration technologies to support their supply chains are: (1) to support their own manufacturing processes from a point-to-point integration to a centralised infrastructure, so their customers can be assured they will receive products in a timely manner, (2) to retain their competitiveness, (3) to support their future needs of any possible type of supply chain integration, and (4) to fulfil the transparency that would facilitate the enhanced levels customer service required. As for SMEs (i.e. suppliers), the main reason that pushes them to adopt integration technologies was external pressure. The case companies have worked with their suppliers (i.e. SMEs) to ensure they adopt the RosettaNet standards to describe electronic transactions, and implement this standard in their ERP systems. This indicates that suppliers were forced and supported by the case companies and the government to automate their information systems. However, most of SMEs are still not able to achieve a high degree of automation so far, as described in Section 5.3.2. The discussion here suggests that the integration needs between SMEs and large organisations are different, and this difference can affect their adoption decision-making.

5.5.1.3 Company Size

It is clear that companies of different sizes manage their information systems differently as they have different handling capability. As reported in Section 5.3.2, among these SMEs (i.e. suppliers), the majority of the micro or small suppliers can only achieve a certain level of automation when adopting integration technologies for their inter-organisational connection. The reasons for this were (1) financial concerns, e.g. costs etc., (2) technical concerns, (3) strategic concerns, and (4) management concerns. Most of SMEs suppliers reported that:

> *"Cost is the major concern, as they do not want to spend too much money on adopting integration technologies if they can develop their own systems that will be compatible to their other systems".*

Some of micro suppliers also reported that:

> *"Since they do not have many systems within the organisations, adopting integration technologies would only add complexity and extra costs".*

However, among those suppliers which were able to achieve a higher level of automation, they were comparatively larger in size, e.g. medium-sized suppliers. The discussion here indicates that there is a relationship between company size and integration technologies adoption.

5.5.1.4 Adoption Factors for SMEs and Large Organisations

As discussed in the literature review in Sections 2.3 and 2.4, in the Tornatzky and Fleischer (1990) framework, there are three elements that influence the process by which innovations are adopted: (1) external environmental context, (2) technological context, and (3) organisational context. This framework has been empirically tested and has been found useful in understanding the adoption of technological innovations. Based on this theory, the researcher identifies the factors affecting the adoption of integration technologies in the companies involved in the Industry Automation Programme. However, suppliers and focal companies relationship context is also identified as a significant influence on potential supply chain integration adoption. This is shown in Table 5.9.

Table 5.9 Adoption Factors for Supply Chain Integration Adoption

Elements	Adoption Factors for Large Organisations	Adoption Factors for SMEs
External Environment Context	• Perceived government pressure	• Competition • External pressure, i.e. trading partner pressure, competitor pressure.
Technological Context	• Perceived benefits • Perceived barriers	• Perceived benefits • Perceived barriers
Organisational Context	• Perceived future prospect	• Company size • Perceived future benefits • IT sophistication • Product characteristics • Government support
Supplier and Focal Companies Relationship Context		• Purchasing amount • Purchasing frequency • Dependency on trading partners

External Environment Context. From the conversation with the SMEs (mainly the suppliers), it was found that when the competition is high in the IT industry, the suppliers are more likely to follow the focal companies to adopt supply chain integration. Moreover, when many suppliers follow the case companies to adopt supply chain integration, others will be more likely to follow. This is because other suppliers can feel the competition pressure. As for large organisations (i.e. the focal companies/case companies), they report that the main pressure they received was from the government, since this project was funded by the Taiwanese government. The case companies need to report their progress to the project committee members at certain times. This situation might be expected to be different for those companies not sponsored by the government.

Technological Context. It was found that both SMEs and large organisations see the perceived benefits as an important factor, since when the perceived benefits of adopting supply chain integration are high, suppliers are more likely to follow the focal companies to integrate their inter-organisational systems. Thus, perceived benefit constitutes a common factor. As for the barriers, both suppliers and focal companies mentioned that these are also very important. However, since this project was funded by the Taiwanese government financially and technically, the perceived barriers are not so relevant in this case, as most of the problems can be eliminated by support from the government, e.g. financial support, technical support, etc..

Organisational Context. It was found that the size of the SMEs can influence their decisions to adopt integration technologies in the following ways:

- The bigger the size of a company, the more likely it will adopt integration technologies to support its supply chain integration.

- When the product value is high, suppliers are more likely to adopt integration technologies to support their supply chain integration.

- When the level of IT sophistication of suppliers is high, they are more likely to adopt integration technologies to support their supply chain integration.

- When the adoption of integration technologies to support their supply chain integration can provide significantly better benefits to the organisations or for future development, SMEs are more willing to adopt it.

- Government support is an important adoption factor, as this project is funded by the Taiwanese government.

Supplier and Focal Company Relationship Context. In addition, it was found that when the purchasing amount and frequency are high from the focal companies, suppliers are more willing to adopt integration technologies to support their supply chains. Thus, this demonstrates that suppliers are highly depended on their trading partners for their integration technologies adoption to support their supply chains. In another words, purchasing amount and purchasing frequency are useful factors that can be used to explain the adoption of supply chain integration.

Based on the findings here, it suggests that SMEs and large organisations in some ways are focusing on different factors when taking decisions for the adoption of integration technologies. However, most factors (i.e. common factors) like perceived benefits, perceived barriers, etc., reported in the literature can be used to explain the adoption of integration technologies by SMEs and large organisations.

5.5.1.5 Time

Many of the case companies involved in the Programme have already implemented ERP, EDI, or even EAI or Web Services technologies. This indicates that these companies are considered the early adopters or even early majority. However, many of the suppliers (i.e. SMEs) involved in the Programme have not adopted ERP or EDI; thus, to fulfil the requirement of the project they have no choice but to adopt ERP and EDI technologies. Thus, these SMEs can be considered the late majority or even laggards. The early adopters, i.e. large organisations, reported that they have gained significant benefits upon the adoption of integration technologies. Some large case companies stated that "by adopting supply chain integration early, they have saved million of dollars each year". Another large organisation also suggested that: "If you have better integration capability, you own more chips to survive or even to win the competition".

The findings here suggest that the timing of adopting integration technologies is important. The earlier you adapt to an integrated IT architecture, the better integration capability you will get, thus resulting in enhanced competitiveness.

To conclude this case study, the empirical data reported indicate that all types of companies today seek to become more agile and responsive, and to maximise their existing IT investments. In order to do so, they need to unlock information and functionality in individual applications and turn them into a shared, enterprise-wide resource. Integration solutions unlock existing information assets and share them across multiple applications and business processes, providing the framework for real-time enterprises and real-time business networks. Integration solutions also enable many companies to create a 'single view' of all their enterprise data, and an infrastructure for ensuring that applications can exchange and update business-critical data no matter where it resides. Another way to look at it is that integration technologies enable an organisation's IT infrastructure and applications to respond rapidly to business changes by providing a dynamic way to streamline, integrate, and manage previously independent business processes. Integration solutions also allow companies to take stand-alone applications and turn them into resources that can be used by other applications or business processes as part of a composite application (applications that are composed of new code, processes, or user interfaces, along with calls to existing and legacy applications and services).

To further illustrate the conceptual model proposed in Figure 3.8 in a comprehensive manner, three more case studies were carried out to support the case study findings reported in this section.

5.6 Case Study Two – AboCom Wireless Mobility (Large Firm)

5.6.1 Background to Organisation (Adopter)

AboCom Systems, Inc., founded in 1995 in Taiwan, is a leading provider of strategic solutions of mobile and Small Office/Home Office (SOHO) data communications. It currently has 651 employees, and has an annual turnover of US$1.4 billions. According to the definition mentioned in Section 1.4, AboCom is considered as a large-sized organisation. AboCom also has a branch office in the USA. Since its inception, AboCom has been positioning itself as the partner of choice for telecommuters in mobile computing. AboCom's Network data communication division has distributed a full range of network data communication devices, including PC Cards, Universal Serial Bus (USB) adapters, modems, and, most recently, gateway devices. In view of the increasing growth of Information Telecom, AboCom has expanded its product offering to include Wintel, Touch Solutions, High Speed Internet Access and Storage. The latest product line, a Wireless Multimedia Residential Gateway solution, provides users with the ability to network computers and other IP-enabled devices. Building on the company's quality products and competitive prices, AboCom has experienced booming sales in the Original Equipment Manufacturer (OEM)/ Original Device Manufacturer (ODM) business sector worldwide. The main goal of AboCom is to deliver superior customer value through innovative products with integrated solutions.

Semi-structured and unstructured interviews took place with the MIS manager, 2 MIS technical personal, the Human Resources Manager, a person from the sales department, and the General Manager. The researcher has visited the company three times to collect the required information and data.

5.6.2 Background to Integration Problem

During the last decade, the tremendous changes in the business arena have pushed AboCom to become more efficient and competitive. AboCom believes that a flexible infrastructure is required to maintain and expand its business to a global level. Such an infrastructure will allow the organisation to easily adapt to its changing business environment and gain a competitive advantage.

AboCom's business activities are complex, due to the variety of products manufactured. Thus, an integrated and flexible IT infrastructure has been necessitated with the existing infrastructure causing numerous problems to the organisation. These problems became an obstacle for AboCom, as they prevented it from implementing its business goals. For instance, AboCom could not support its goal of closer collaboration and coordination of inter-organisational business processes due to the non-integrated nature of its applications. This held the organisation back from achieving competitive advantage and cost reduction. To better understand these problems, they are classified into: (1) technical, (2) managerial, and (3) financial.

- **Technical Problems.** The existing IT infrastructure is heterogeneous and consists of hundreds of incompatible systems. As a result, AboCom faces significant integration problems when attempting to migrate its existing custom-built applications and update the day-to-day software. In addition, there was a redundancy of data and functionality, as many applications store similar data or run systems that overlap in functionality. The reasoning is that each business unit or subsidiary has its own IT infrastructure. Furthermore, subsidiaries use programs with similar functionality to automate their business processes. In each subsidiary, applications were customised in a unique way. In most subsidiaries, many systems store data for the same entity, resulting in data redundancy. The reason for this is that applications cannot share common data or objects due to integration problems. Additionally, the non-integrated infrastructure caused many problems to the organisation, since it could not achieve supply chain and eProcurement integration. Therefore, AboCom could not take advantage of IT and support closer collaboration with its suppliers and customers.

- **Managerial Problems.** AboCom's suppliers, vendors and customers all have different needs, thus, AboCom could not avoid or neglect changing its whole systems according to these needs. Thus, with a non-integrated system, it was hard to manage AboCom's supply chain. Moreover, since multiple applications store data for the same entity, management could not retrieve the most updated data for this entity, and therefore faced problems in decision-making. AboCom requires flexible, cross-organisational core business processes, such as (1) development, (2) controlling, (3) sales, (4) quality management, and (5) finance and accounting, which must be based on a homogeneous and flexible IT infrastructure. The latter will allow the organisation to be more flexible in adapting to the changes of the business environment. Existing IT infrastructures cannot efficiently support core business processes, and this is therefore becoming an obstacle for achieving business goals. The strong need in the manufacturing industry for the integration of inter-organisational business processes requires the integration of new systems into existing infrastructures. In order to streamline business processes between the organisation and its trading partners, there is a need for better collaboration among these partners by fully integrating the organisation. There is also a strong need to integrate Supply Chain Management (SCM) and Customer Relationship Management (CRM) systems to improve coordination and relationship with suppliers and customers.

- **Financial Problems.** AboCom's suppliers and customers demand closer collaboration with the organisation. However, the insufficient IT infrastructure could not accomplish a tighter collaboration at both intra-organisational and inter-organisational level. This situation resulted in a loss of sales, since AboCom could not efficiently support its customers or coordinate its activities with its suppliers. Another important financial problem was the high operational and maintenance costs of the existing IT infrastructure, which included numerous systems with overlapping functionality.

5.6.3   Motivation to Integration Technologies Adoption

Enterprises seek new ways to gain competitive advantage and believe that integration will support this strategy, as integration enables the sharing of data and business functions across applications. The MIS manager of AboCom said that:

> *"Adopting integration technologies does not guarantee that AboCom will gain competitive advantages, but not having it will become a problem. In order to compete, efficiency is very important. Adapting to an integrated IT infrastructure is a way to increase the efficiency, so we can provide our customers with better services".*

AboCom's traditional enterprise applications were custom-built to address specific business needs. As enterprises have grown, the need to share information across departments and business areas becomes more critical. Thus, AboCom is turning to integration to provide a method for interconnecting these distributed and often proprietary systems. In doing so, ERP, EAI, EDI and Web Services technologies are adopted by AboCom to support its inter- and intra-organisational integration.

There are four major reasons why AboCom is implementing integration technologies:

- **New systems have not replaced legacy systems.** New enterprise applications such as SAP, Seibel, etc. which have been deployed typically do not replace existing legacy applications, but rather complement or extend them., often generating a need for integration or connectivity between them.

- **Need to consolidate and globalise.** Mergers and acquisitions have left AboCom with a broad array of mission-critical systems that simply cannot be abandoned or replaced. Instead, integrating them and putting systems in place to exchange information among AboCom's various applications becomes a much more realistic solution.

- **Search for increased productivity.** The economic situation has forced AboCom to search for ways to increase productivity and reduce costs. By using integration platforms to automate existing business processes and applications, AboCom is able to streamline its business while increasing productivity and reducing costs.

- **Raised expectations from Web experiences.** AboCom's customers now expect it to have a consolidated view of their accounts, transactions, and any other related information, regardless of where those data actually are. In order to stay competitive, AboCom needs to provide better availability of data and applications to both internal users (such as customer service representatives or sales people) and to external users (such as customers or partners).

Additionally, AboCom recognised the need for a flexible and manageable IT infrastructure when it attempted to develop wireless mesh network systems (i.e. Web Services). Such a network, being a peer-to-peer multi-hop network providing a reliable and flexible system that can be extended to thousand of devices, has been widely deployed in the Wireless Metropolis Area Network (WMAN) application. According to AboCom, the mesh networks system is compatible with the existing infrastructure of the Taiwanese telecom industry, ISP, and content providers business. Through the highly efficient network quality of mesh network system, users will be enticed to enjoy high quality Internet access and online video content service. With the introduction of its new Wireless Multimedia Residential Gateway device, AboCom sought to distinguish itself as the ODM/OEMs, network operators, and retail chains. As AboCom custom-builds each gateway according to customer requirements, the company's primary challenge was to provide its diversified customers with a comprehensive list of options for their gateway devices, while using one single operating system platform to maintain a streamlined, cost-effective development process. The gateway device platform solution had to include the following key features:

- Robust security features to help ensure that Internet connectivity and network data are protected from unauthorised access,

- Centralised storage where users can save and access digital media, including videos and MP3 files on the hard disk,

- Voice-Over IP (VoIP) capabilities,

- Multimedia services, including encoding and decoding capabilities for capturing and broadcasting TV signals to digital devices such as computers and home entertainment centres,

- Wireless capabilities.

AboCom was able to meet the broad spectrum of customer requirements by building a Wireless Multimedia Residential Gateway platform solution based on Microsoft Windows CE .NET 4.2. Windows CE .NET is a comprehensive, extensible operating system that includes a large set of network and communication protocols, security features, device management functionality, applications, and an intuitive sample user interface. The operating system enables AboCom to customise its gateway products quickly and cost effectively according to customer requirements. The real-time communications service in Windows CE .NET 4.2 enables the AboCom gateway to relate instant messaging and voice calls, including VoIP bridging from an IP device to a regular Public Switched Telephone Network (PSTN) phone.

Easy integration of third-party software is a critical factor for efficient development of a gateway device. AboCom carefully considered its options before finalising its choice to Windows CE .NET. The MIS manager in AboCom reported that:

> *"We thought about VXWorks, but it wasn't powerful enough for our gateway.*
> *Linux was another contender, but it could not meet the same level of*
> *standardisation, versatility and stability as Windows CE .NET. Linux is*
> *particularly difficult from a third-party application integration standpoint.*

Linux has so many different versions. You have to make sure each device driver is compatible with a particular version of Linux. If we are not lucky, the device maker does not want to support the device driver for our specific version of Linux. That creates lots of problems for those of us who create products. With Windows CE .NET, there is one version, and because it's from Microsoft, it's easy to support and easy to get industry support".

Although AboCom typically focuses on the hardware and driver layers, the company does integrate third-party software into the gateway when customers request it, a process made easier by working with the standard Windows application programming interfaces (APIs). The Platform Builder, one of the Windows CE .NET tools, also facilitates this process. AboCom noted that:

"It helps our developers to build components, and it also helps our customers. We can use Platform Builder to generate a Software Development Kit (SDK) for our customers, which they then use to develop software that is compatible with the device".

The empirical data extrapolated from AboCom have revealed many factors that stimulate the adoption of an integrated infrastructure. These factors include:

- Internal pressure: the limitations of existing IT infrastructure;

- External and competition pressures: increased competition and a requirement for closer collaboration with trading partners;

- Technical factors: easy integration, ease of use and support.

5.6.4 Benefits of Integration Technologies Adoption

The author asked the interviewees to determine the benefits from the implementation of integration technologies. Table 5.10 presents interviewees' answers, and categorises integration technologies benefits according to the model proposed by Shang and Seddon (2000) (see Section 2.2.5.2). Interviewees share similar perceptions and reported that the integrated infrastructure resulting from the implementation of integration technologies increased organisation performance, and systems efficiency and functionality. The main findings include:

- **Operational Benefits.** Integration technologies reduce the cost of managing, running and maintaining the IT infrastructure. The integration has an impact on reducing the overall operational cost at AboCom due to business process reengineering and organisational restructuring. This has resulted in quicker response to change, significantly minimised errors, and increased productivity since processes have been optimised and fully automated and integrated. Although the adoption of integrated IT infrastructure has helped the company to satisfy most of its customers, there are still some unsatisfied. The MIS manager said that:

> *"It is hard to please every customer, thus I would only say the adaptation to the integrated IT infrastructure has pleased some of the customers, not all of them appreciate the improved efficiency. The hardest thing is to please the customers, they are never satisfied with everything. We can only seek ways to improve our services in order to make the customers happy".*

- **Management Benefits.** The adaptation to the integrated IT infrastructure has resulted in more organised business processes and was allowed AboCom to better understand and control them. In doing so, business processes and data quality have been improved as they support the decision-making process through the integrated infrastructure, which resulted in increased performance and management, e.g. quick access to information, improved inventory control, reduced processing time, and simplified transaction flow.

- **Strategic Benefits.** As mentioned by the MIS manager before, not adopting integration technologies will become a problem. Thus, this means that the adaptation to an integrated IT infrastructure does give the company competitive advantages. The MIS manager also stated that the adoption of integration technologies has significantly increased the efficiency of business process, hence increasing customer satisfaction. This has resulted in closer collaboration with customers and suppliers, and better communication among partners. In addition, the MIS manager mentioned that the adoption of integration technologies to support their IS has maybe achieved a higher return on investment, but the actual figures were not given. The MIS manager reported that:

> *"It is hard to judge whether the adoption of integration technologies has actually helped us to achieve a higher return on investment as I can not give you an actual figure".*

- **Technical Benefits.** Many technical benefits were identified. For example, reduced development complexity, automated business processes, open standards provided, reduced integration costs, reduced integration complexity, etc. (see Table 5.10). The EAI solution supported AboCom in reducing the redundancy of data and systems. Fewer data and applications result in less maintenance effort. The Web Services solution supports AboCom in reducing integration costs and achieving reusability and flexibility. The ERP solutions support AboCom in automating the internal business processes. Thus, the use of integration technologies for the development of integrated IT infrastructure has achieved a more flexible and manageable solution to support AboCom in different ways.

- **Organisational Benefits.** The integrated IT infrastructure has allowed the organisation to do business more effectively. This is attributed to business processes being organised and fully automated and integrated. Thus, manual tasks have been significantly reduced, and unnecessary or redundant tasks have been eliminated. In doing so, organisation is able to gain an instant, real-time view of all its data and operations, which can lead to better decision-making. Integration technologies also provide the flexibility to adapt business processes quickly to accommodate growth and meet new business challenges as they arise.

Table 5.10 Classification of AboCom's Integration Technologies Benefits

Key: High (●), Medium (◐), Low (○)

Category	Integration Technologies Benefits	Improvement
Operational	Reduce operational costs	◐
	Achieve customer satisfaction	◐
	Minimise errors, delays and increase accuracy of data	●
	Quicker response to change	●
	Increase productivity	◐
Managerial	Improve inventory control	◐
	Quick access to information	●
	Increase revenue	◐
	Reduce processing time and provide faster delivery of products or services	◐
	Simplify transaction flow	◐
Strategic	Increase business and management efficiency	◐
	Achieve higher ROI	◐
	Increase competitive advantage	◐
	Increase collaboration among customers, services providers and intermediaries	●
	Increase business opportunities	●
Technical	Offer solutions to problems of legacy systems	◐
	Minimise cost of ownership and development costs	○
	Reduce development complexity, times and risks	●
	Automate business processes	●
	Provide open standard	●
	Reduce integration cost	●
	Reduce integration complexity and speed up application integration	●
	Permit full-scale integration	◐
	Provide multiple connect points for other systems to integrate with	●
	Offer ease of integration with other pieces of software	●
	Provide real-time service-oriented architecture	●
	Simplify design development, maintenance and usage	◐
	Provide platform and language independence	●
	Achieve reusability and flexibility	●
	Provide stability using dynamic integrated interface to integrate systems	●
	Achieve interoperability	●
	Able to unite all major systems vendors (i.e. vendor neutral)	●
	Reduce time and cost to launch applications	●
Organisational	Increase flexibility	◐
	Quick response to business needs	◐
	Reduce time to market	◐

5.6.5 Barriers to Integration Technologies Adoption

The adoption of integration technologies has impacted on AboCom. Similar to the benefits classification, the interviewees were asked to comment on the barriers for the adoption of integration technologies. Table 5.11 summarises and classified the barriers according to the model proposed by Shang and Seddon (2000).

Table 5.11 Classification of AboCom's Integration Technologies Barriers

Key: High (●), Medium (◕), Low (○)

Category	Integration Technologies Barriers	Significance
Operational	Face operational challenges	◕
Managerial	Face difficulty in managing relationships with other organisations	◕
Strategic	Lack of business perspective	○
Technical	Lack of large-scale implementation examples and experiences available	◕
	Lack of security protocols and standards	○
	Lack of user interface encapsulation mechanisms	●
	Concern over security	◕
	Concern over maturity of integration technologies	●
	Concern over transaction distribution management	◕
	Add complexity to business transaction protocol implementation	●
	Lack of system reliability at any moment	○
	Concern over whether old generation solutions are agile enough to react to changes	○
	Lack of XML-based management protocol	○
	Concern over maturity of Web Services payment methods	●
	Inexperience in architecting Web Services	●
Organisational	Increase organisational complexity	◕
	Difficult to change internal organisational culture to embrace Web Services	○

The MIS manager from AboCom said that:

> *"The most important barrier to integration technologies adoption at AboCom deal with the problems with the SMEs suppliers, since their ability to integrate is low. Most of the time, orders are still done manually via fax or telephone. Additionally, some suppliers are still having concerns to share and integrate their data and processes".*

Apart from the above mentioned integration technologies barriers, according to interviewees there are more barriers to integration technologies adoption at AboCom that deal with:

- Difficulty in managing relationships with the SMEs suppliers;

- High complexity in understanding the business processes; and

- High cost of business process reengineering and organisational restructuring.

5.6.6 Investigating Factors Affecting AboCom's Adoption Decision

The interviewees were asked to rate the importance of the adoption factors reported in the literature, and to state any other factors that they think are important to the integration technologies adoption. The purpose of this section is to gain a comprehensive understanding on the adoption factors affecting the integration technologies adoption decision in large organisation (as explained in Chapter 3 Section 3.3).

The interviewees were also asked to pick 5 factors they think are most important to its integration technologies adoption decision making, these 5 factors are: (1) competitive pressure, (2) customer power, (3) perceived benefits, (4) perceived financial costs, and (5) IT infrastructure. The interviewees said that:

> *"The reason to adopt integration technologies is to increase business efficiency and to win in the competition. Thus, competitive pressure and perceived benefits are important, as we only adopt integration technologies when we are sure that this will give us additional benefits". "Customer power is important, as we rely on customers to make profits; thus, try to provide a better service to them is the only way to stay in the competition. Of course, costs are always important, as every company is trying to cut down the cost, thus the profit margin will be bigger".*

Table 5.12 shows the integration technologies factors affecting AboCom's decision.

Table 5.12 Integration Technologies Adoption Factors

Key: High (●), Medium (◐), Low (○)

Factors	Importance
Adopter Characteristics	◐
Availability of Standards	●
Barriers	◐
Business Complexity	○
Competitive Pressures	●
Customer Power	●
Dependency on Partners/ Trading Partners Readiness	●
Environmental Characteristics	●
Evaluation Framework for Integration Technology and Packages	●
External Pressure	●
Extent of Organisational Change	○
External Environment Characteristics	●
IS Innovation Type	●
IT Sophistication	●
IT Infrastructure	●
Internal Environment Characteristics	●
Internal Pressure	●
Innovation Characteristics/ Perceived Innovation Characteristics	●
Organisational Characteristics	◐
Organisational Readiness	◐
Perceived Financial Cost/ Financial Resources	●
Perceived Benefits (Direct and Indirect)	●
Perceived Technical Competence/ Technological Skills Readiness	●
Perceived Industry Pressure	●
Perceived Government Pressure	○
Security/ Control Procedures	○
Support/ Organisation Support	●
Stakeholders	●
Supplier Trust	○
Supplier Commitment	○
Technical Factors	◐

5.7 Case Study Three – Hi-Touch Image Technologies Ltd. (SME)

5.7.1 Background to Organisation (Adopter)

Hi-Touch Imaging Technologies designs and manufactures the Hi-Ti brand of digital photo printers, using dye-sublimation technology to offer both consumer and commercial print solutions. Hi-Touch currently has 650 employees worldwide, and has an annual turnover of US$1.5 millions. Thus, Hi-Touch is considered as a small to medium-sized company according to the definition mentioned in Section 1.4. Hi-Touch Imaging Technologies was established in Taiwan in 2001, with cutting edge research and development teams, specialising in optical and chemical knowledge related to digital photography, which has been central to their ability to create high quality, digital photo printers. In that time, Hi-Touch has seen rapid growth, with branches in the UK, USA, Netherlands, Middle East, India, Russia and China, trading across the globe.

Semi-structured and unstructured interviews took place with the MIS manager, a technical person from the MIS department, a person from the sales department, the Product Manager and a person from the Finance Department. The researcher visited the company a couple of times to collect the required information and data.

5.7.2 Background to Integration Problem

Each subsidiary has its own IT infrastructure, which is operated and coordinated independently. The non-integrated nature of Hi-Touch's IT infrastructure has caused some problems and inconveniences to the organisation. To better understand these problems, they are classified into: (1) technical, (2) managerial, and (3) financial.

- **Technical Problems.** The MIS manager from Hi-Touch reported that "Hi-Touch prefers to buy off-the-shelf software (i.e. ready- made software), and to further develop these software to suit their needs, as this way is much cost saving". Thus, the organisation consists of many applications and two ERP systems from different vendors. Obtaining data from custom systems is difficult, as the majority of these systems have incompatible and heterogeneous data structures and formats. In addition, Hi-Touch has 5 subsidiaries around the world, and they all have different IT infrastructure and install different applications and systems. Thus, Hi-Touch found it hard to manage these systems without an integrated solution. However, due to the lack of knowledge and financial costs concerns, they have not yet adopted all the necessary integration technologies to support their systems or data integration.

- **Managerial Problems.** The diversity of information systems causes delays in giving information, as applications are not integrated, and much work has to be carried out manually. For instance, data from one system has to be printed out and then re-entered in a different format to a target system. The reason for this is that the target system has its own data structure, and/or it is based on different operating systems. Nonetheless, the delays in delivering information cause problems in decision-making and management. When the MIS manager and one of the technical persons from Hi-Touch were asked to comment on their management problem, they said:

  "The biggest management problem we have encountered was that every site (i.e. subsidiary) has different needs for its data structures, data formats and systems. It is hard to come to an agreement on one unique format/system/application which could suit everyone's needs. With a non-integrated IT infrastructure, the IT technicians need to modify and write the source code many times according to their needs (i.e. if there are any changes)".

What the manager meant was that in each subsidiary, applications were customised in a unique way to suit needs. In most subsidiaries, many systems store data for the same entity, which results in data redundancy. The reason for this is that applications can not share common data or objects due to integration problems. The non-integrated infrastructure leads managers to inefficient decisions, important information is often missing, and/or data can not be retrieved from applications. For example, there is often a delay in confirming order information and sending information dealing with product availability. Therefore, in many cases, the management can not take accurate decisions regarding the replacement of products. This inability thus leads to loss of sales and low customer satisfaction.

- **Financial Problems.** Hi-Touch has realised that the non-integrated nature of systems cost the organisation money and time. This is attributed to the organisation having to spend high amounts of money to support and maintain all these systems. Additionally, the inability of Hi-Touch to serve customers efficiently has an extra cost, as it leads to loss of sales, and thus customers often turn to competitors.

5.7.3   Motivation to Integration Technologies Adoption

During the last decade, the tremendous changes in the global business arena have led Hi-Touch to adopt e-business practices and applications to gain competitive advantages. The company recognised that integration is a significant parameter that influences the success of e-business applications and supports it in achieving a competitive advantage. Although Hi-Touch has the vision that it needs to automate its business process and integrate the heterogeneous data structures and formats, it   has only managed to adopt EDI partially to communicate with their partners, suppliers and customers (mainly for purchasing, i.e. orders), as well as the ERP system from DATA SYSTME (ERP vendor) to manage its internal business processes. The main reason for this is due to the high costs associated with the adoption of integration technologies, e.g. EAI or even EDI is expensive.

Hi-Touch reported that even though it has adopted EDI to solve its integration problem, it still requires altering target and source applications all the time when there are any changes. Additionally, EDI has a high cost, and the nature of EDI standards in use (UN/EDIFACT) is complicated, which adds complexity. This is why Hi-Touch is slowly moving to EDI over Internet technology, but this part has not been implemented completely. Hi-Touch has also adopted ERP systems to support its intra-organisational integration. However, it claimed that ERP systems have failed to fully support Hi-Touch's intra and inter-organisational integration, since they co-exist alongside other applications and the version of ERP systems Hi-Touch used is the simplified version. Hi-Touch's ERP systems do not support real-time capabilities and there are many compatibility, problems among ERP systems, and as they do not support of all these systems under an e-business architecture that requires real-time data, this is an obstacle. Therefore, the organisation believes that the way forward is to develop an integrated IT infrastructure by redesigning its IT infrastructure, and phasing out all redundant systems and data. However, this is not an easy task for a company with limited resources like Hi-Touch.

Hi-Touch states that it does not have enough budget to implement integration technologies at a moment, although they know it is essential, as the non-integrated IT infrastructure has caused Hi-Touch many problems: (1) high cost of maintenance, (2) not manageable, (3) not flexible, (4) results in insufficient decision-making, and (5) leads to low customer and partner satisfaction. EDI is as far as it goes so far, but Hi-Touch hopes to fully automate its IS in the future to increase its efficiency. The technical person from the MIS department said that:

> *"It is not up to me to decide whether to adopt integrated IT infrastructure, although I know it is very important issue. In my company, the decision-making process is autocracy. The boss is the one who makes the decision, and all he wants is to cut down the costs as much as possible. Our management is not as systematic as large organisations' do. I suggest that if the company continue to grow, Hi-Touch will probably need to consider adopting EAI or Web Services in the future if the budget is allowed".*

Therefore, there is a need for rapid transformation from closed internal processes to open externalised processes. However, this target can be achieved through the development of an integrated, adaptive and consistent IT infrastructure across Hi-Touch Technologies Ltd.

5.7.4   Benefits of Integration Technologies Adoption

The researcher asked the interviewees to determine the benefits from the implementation of integration technologies. In this case, they were asked to comment on the benefits of adopting ERP and EDI. Table 5.13 presents interviewees' answers categorised according to the model proposed by Shang and Seddon (2000) (see Section 2.2.5.2). It appears that interviewees share common perceptions regarding integration technologies benefits. The adoption of EDI and ERP clearly automated business processes and minimised errors and also provided more understanding and control of business processes, with activities having been improved through reengineering.

However, since Hi-Touch does not adopt any other types of integration technologies (e.g. EAI or Web Services) apart from EDI and ERP, the benefits of using EDI and ERP are thus to some extent limited. Adopting EDI and ERP does not support Hi-Touch to integrate its IS fully; instead, it helps Hi-Touch to automate its internal business process and to speed up the purchasing (i.e. ordering) transaction. For example, reduce operational costs, and minimise errors and delays and increase the accuracy of data (see Table 5.13 for the benefits of using EDI and ERP).

Table 5.13 Classification of Hi-Touch's Integration Technologies Benefits

Key: High (●), Medium (◖), Low (○)

Category	Integration Technologies Benefits	Improvement
Operational	Reduce operational costs	●
	Achieve customer satisfaction	◖
	Minimise errors, delays and increase accuracy of data	●
	Increase productivity	○
	Quicker response to change	○
Managerial	Improve inventory control	◖
	Quick access to information	◖
	Increase revenue	◖
	Reduce processing time and provide faster delivery of products or services	◖
	Simplify transaction flow	◖
Strategic	Increase business and management efficiency	◖
	Increase competitive advantage	○
	Achieve higher ROI	◖
	Increase collaboration among customers, services providers and intermediaries	○
	Increase business opportunities	○
Technical	Offer solutions to problems of legacy systems	○
	Minimise cost of ownership and development costs	◖
	Reduce development complexity, times and risks	◖
	Automate business processes	○
	Provide open standard	○
	Reduce integration cost	○
	Reduce integration complexity and speed up application integration	○
	Permit full-scale integration	○
	Provide multiple connect points for other systems to integrate with	○
	Provide real-time service-oriented architecture	○
	Offer ease of integration with other pieces of software	○
	Simplify the design development, maintenance and usage	◖
	Provide platform and language independence	○
	Achieve reusability and flexibility	○
	Provide stability using dynamic integrated interface to integrate systems	○
	Achieve interoperability	○
	Able to unite all major systems vendors (i.e. vendor neutral)	○
	Reduce time and cost to launch applications	◖
Organisational	Increase flexibility	◖
	Quick response to business needs	○
	Reduce time to market	◖

Table 5.13 indicates that ERP and EDI have contributed limited benefits to Hi-Touch, especially in the area of integrated IT infrastructure. Thus, it is important that Hi-Touch considers other types of integration technologies, such as EAI or Web Services, in the future to integrate fully their intra and inter-organisational IS.

5.7.5 Barriers to Integration Technologies Adoption

The adoption of integration technologies has impacted on Hi-Touch. Similar to the benefits classification, the interviewees were asked to comment on the barriers for the adoption of integration technologies.

One of the employees from the MIS department said that:

> *"Technical problems can always be solved, the most difficult part is to persuade the employees to change, or even the boss to accept the fact that integrated IT infrastructure is important, as without an integrated IT infrastructure, there will be many problems and time-wasting. However, most of the employees do not understand why an integrated IT infrastructure is important. Therefore, they are reluctant to change, as they are afraid that they will need to learn more things i.e. more work needing to be undertaken".*

Employees from the financial and sales department added that:

> *"Of course, money concern is another important barrier that delays the boss from adopting integration technologies. What the boss wants is to cut down costs as much as possible".*

Upon the adoption of ERP and EDI, many integration problems mentioned in Section 5.7.2 remain to be solved. For example, the technical person from Hi-Touch said that:

> *"We still have to modify the source codes many times when there are changes made. Data redundancy problem still exists".*

The above statements show that the major barrier to EDI and ERP is that they do not fully support intra-organisational and inter-organisational integration. Thus, integration problems still exist, such as data redundancy, which does not simplify the design development, and maintenance and usage, etc..

Table 5.14 summarises and classifies the barriers according to the model proposed by Shang and Seddon (2000).

Table 5.14 Classification of Hi-Touch's Integration Technologies Barriers

Key: High (●), Medium (◐), Low (○)

Category	Integration Technologies Barriers	Significance
Operational	Face operational challenges	◐
Managerial	Face difficulty in managing relationships with other organisations	●
Strategic	Lack of business perspective	◐
Technical	Lack of large-scale implementation examples and experiences available	●
	Lack of security protocols and standards	◐
	Concern over security	●
	Concern over maturity of integration technologies	◐
	Concern over transaction distribution management	●
	Add complexity to business transaction protocol implementation	●
	Lack of system reliability at any moment	●
	Concern over whether old generation solutions are agile enough to react to changes	●
	Lack of XML-based management protocol	●
Organisational	Difficult to change internal organisational culture	●
	Increase organisational complexity	●

Table 5.14 shows that the adoption of ERP and EDI has not significantly solved most of the integration problems that Hi-Touch is facing, as mentioned in Section 5.7.2. Thus, Hi-Touch reported that they want to look for other integration solutions to solve their current integration problems in order to increase its competitiveness. However, this is not an easy task for Hi-Touch. The manager stated that they need more time, budget and advice from knowledgeable experts to plan for further integration technologies adoption, e.g. EAI or Web Services.

5.7.6   Investigating Factors Affecting Adoption Decision

The interviewees were asked to comment on the factors affecting their decisions for the EDI and ERP adoption. Apart from the factors reported in the literature, as mentioned in Section 3.2.4, the researcher asked the interviewees to state any additional factors. The interviewee said that "The factors mentions here are very detailed already, we can not think of any others". Thus, the researcher asked the interviewees to comment on the identified factors based on the high, medium and low measurements. The results are shown in Table 5.15.

Table 5.15 Integration Technologies Adoption Factors

Key: High (●), Medium (◐), Low (○)

Factors	Importance
Adopter Characteristics	●
Availability of Standards	●
Barriers	●
Business Complexity	○
Competitive Pressures	●
Customer Power	●
Dependency on Partners/ Trading Partners Readiness	◐
Environmental Characteristics	○
Evaluation Framework for Integration Technology and Packages	○
External Pressure	●
Extent of Organisational Change	●
External Environment Characteristics	◐
IS Innovation Type	○
IT Sophistication	◐
IT Infrastructure	●
Internal Environment Characteristics	●
Internal Pressure	●
Innovation Characteristics/ Perceived Innovation Characteristics	○
Organisational Characteristics	●
Organisational Readiness	◐
Perceived Financial Cost/ Financial Resources	●
Perceived Benefits (Direct and Indirect)	●
Perceived Technical Competence	◐
Technological Skills Readiness	◐
Perceived Industry Pressure	○
Perceived Government Pressure	○
Security	●
Control Procedures	◐
Support/ Organisation Support	◐
Stakeholders	○
Supplier Trust	○
Supplier Commitment	○
Technical Factors	◐

Again, interviewees were asked to choose the 5 most important factors affecting their integration technologies adoption decision, these factors are: (1) financial costs, (2) competitive pressure, (3) IT sophistication, (4) external pressure, and (5) organisational characteristics. The interviewees reported that the major concern to adopt an integration technology or not in Hi-Touch depends heavily on the costs of implementation. For example, unlike large organisations which can afford to adopt an ERP system from SAP, Hi-Touch reported that it can not afford to do so, as it is too expensive. The MIS manager said that:

> *"SAP is the brand for ERP system, but the only thing is that its ERP system is very expensive, which we can not actually afford. This is why we tend to go for a cheaper version of ERP system e.g. ERP system from DATA SYSTEM. I do not think that most SMEs can actually afford to adopt an expensive technology if they actually want to make profits".*

The above statement indicates that the SMEs' characteristic limitations, like limited knowledge and finance resources, have affected their adoption decisions in relation to their integration technologies adoption (i.e. these limitations are a real obstacle to SMEs).

In the next sections, additional case studies were undertaken in non-adopters SMEs to further analyse the reasons why SMEs do not have or have the intention to adopt integration technologies. These case studies have acted as additional information to assist analysis of adoption factors affecting SMEs' decisions on integration technologies adoption.

5.8   Case Study Four – eSynergy Technologies Ltd (SME)

5.8.1   Background to Organisation (Non-Adopter)

eSynergy had been dedicating itself to be a Computer Integration Manufacturing (CIM) leading company in IC and the TFT-LCD fabrication-related field. eSynergy's mission is to provide the customers with total CIM solution, with solid teamwork implementation, professional domain know-how, and on-time delivery, to create the value and profit together. eSynergy currently has 70 employees worldwide and an annual turnover of US$0.3 millions. eSynergy's main business areas include software development, computer integration manufacturing, and manufacturing execution systems.

Semi-structured and unstructured interviews took place with the general manager, a software developer, and 2 general staff. Although eSynergy Technologies Ltd does not adopt integration technologies, the main purpose of this case study was to find out the reasons why it did not adopt any of them.

5.8.2 Background to Integration Problems

eSynergy's manger claims that there is no problem for the business activities. However, the researcher realised there are some problems after interviewing the employees from the organisation. What the manager said was different from the employee responses. The employee said that:

> *"When the manager says no problem, he is trying to hide the serious problem behind".*

After interviewing the employees from eSynergy, the researcher found that the company's working process is very slow, and there are some customers complaining that engineers cannot response quickly to their requests. Since eSynergy does not have a standard operation procedure, the employees found it hard to deal with each project as they need to learn every new project from the beginning (i.e. they do not have a flowchart to follow). The interviewees also mentioned that they spend much times on restarting a new case/project, therefore overtime is required almost every day. For this reason, the employees' turnover rates (especially for those technical people) are high in eSynergy, and most of them leave to join other companies (most of which are eSynergy's customers or partners). Because of this, as reported by the interviewees, most of the staff in eSynergy do not like to learn new things. The interviewees said that:

> *"Most of the time, we are forced to learn new things which we don't really want to. The main reason is that we don't know when we are going to leave the company, maybe tomorrow".*

This is the main reason why eSynergy does not adopt any integration technologies, since most of the employees are looking for the chance to migrate to other companies, e.g. large companies.

The non-integrated nature of eSynergy has also caused some other problems and inconveniences to the organisation. To better understand these problems, they are again classified into: (1) technical, (2) managerial, and (3) financial. However, the researcher found that most of eSynergy's problems are from the management perspective.

- **Technical Problems.** Most of the eSynergy's information and data are processed in a very traditional way. Most of the Purchasing Orders are still handled by paper, fax and telephone. One of the interviewee from the sales department said that:

  > *"We often deal the purchasing order through the paper work. When a business deal is made, we need to record the purchasing order document in writing, and this must be done within the company. Thus, we need to come back to the company to do this and often end up leaving the office late".*

The above statement demonstrates that with a non-integrated IT infrastructure, this often results in time delays in delivering information (i.e. can not obtain real-time information), as much work needs to be carried out manually. This often causes delays in decision-making, thus resulting in an inflexible management style. For instance, data from one system have to be printed out and then re-entered in a different format to the main system.

- **Managerial Problems.** The MIS manager from eSynergy reported that "eSynergy's employees are too busy to learn new things". However, the employees from eSynergy said that "They do not wish to learn new things as this will add more work load to our everyday job. We already work overtime almost every day". The above statements show that eSynergy has a serious management problem as its employees refuse to learn new things. The high turnover rate is another serious management problem too, as the manger revealed that:

  > *"The human resources management is very difficult because eSynergy is close to the Hsin-Chu Science Park where most of the large companies are situated. Most of these large organisations provide better compensation to employees. Thus, they can attract better employees to their companies. As for us or for most of the SMEs, it is hard to recruit strong technical-based employees as these employees, will rather go for the large organisations".*

  > *"We do know too busy is our big problem, but since most of our employees have the engineer's background, we don't know too much about management. The main purpose of our company is to make profits so as to survive. We are only meeting micro-profit era in the IC and TFT-LCD industry. We do realise that the high technology market changes every day, every hour and every minute, and is a very competitive market. If we cannot step on, we might be replaced soon or later by other competitors in this*

highly competitive market. However, there is nothing much we can do now, as most of the employees here in the company are pretty much occupied with many things. Integration technologies adoption can be time consuming, and will not be our first priority at the moment".

With the non-integrated infrastructure, eSynergy often faces the following problems: (1) insufficient decision making, (2) important information if often missing, and (3) data cannot be retrieved from employees' and customers' requests. For example, there is often a delay in confirming order information and sending information dealing with product availability. In many cases, the management cannot take sufficient decisions regarding the replacement of products. Thus, this inability leads to customer and employee complaints and dissatisfactions.

- **Financial Problems.** eSynergy has understood that the non-integrated nature of systems costs the organisation money and time. This is attributed to the organisation having to spend high amounts of money to support and maintain them all. Additionally, the inability of eSynergy to serve customers efficiently has incurred extra costs to the company as it leads to loss of sales. As suggested by one of the interviewees "*no money, no improvement, and no improvement becomes no sales*".

5.8.3   Reasons for Not Adopting Integration Technologies

Firstly, the failure of Synergy to adopt any of the integration technologies can be explained by its (1) manpower, (2) the business model, and (3) micro profit.

- **Manpower.** Since eSynergy provides services to its customers, most of the manpower is in-house, supporting the IC and TFT-LCD manufacturing.

- **Business Model.** eSynergy's business activity is too simple, thus there is no need to adopt integration technologies.

- **Micro Profit.** The main organisation activities are simply in program writing for the manufacturing, and the business activities are all in project leading and in a new business setting. eSynergy is not involved in any after-sales services, and has no continuing relationships with its customers after a project is finished. The interviewee from eSynergy said that:

  "We are a kind of services provider, and there is no need to adopt the integration technologies in this kind of simple business activity".

To better understand the reasons for eSynergy not adopting integration technologies to support its IS, these are categorised into: (1) managerial, (2) technical, and (3) financial reasons.

- **Technical Reasons.** eSynergy is a kind of project-based company, and most of its engineers are located in the customers' companies. Every employee acts as an individual co-operator and only communicates with each other by MSN messager. Thus the business processes are rather simple in eSynergy, and hence the manager from eSynergy suggested that there is no need to invest in integration technologies at the moment. eSynergy had once introduced on ERP system, but the result was unsuccessful. The reasons were: (1) most employees failed to learn and use the ERP system properly, and (2) the ERP system provider chosen had a financial crisis, thus eSynergy was forced to terminate the contract. Due to the limited resources within the company, eSynergy is not yet able to adopt an ERP system again, as it does not wish to fail, and cannot afford to fail again. This limitation also restricts eSynergy from taking decisions to adopt any other types of integration technologies to support its IS or data integration. In addition, the purchasing process is simple since there is not a variety of products (i.e. eSynergy only provides services), and the purchasing orders are rather simple than complicated (i.e. not much information needs to be addressed in the purchasing orders). Thus, eSynergy finds it unnecessary to standardise its purchasing process.

- **Managerial Reasons.** eSynergy is a relatively new company and was founded in 1997. Thus, the company is still in the early stage of development. The manager from eSynergy said that:

    "At this stage, the company is trying to survive, and the IC and TFT-LCD businesses are getting tougher than before. Therefore, we do not have sufficient budget to invest in integration technologies. Moreover, since the employees' turnover is high at the moment and after our prior failure on ERP adoption, it is hard to resume ERP adoption, as we do not have suitable engineers with appropriate skills to manage the ERP system, and most of the existing engineers are pretty much occupied with other jobs".

The above statement indicates that eSynergy will not invest in any integration technologies if the immediate benefits cannot be realised or a quick return on investment is not guaranteed.

- **Financial Reasons.** As mentioned before, eSynergy does not wish to invest in further development (e.g. integration technologies adoption), as the company does not have sufficient budget for it. Additionally, the prior failure experience in adopting ERP systems which resulted in time-wasting and money lost has delayed eSynergy's decisions in further adopting integration technologies to support its IS. In this highly competitive hi-technology market, a quick return on investment is essential, especially for a company size like eSynergy (i.e. SME), and this is the only way to survive.

Contrast to eSynergy, the manger in Industrade is enthusiastic in adopting integration technologies as a way to support its IS integration. It is currently working on its intra-organisational integration, and is planning and preparing to adopt Web Services to support its inter-organisational integration. This case study is described in the following section (Section 5.9).

5.9 Case Study Five – Industrade Technologies Ltd (SME)

5.9.1 Background to Organisation (Non-Adopter: Planning to Adopt)

Industrade Technologies Ltd. is a trade company founded in the 1980s, with a capital of US$600, 000 dollars, and currently has 15 employees worldwide. It is thus considered as a small-sized company according to the definition given in Section 1.4. Industrade is an equipment supplier specialising in high technology components and devices for most manufacturers in the Taiwan semiconductor industry, such as Delta and Inventec. Its main products include electronic semiconductor devices and heat-treatment, and most of this equipment is imported from European companies such as ABB, Naberthern, IXYS, and SMSC Corporations. Industrade has been growing rapidly in the Asia market, and is planning to set up branches in Thailand, China, Vietnam, and Indonesia in the near future. To do so, Industrade believes that intra and inter-organisational integration is important, as this can help it to automate its business process, thus resulting in improved efficiency and competitive advantages. Industrade is a SME which has begun to see integration technologies as a way of gaining competitive advantage, rather than simply as a tool to support its business operations.

Semi-structured and unstructured interviews took place with the MIS manager, who is the main person in charge of all technical issues in the organisation (e.g. systems set-up, design and software purchasing, etc.), and is the key decision-maker besides the general manager.

5.9.2 Background to Integration Problems

Industrade consists of many applications and systems from different customers, and their non-integration has caused problems and inconveniences, as reported by the MIS manager:

> *"Most of our key customers asked us to set-up a platform that is compatible to their systems. Therefore, we need to develop different systems to meet different customers' requirements. This is time-consuming, as we need to employ someone with technical background to maintain each of our customers' system. An example from one of our partners, Silicon Application Company (SAC), it employed an extra 23 employees just to maintain its 23 different customers' systems. For this reason, I believe that adapting to an integrated IT infrastructure is crucial. However, we have no control (i.e. powerless) over our suppliers and customers, and cannot force them to use the same systems as we do. Thus, integration is not an easy task for us".*

Industrade realised the need to integrate its IT infrastructure as a way to gain a better control over its subsidiaries, customers and suppliers. However, it is hard to perform such a task, due to its lack of finance, and expertise, as reported by the manager:

> *"Integration Technology is still a long way to go because many companies develop their own systems, e.g. Web services, RosettaNet, and ebSML, and it is hard to integrate all these disparate systems. Despite all the difficulties to integrate these disparate systems, there is still a need to do so. This is why we are integrating our internal systems at the moment, because we take this process as a preparation for our future inter-organisational integration".*

5.9.3 Motivation to Integration Technologies Adoption

Semiconductor was a fast growing industry in Taiwan in 1980s, with many business opportunities. However, these business opportunities have decreased dramatically in the past few years due to the semiconductor industrial migration, with many of the manufacturers moving their factories to other Asian countries like China, Vietnam,

Malaysia and Thailand. In this case, Industrade has lost many of its customers (i.e. loss of competitive advantages), and has begun to realise that there is an urgent need to seek business opportunities outside Taiwan, as well as to build up a closer relationship with its existing customers (i.e. to provide a better service to them). To do this, the manager in Industrade recognised the importance of adopting integration technologies to support its intra and inter-organisational IS. Thus, Industrade set up an internationalised business plan three years ago regarding the adoption of integration technologies to support its intra and inter-organisational business processes. The plan was first to integrate its internal systems, then its external systems. However, this plan did not succeed due to costs concerns over the integration solutions available in the market at that time, e.g. mySAP and Oracle ERP too expensive.

Until Recently, Industrade has been introduced to a new software package from SAP Business One (B1). SAP B1 is a simple, 'off-the-shelf' integration software based on a Web Services platform (i.e. Web Services technology), which provides a cheaper, easier, and quicker adoption process for SMEs. SAP B1 provides the integration abilities that cover finance, sales, purchase, warehouse, distribution, production, invoice management, customer relations management, and human resources management, thus resulting in quicker decision-making process and increased efficiency. The Industrade MIS manager reported the reasons for adopting such software: (1) SAP is a well-known integration technology provider, (2) many IT companies adopt software from SAP, (3) reasonable and affordable price for small businesses, and (4) SAP B1 provides a platform which supports EAI and Web Services technologies. The manager said:

> *"We were going to adopt mySAP, but decided not to since it suits large organisations better than small business. However, SAP B1 is different, it is in a reasonable price, and it provides us with a platform that supports EAI or Web Services technologies, which can be used to help our inter-organisational integration in the future. We are currently the second user of SAP B1 in Taiwan".*

The manager also reported benefits of SAP B1:

- It has the same interface with Microsoft Windows, thus shortening users' learning period, and increasing productivity.

- It emphasises easy and quick access to users.

- It allows non-technical users to use this system, and there is no need to hire employees with technical background to maintain such a system.

- The characteristics of SAP B1 are integrated, localised, 'drag and relate', workflow warning system, and strongly adaptive with other system.

Industrade has purchased the software already, and is planning to implement this software in September 2005. It is currently preparing for B1 adoption by undergoing a Business Process Reengineering (BPR) with the assistance from a SAP consultant in Taiwan. The MIS manager reported that Industrade can only afford to adopt SAP B1 for intra-organisational integration (i.e. ERP) at the moment, due to the limited resources (e.g. costs, time, knowledge, etc.), but will consider inter-organisational integration in the future when the budget is allowed and technical ability is mature.

5.9.4   Barriers to Integration Technologies Adoption

One problem is that since adopting ERP system needs Industrade to provide a clear flow chart of its business processes, which is difficult for Industrade because it does not have a formal decision-making process, and a formal flowchart to follow. The MIS manager reported that "We really have a tough time in uniting and identifying our business processes, thus many meetings were arranged to re-engineer all of our management processes. For this reason, many employees feel under-pressure, i.e. overloading".

Employees' resistance to change was another serious barrier to Industrade's ERP adoption; as reported by the MIS manager, most employees found it difficult to understand all the technical terms and issues because different terms are used in different software companies (e.g. 'bill' is used in the IBM financial system, whereas 'invoice' is used in the SAP financial system, etc.). A lot of employees fear that they will not be able to operate in an integrated environment, as they are short of hard skills. The MIS manager reported:

> *"It is easier to solve technical problems than to change human behaviour. Most employees are wondering that whether adapting to an integrated IT infrastructure can really add value to the company, and make things easier for them".*

Despite the barriers mentioned above, the MIS manager believed that education will help employees understanding the reasons for adopting integrated solutions, and thus reduce resistance to change. Training can also help employees adapt to using a system, as they will advance their knowledge and learn how to handle and operate an integrated solution.

In addition, the researcher asked the MIS manager to report any other relevant integration technologies barriers, and these are summarised in Table 5.16.

Table 5.16 Classification of Industrade's Integration Technologies Barriers

Key: High (●), Medium (◖), Low (○)

Category	Integration Technologies Barriers	Significance
Operational	Face operational challenges	◖
Managerial	Face difficulty in managing relationships with other organisations	●
Strategic	Lack of business perspective	◖
Technical	Lack of large-scale implementation examples and experiences available	○
	Lack of security protocols and standards	◖
	Concern over security	●
	Concern over maturity of integration technologies	◖
	Concern over transaction distribution management	●
	Add complexity to business transaction protocol implementation	●
	Lack of system reliability at any moment	●
	Concern over whether old generation solutions are agile enough to react to changes	○
	Lack of XML-based management protocol	○
Organisational	Difficult to change internal organisational culture	◖
	Increase organisational complexity	○

Although more time, budget and expertise are required for integration technologies adoption, the manager is still very positive. He said: "We see this transformation is a learning process, and will try to overcome the problems as much as we can".

As for the benefits, since Industrade is going to adopt SAP B1 in September 2005, benefits of adopting integration technologies are therefore unclear at this stage. The manager reported that it needs a time of at two years to realise its benefits, but it is expecting an improvement in business efficiency. Industrade has run the system SAP B1 as a pilot for 2 months, and reported that efficiency has been improved, which is 5 times better than before. Industrade is expecting that adopting SAP B1 will (1) automate business processes and minimise errors, and (2) provide better understanding, and control of business processes. The MIS manager claimed that integration technologies adoption is necessary (i.e. basic requirement to gain competitive advantage), especially for companies in the IT industry, and is the way to remain competitive.

5.9.5 Investigating Factors Affecting Adoption Decision

The interviewee was asked to comment on the factors (as reported in Section 3.2.4) affecting the decisions for SAP B1 adoption, as shown in Table 5.17.

The interviewee addressed that the most important factors affecting Industrade's adoption decision are: (1) adopter characteristics, (2) organisational characteristics, (3) availability of standards, (4) internal environment, and (5) IT sophistication. Among these factors, adopter and organisational characteristics are the most important for the decision. This is because the manager in Industrade is the key decision-maker (i.e. top-to-bottom decision-making process), his characteristics can influence the way it approaches integration technologies adoption. Unlike Hi-Touch and eSynergy, where their managers emphasise the cost issue more than anything else, the manager in Industrade focuses more on gaining competitive advantages and improving the business operations.

In this and the previous section (Section 5.8), the researcher has discussed two different SME cases as integration technologies non-adopters, where one has the intention to adopt, and the other does not. The results derived from these two case studies provide a comprehensive view on integration technologies adoption by SMEs, which can help the researcher to better understand the differences between SMEs and large organisations in their adoption. In the next section, these differences among a large organisaiton (AboCom), and SMEs (Hi-Toucfh, eSynergy, and Industrade) for their adoption decisions will be analysed.

Table 5.17 Integration Technologies Adoption Factors

Key: High (●), Medium (◓), Low (○)

Factors	Importance
Adopter Characteristics	●
Availability of Standards	●
Barriers	●
Business Complexity	○
Competitive Pressures	◓
Customer Power	◓
Dependency on Partners/ Trading Partners Readiness	◓
Environmental Characteristics	◓
Evaluation Framework for Integration Technology and Packages	○
External Pressure	◓
Extent of Organisational Change	●
External Environment Characteristics	◓
IS Innovation Type	○
IT Sophistication	●
IT Infrastructure	●
Internal Environment Characteristics	●
Internal Pressure	○
Innovation Characteristics/ Perceived Innovation Characteristics	●
Organisational Characteristics	●
Organisational Readiness	◓
Perceived Financial Cost/ Financial Resources	●
Perceived Benefits (Direct and Indirect)	●
Perceived Technical Competence	◓
Technological Skills Readiness	◓
Perceived Industry Pressure	○
Perceived Government Pressure	○
Security	●
Control Procedures	◓
Support/ Organisation Support	◓
Stakeholders	○
Supplier Trust	●
Supplier Commitment	●
Technical Factors	◓

5.10 Analysing Difference between Large and Small Organisations in relation to Integration Technologies Adoption

Following the above description of the case studies on AboCom (Section 5.6), Hi-Touch (Section 5.7), eSynergy (Section 5.8) and Industrade (Section 5.9), similarly to Section 5.5.1, this section examines whether the identified parameters in Chapter 3, Figure 3.2 are appropriate to explain the adoption of integration technologies in SMEs and large organisations. These parameters are now analysed respectively in the following sections.

5.10.1 Nature of Organisations

As reported in Sections 5.6 and 5.7, the nature of SMEs and large organisations has impacted on the way they approach integration technologies adoption. For Hi-Touch and Industrade (SMEs), they prefer to go for an 'off-the-shelf' software package, as this is a much cheaper and more convenient option. Most of the time, Hi-Touch does not have sufficient knowledge to develop the system on its own, and development is very time-consuming. This indicates that the nature of a SME is to have limited resources (see literature reviewed in Section 1.4). As for a large firm like AboCom, it has adopted various types of integration technologies to support its IS integration. The purpose of the adoption of such technologies is to improve business efficiency, to provide customers with better services, and to build a closer relationship with suppliers, customers and partners. AboCom realised that not adapting to an integrated IT infrastructure will probably result in competitive disadvantages. The results from these two case studies show that the characteristics of SMEs and large organisations are significantly different, and this difference can affect their integration technologies adoption decision-making. Hence, SMEs and large organisations are focusing on different adoption factors when taking decisions.

5.10.2 Integration Needs

The basic integration need for AboCom, Hi-Touch and Industrade is similar, so as to increase business efficiency. However, AboCom, Hi-Touch and Industrade have different views in achieving this goal. For Hi-Touch, it focuses on the costs issue more than anything else. For Industrade, it focuses on gaining competitive advantages. As for AboCom, it understands the importance of adapting to an integrated IT infrastructure to solve its integration problems, as stated in Section 5.6.2, and it realised the adaptation to an integrated IT infrastructure is essential to secure its competitiveness. The analysis of these three case studies suggests that not only the integration needs between SMEs and large firms are different, but also their perceptions towards integration are different. SMEs and large organisations focus on different matters (i.e. their perceptions) towards their integration technologies adoption. For Hi-Touch, it sees the adaptation to an integrated IT infrastructure will add extra complexity and incur extra costs for the company. Thus, Hi-Touch often ignores the problems or issues with a non-integrated IT infrastructure. Industrade has the same concerns as Hi-Touch, such as time, finance, and expertises concerns, however, these difficulties have not diminished its intention to adopt integration technologies to support its IS.

As for AboCom, it understands the integration problems caused by a non-integrated IT infrastructure, and is motivated to adapt to an integrated architecture. AboCom knows that without an integration solution, the company will probably end up with competitive disadvantages. AboCom realises building a closer relationship with its trading partners and customers is a very important issue, and is the key to success. Hence, the discussion here suggests that the integration needs and perceptions towards integration technologies are different between SMEs and large organisations. This difference can affect the adoption factors that SMEs and large firms are focusing on when taking a decision for their integration technologies adoption.

5.10.3 Company Size

It is clear that companies with different sizes approach integration technologies adoption differently referring to the case studies reported in Sections 5.6, 5.7, 5.8 and 5.9. It is obvious that companies with different sizes have different concerns for the integration technologies adoption. For example, Hi-Touch and Industrade can not afford expensive technologies such as an ERP system from SAP and tends to go for 'off-the-shelf' software, whereas AboCom has adopted an ERP system from SAP, and many other types of integration technologies such as EAI and Web Services. AboCom states that with its complex business activities and variety of products manufactured, avoiding data redundancy and building a closer relationship with its trading partners and customers (i.e. improved supply chain management) are the only way to remain competitive. Thus, adopting integration technologies to support AboCom's IS is essential. On the other hand, eSynergy claimed that its business activity is too simple, thus there is no need to adopt integration technologies. eSynergy argues that adopting integration technologies will only add complexity and extra costs to the organisation. The discussion here indicates that company with different sizes have different views and perceptions regarding adoption. This difference can affect the factors that SMEs and large firms are focusing on when taking an adoption decision.

As reported in Sections 5.6.5, 5.7.5 and 5.9.5, AboCom, Hi-Touch and Industrade have reported 5 most important factors affecting their integration technologies adoption decision. This is shown in Table 5.18.

Table 5.18. Adoption Factors for Integration Technologies Adoption in SMEs and large Organisations

Elements	Adoption Factors for AboCom (Large Firm)	Adoption Factors for Hi-Touch and Industrade (SMEs)
External Environment Context	• Competitive pressure • Customer power	• Competitive pressure • External pressure • Internal environment
Technological Context	• Perceived benefits	• Available of standards
Organisational Context	• Perceived financial costs • IT infrastructure	• Perceived financial costs • Adopter characteristics • IT sophistication • Organisational characteristics

Table 5.18 indicates that most factors (i.e. common factors) are used by SMEs and large firms to explain their integration technologies adoption decision, for example factors like perceived benefits, competitive pressure and perceived financial costs. However, Tables 5.12, 5.15 and 5.17 suggest that SMEs and large organisations in some ways are still focusing on different factors when taking decisions for the adoption of integration technologies (only two or three different factors between them).

5.10.4 Time

AboCom reported that it started the implementation for EDI and ERP systems 4 years ago, and that only in the recent 1 to 2 years EAI and Web Services technologies have been adopted. As for Hi-Touch, it started its ERP system implementation 3 years ago, together with the EDI technology. Industrade is going to adopt ERP system in September 2005. When the interviewees were asked to comment on whether the early adoption of integration technologies as resulted in competitive advantages, AboCom replied that:

> *"The early adoption of integration technologies has helped the company remain in the competition. It is hard to say whether this has given us competitive advantages, but certainly gives us many advantages. The early adoption was partly due to the pressures from our customers, as they demand more efficient business processes. In order to fulfil our customers'*

>*needs, the MIS team decided to develop and adopt essential integration*
>*technologies to support our IS integration".*

Hi-Touch said that:

>*"I don't think that we can be considered as early adopters, as we are still*
>*lagging behind many companies in terms of integration technologies*
>*adoption. We have so far only been able to install ERP systems and partial*
>*EDI systems. EAI and Web Services technologies are still a bit new to us.*
>*We need to gather more information about these technologies and make*
>*sure that adopting these integration technologies can actually cut down the*
>*system maintenance costs and operational costs. However, due to the*
>*budgets concern, at the moment, it is not possible for us to consider any new*
>*integration technologies. Maybe in the future, you never know".*

Industrade claimed that:

>*"Yes, I think early adoption of integration technologies will give our*
>*company competitive advantages. Despite the leading position for large*
>*firms, as far as I know, for a company size like us (with only 15 employees),*
>*we are in the leading position in adopting integration technologies in*
>*Taiwan. Most of other small businesses have not yet realised the benefits of*
>*integration technologies".*

Based on the findings here, it suggests that timing can affect the different adoption factors between SMEs and large firms when taking decisions for their integration technologies adoption. For example, IT maturity might be a factor/concern for SMEs, but not necessarily for large firms, as no matter whether the technology is mature or not, the early adopters will still be likely to take the initiative to adopt such technology. In this case, Hi-Touch and Industrade can be categorised in the late majority or laggards groups compared to large firms.

5.11 Conclusion

This chapter presents and analyses the integration technologies adoption practices in one Industry Automation project which has 15 large organisations and many of their suppliers (SMEs) involved, and in one large company and three SMEs (adopter and non-adopters). Based on the empirical data reported in this chapter, the enquiry now is able to draw conclusions. However, before any conclusions can be presented, it is important to appreciate the positioning of such conclusions within the context of the empirical research methodology presented in the preceding chapter. As a result, the following represents those conclusions derived from the empirical research presented in this chapter.

Empirical data revealed from these case studies confirm that the parameters identified in the conceptual model in Section 3.2.5 affect the different adoption factors among AboCom , Hi-Touch and Industrade (also suppliers and the case companies) when they take decisions for integration technologies adoption. Additionally, the empirical data also confirmed that the adoption factors for integration technologies can be placed into three categories: common factors, factors explicit to SMEs and factors explicit to large organisations, as proposed in Section 3.4. The common factors that influence integration technologies adoption have been reported, such as perceived benefits, perceived barriers, perceived financial costs and competitive pressure. Factors explicitly for SMEs are IT sophistication, organisation characteristics, external pressure and dependency on trading partners. Factors explicitly for large organisations are IT infrastructure, technical factors, internal pressure and perceived future prospect. The identified factors will be further analysed in Chapter 6, and also the factors that have been reported and analysed in this chapter are taken into consideration in Chapter 6 to revise the conceptual model proposed in Figure 3.8.

A number of interesting issues emerged after analysing the 'stories' of the focal companies and the suppliers involved in the Industry Automation Programme case and the three additional case studies. The most predominant issue was that the large organisations (i.e. focal companies) have realised that, nowadays, the competition among enterprises is about the efficiency of the supply chain, which stress tighter cooperation relationship of overall supply chain process. This was done by organisations adopting integration technologies such as EAI and ERP to support their supply chain integration. However, most of their suppliers do not have this vision, and do not have sufficient knowledge or resource to support their integration technologies adoption. Therefore, this was where the Industry Automation Project came from to support the focal company and, in the mean time, to push their suppliers (most of them are SMEs) to adopt integration technologies to support the efficiency of their supply chains. In doing so, additional adoption factors for SMEs were found, such as purchasing amount and purchasing frequency. When these are high from the focal companies, their suppliers are more willing to adopt integration technologies to support their supply chains, so as to increase business processes efficiency to satisfy their customers (focal companies).

Another issue was that since the Industry Automation Programme case was supported by the Taiwan government financially and technically, most of the barriers to integration technologies adoption by SMEs to support their supply chains were eliminated. For example, technical support, support from their focal companies, financial support, etc.. The situation might be different for those SMEs without all this appropriate support, as most SMEs might just ignore support to face their problems. This was further illustrated in the Hi-Touch, eSynergy and Industrade case studies, where the researcher found that the managers in SMEs play an important role in decision-making. The main reasons why eSynergy has not adopted integrated technologies were due to the fact that they do not have sufficient resources, and the manager in eSynergy does not want to face the problems they would have. The culture of eSynergy is more towards autocracy, where the manager is the key decision-making person, and its main goal is to stay in the competition (i.e. to survive). Thus, eSynergy does not want to risk and to spend more budgets on integration technologies investment as it does not want to fail. As mentioned in the eSynergy case study, it tried earlier to adopt the ERP system, but it did not succeed. Thus, eSynergy is afraid of failing, and can not afford to fail again. Similar to eSynergy, the main goal of Hi-Touch is to survive. The manager in Hi-Touch thinks that the adoption of integration technologies will be time-consuming and costly, and the existing systems are good enough to manage the current business processes. Additionally, Industrade also mentioned that due to the limited resources, it can only manage to integrate its internal IS, rather than external. These demonstrate the different factors and concerns focused on between SMEs and large organisations when taking decisions for their integration technologies adoption. The researcher found that most SMEs lack a future perspective compared to large organisations, where they realised that the future competition is among supply chains and not the enterprises. Therefore, the adoption of integration technologies to support their supply chains is seen as an important issue for the future success of the large organisations.

Managing people is another key issue or limitation for SMEs in terms of their integration technologies adoption. As reported by Hi-Touch, eSynergy and Industrade, the most difficult problem is not the technical area, but the management problem. How to manage people is a very difficult task for companies like Hi-Touch and eSynergy with a high employee turnover rate. Both companies found it hard to retain knowledge in their organisations. This explains why SMEs often lack 'know-how', as reported in the literature discussed in Section 1.4.

The key conclusions elicited from the adoption of integration technologies in the Industry Automation Programme (includes suppliers and focal companies), eSynergy, Industrade, AboCom, and Hi-Touch, are summarised in the following paragraphs.

- The cases presented in this chapter suggest that the nature of SMEs and large organisations is significantly different, and this can affect their adoption decisions. For example, Hi-Touch and Industrade prefer to go for off-the-shelf software package, as this way is bother-free and less time-consuming, and is a much cheaper option. As for a large organisation like AboCom, it has fewer limitations compared to SMEs, thus its focus for integration technologies adoption is different from theirs, e.g. providing better services to customers, increase efficiency etc.

- The tremendous changes in the business arena require flexible organisations that can easily adapt to the needs of the business environment. Pressures from the business environment, such as increased competition and trading partner's pressures, appear to have affected the decision of AboCom and the focal companies in the Industry Automation project for integration technologies adoption. Empirical data indicate that AboCom and the focal companies (mainly large organisations) have moved to integration technologies adoption such as EAI and Web Services to address: (1) increased competition, and (2) pressures from their partners for closer collaboration. The empirical data also reveal that SMEs like Hi-Touch, Industrade and the suppliers have not yet been able to adapt to fully-integrated their IT infrastructure, e.g. adoption of EAI or Web Services. The main reason for this was that the managers from SMEs see the adaptation to an integrated IT infrastructure will add extra complexity and incur extra costs to the company. Thus, this confirms that the integration needs and perceptions regarding integration technologies are different between SMEs and large organisations. In other words, large firms use IS/IT to add value rather than simply to reduce costs. SMEs' exploitation of IS tends to mimic the early use in large firms – cost reduction. However, SMEs may use IS to co-ordinate internal activities, to add value via collaboration, particularly with customers, and occasionally, to innovate. This difference can affect the adoption factors that SMEs and large firms are focusing on when taking a decision for integration technologies adoption.

- The case studies reported in this chapter also reveal that companies with different sizes have different views and perceptions regarding integration technologies adoption. This difference can affect the factors that SMEs and large firms are focusing on when taking an adoption decision.

- Empirical evidence elicited from all the case studies shows that the early adoption of integration technologies has helped the company to remain in the competition. The case companies reported that the adoption of integration technologies to support the efficiency of their business processes is an important issue, as the competition will only get tougher and to hold more chips in hand is the only way to succeed in the future. Adapting to an integrated IT architecture early will help the company to avoid any problems caused by a non-integrated IT infrastructure.

- A number of factors were found associated with the adoption of integration technologies explicit for SMEs, large organisations, and for both (i.e. common factors). The empirical data show that factors for Hi-Touch and Industrade (i.e. SMEs) are IT sophistication, internal environment, external pressure, adopter characteristics, availability of standards, and organisation characteristic. As for AboCom and the case companies from Industry Automation Programme (i.e. large organisations), they focus more on factors such as customer power, and IT infrastructure. The common factors are competitive pressure, perceived benefits, perceived barriers, and perceived financial costs. The classification of factors will be discussed in more detail in Chapter 6.

Chapter 6: Revised Conceptual Model

Summary

The previous chapter explored the research issues identified in Chapter 3, which dealt with the factors that influence the adoption of integration technologies between SMEs and large organisations. In doing so, Chapter 5 presented and analysed case studies, which were conducted in one supply chain integration project named Industry Automation Programme, one large organisations, and three SMEs (adopter and non-adopters). The issues in practice and the empirical evidence that resulted from the analysis indicate the need for modifications to the conceptual model proposed in Figure 3.8. This chapter takes into consideration the empirical data to revise the conceptual model and to validate the research questions identified in Chapter 3. In doing so, satisfying the aim of this thesis by offering decision-makers and researchers a frame of reference for the adoption of integration technologies in SMEs and large organisations.

6.1 Introduction

A review of the innovation and diffusion literature indicates a considerable amount of research where attention is given to a range of features which may support integration technologies adoption, e.g. of EAI, EDI and Web Services. However, according to the literature where it addresses that due to SMEs' very distinct type of characteristics, they use IT to support their business differently from large counterparts (Iacovou, Benbasat & Dexter, 1995; Kuan & Chau, 2001). SMEs are different from other types of organisations, where by their natural resources are limited by such as time, financial and expertise constraints (Barney, 1991; Thong, 2001; Welsh & White, 1981). For this reason, it is expected that SMEs may focus on different factors from larger organisations when taking decisions for their integration technologies adoption. Thus, taking into account the specific characteristics of SMEs which made them distinct from other types of organisations, in an attempt to study the adoption of integration technologies areas, a number of research questions are raised as reported in Chapters 2 and 3. These research questions are investigated in Chapter 3 and supported the researcher to identify the parameters for the integration technologies adoption in SMEs and large organisations. These parameters are: nature, integration needs, time and company size. A conceptual model was thus proposed in Chapter 3 Figure 3.8 that can be used to explain the adoption of integration technologies, taking into consideration the different adoptions factors that SMEs and large organisations focus on.

The conceptual model was examined through empirical evidence reported in Chapter 5, which suggests that the empirical data complement the identified parameters: nature, integration needs, company size and time shown in Figures 3.2 and 3.8. As reported in the literature, IS research is often criticised for insufficient reference to theory in explanations of findings (Caldeira & Ward, 2003). Therefore, further analysis in this chapter describes how the findings from the study can be understood with reference to resource-based, and diffusion of innovation theories reported in Chapter 2 and 3. This results in the identification of sub-parameters. In addition, based on the empirical data and the theoretical analysis, a number of adoption factors are found. These adoption factors are then classified into common factors, factors explicitly for SMEs and factors explicitly for large firms (as reported in the proposed conceptual model in Figure 3.8) to support a more comprehensive view of this area. Apart from the factors reported in the literature, an additional factor (perceived future prospect) was found, based on the empirical data analysis.

Chapter 5 has offered much empirical data that has been used to assess the conceptual model presented in Section 3.4 Figure 3.8 for the adoption of integration technologies in SMEs and large organisations. The aim of this chapter is to take into account and further analyse the empirical data that derived from the previous chapter (Chapter 5), offer revisions to the conceptual model for integration technologies adoption in SMEs and large organisations as well as report any additional findings. Section 6.2 summarises and further analyses the key issues elicited from the analysis of the case studies reported in Chapter 5, exemplifying their need to be considered in any revisions to the conceptual mode. Thereafter, Section 6.3 revises the conceptual model for integration technologies adoption in SMEs and large organisations. Modifications are made to the conceptual model by adding factors that are derived from empirical research and theoretical analysis. These factors focus on: (1) factors explicitly for SMEs: external pressure, IT sophistication, dependency on trading partners, and government regulation; (2) factors explicitly for large organisations: IT infrastructure, IS complexity, internal pressure, and perceived future prospects; and (3) common factors: perceived benefits, perceived barriers, perceived financial costs, and competitive pressure.

Hence, this chapter results in the proposition of a novel conceptual model for the adoption of integration technologies in SMEs and large organisations. Such a model can be used by organisations or researchers as a tool for decision-making when adopting integration technologies.

6.2 Lessons Learned from Case Studies and Further Analysis of the Empirical Data

A synopsis of the main findings elicited from Chapter 5 is given in this section, allowing others to relate their experiences to those reported in Chapter 5. It is not the intention of this section (or this thesis) to offer prescriptive guidelines for integration technologies adoption, but rather to describe case study perspectives that allow others to relate their experiences to those reported. Hence, this thesis offers a broader understanding of the phenomenon of integration technologies adoption, taking into consideration the differences between SMEs' and large organisations' nature, company size, integration needs and adoption timing, and make use of resource-based and innovation diffusion theories to analyse and interpret such differences. However, this research does not intend to compare the adoption of integration technologies between SMEs and large organisations, as it is inappropriate to compare two very different types of companies, as the result ought to be different. Rather, this research aims to apply the resource-based and diffusions of innovation theories to interpret and analyse the different adoption factors that SMEs and large organisations focused on when taking decisions for their integration technologies adoption. This results in a richer picture of integrated technologies adoption.

A number of interesting issues have been extrapolated from the empirical data, and an additional factor was discovered that was taken into account during the adoption of integration technologies by the case organisations reported. The key issues that derived from empirical data are summarised and further analysed in the following sub-sections.

6.2.1 Nature Resources of Organisations

All types of companies today seek to become more agile and responsive, and to maximise their existing IT investments. To do this, they need to unlock information and functionality in individual applications and turn them into a shared, enterprise-wide resource. Thus, integration of enterprise applications and data to simplify and automate business processes has become an important focus for many organisations. Nonetheless, as stated in Section 2.4, the unique characteristics of small businesses are exemplified in the condition known as resource poverty, where small businesses operate under severe time constraints, financial constraints, and expertise constraints. Pettiigrew, Whipp and Rosenfeld (1989) and Caldeira and Ward (2003) also emphasise the internal and external resources to analyse the IS/IT implementation in SMEs. They state that the internal resources include (1) financial resources, (2) human resources, (3) management perspectives and attitudes, (4) IS/IT competences, (5) organisational structure, (6) power relationships, and (7) user attitudes. The external resources cover (1) external expertise (e.g. vendors' support or consultant effectiveness), (2) technology available, and (3) business environment (e.g. clients, and suppliers, pressure to adopt IS/IT).

The empirical data complement the viewpoint reported in the literature and indicate that different types of organisations (micro, small, medium and large organisations) approach integration technologies adoption differently due to their internal and external resources constraints. According to the Industry Automation Programme, most of their SMEs suppliers are not able to achieve a high level of automation when adopting integration technologies due to their limited abilities (lack of know-how) and resources. Hi-Touch, Industrade and eSynergy also reported that the limited finance, time and expertise resources have inhibited their integration technologies adoption. For this reason, eSynergy has not yet adopted any type of integration technology to support there is, and Industrade is only able to integrate its internal IS.

Although Hi-Touch has adopted EDI technology, EDI, as reported in Chapter 2, has many drawbacks and can not fully support organisations to integrate their intra and inter-organisational systems. Thus, Hi-Touch has not managed to overcome all of its integration problems. Furthermore, the empirical data also demonstrates that the financial constraint seems to be the biggest concern to Hi-Touch, eSynergy, and Industrade, and this tends to delay their integration technologies adoption. AboCom also reported that its SMEs suppliers' abilities for integration are low, and this has caused a problem to AboCom, as many transactions still need to be handed manually by telephone or fax. Nonetheless, the empirical evidence also illustrates that the lack of sufficient integrated technologies knowledge of most SME managers (e.g. suppliers, Hi-Touch, and eSynergy) has caused delay in their integration technologies adoption decision-making, since they are the major decision makers as well as the key persons in the survival of the business (Rizzoni, 1991; Thong & Yap, 1994). Contrast to Hi-Touch and eSynergy, manager in Industrade is intended to integrate their intra and inter-organisational systems. In order to meet this goal, Industrade is currently working on integrating its intra-organisational systems, and is preparing to integrate its inter-organisational systems by considering EAI and Web Services technologies in the near future. Therefore, this indicates that the decision on whether to adopt an integration technology is heavily depended on SMEs managers' perceptions, knowledge and intentions (i.e. highly depended on adopter or organisational characteristics).

Thus, the evidence discussed here in this section provides the answer to the research question: Are the nature resources of SMEs a real obstacle to the adoption of integration technologies?

6.2.2 Integration Needs

According to the Industry Automation Programme case, large organisations and SMEs have different needs in integration technologies adoption. The large companies involved in the project reported that they adopt integration technologies to assist their supply chains as (1) to support their own manufacturing processes, (2) to retain their competitiveness, (3) to support their future needs for any possible type of supply chain integration, and (4) to fulfil the transparency that would facilitate the enhanced levels of customer service required. As for their SMEs suppliers, they reported that the main drive for them to adopt integration technologies was from the external pressures such as from the trading partners and the government. SMEs suppliers claimed that some of the case companies are their biggest customers, thus they have no choice but to respond to their requests to integrate their IT infrastructure. Hi-Touch described that despite whether there is a need to adapt to an integrated IT infrastructure, cost is always the concern. eSynergy also revealed that failure is not allowed, as the main goal for them is to survive, thus they cannot afford to fail. In this kind of situation, SMEs' integration need is most likely lead to an integration technologies non-adoption. The empirical evidence here suggests that the integration needs for SMEs and large organisations can be classified into: (1) passive mode, and (2) active mode. When organisations' integration needs are more towards active mode (e.g. needs come from their technical, managerial needs, etc.), they are more likely to adopt them, and less likely not adopt integration technologies. When organisations' integration needs are more towards passive mode (e.g. being forced), they have equal chances to either adopt and not to adopt integration technologies, and this decision is highly depended on the perception of SMEs' managers. The relationship between integration needs and integration technologies adoption is explained in Figure 6.1. Thus, the empirical evidence here provides answer to the research question: To what extent do SMEs' integration needs differ from large companies'?

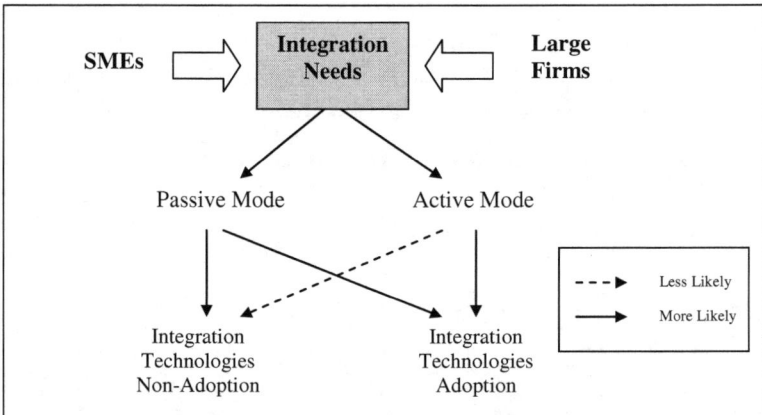

Figure 6.1 Relationship between Integration Needs and Integration Technologies Adoption

6.2.3   Company Size

The empirical data suggest that companies of different sizes have different perceptions in relation to their integration technologies adoption. For instance, a small-sized company like eSynergy reported that its business activity is simple, and adopting integration technologies will only add complexity and extra costs to the company. For a company like AboCom, its business activities are complex, and integration technologies enable its

IT infrastructure and applications to respond rapidly to business changes by providing a dynamic way to streamline, integrate, and manage previously independent business processes. This suggests that there is a relationship between business complexity and company size. The empirical data indicate that the larger size the company is, the more complex the business activities can get. Moreover, when the business activities are more complex in an organisation, the more likelihood that such an organisation will adopt integration technologies. When the business activities are less complex in an organisation, the more likelihood that such an organisation will not adopt integration technologies (see Figure 6.2). Hence, the evidence here provides the answer to the research question: What is the relationship between integration technologies and their adoption in companies of different sizes?

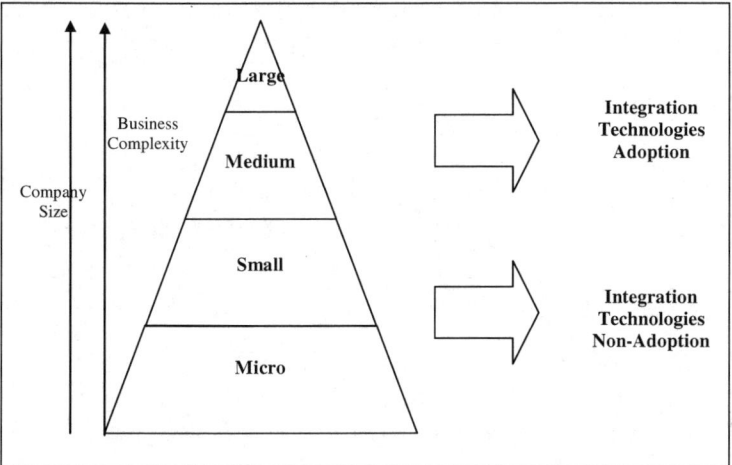

Figure 6.2 Relationship between Company Size and Integration Technologies Adoption

6.2.4   Time

AboCom reported that the benefits of adopting integration technologies are obvious, and not adopting will become a problem for the organisation. The big multinational companies involved in the Industry Automation Programme case study also stated that early adoption of integration technologies, e.g. EAI or Web Services, gives the companies a future prospect. Also, integration technologies like Web Services and EAI are the trend, and the technologies are actually pretty mature now. The SMEs' suppliers involved in the Industry Automation Programme case study and Hi-Touch indicate that their IT abilities are relatively low, and having less financial support compared to those large organisations, they thus tend to go for off-the-shelf software packages. Hi-Touch reported that it does feel the pressure from the external environment; however, its financial status is still its biggest concern in relation to its integration technologies adoption. Thus, it tends to delay adoption.

In the analysis of the case data, timing was identified to have influence on adoption decision-making. Consequently, such differences led to divergent adoption policies and practices. To further illustrate the integration technologies adoptions between SMEs and large organisations in a comprehensive manner, a single-dimension typology to distinguish each integration technologies adopter is considered through the themes of Initiator, Facilitator and Consumer.

- **Initiator.** Integration technologies *initiator* refers to organisations that have recognised the need for adopting integration technologies, have less constraint for financial support, have higher level of IT sophistication, and do not experience excessive pressure through external factors. These firms normally adopt integration technologies internally to strengthen their core business competitiveness. This type of adoption later transforms into increased interaction with their business partners. In this case, larger case companies (i.e. focal companies) are representative of such an initiator, referred to in the Industry Automation Programme case study reported in Section 5.5. This type of adopters can also be categorised as innovators or early adopters (see Section 3.2.4).

- **Facilitator.** Integration technologies *facilitator* refers to organisations that have recognised the potential growth of the market, are financially and technically capable to develop integration technologies products, and make it their core business at strategic level. These firms may adopt integration technologies internally to support their business objectives and operation. In this case, AboCom is representative of such a *facilitator*, referred to in the AboCom case study reported in Section 5.6. The adopters classified in this group can also be categorised as the early majority.

- **Consumer.** Integration technologies *consumer* refers to adopters which have already received or recognised the pressure from business environment, have less IT capability and financial support, and use integration technologies to support their core business. In this case, SMEs like Hi-Touch, Industrade, and suppliers from the Industry Automation Programme are representative of such a *consumer*, referred to in the Industry Automation Programme case study reported in Section 5.5, and the

Hi-Touch, and the Industrade case studies reported in Sections 5.7 and 5.9. The adopters classified in this group can also be categorised as the late majority or laggards.

Table 6.1 summarises the discussion above. Thus, the discussion and evidence here provide the answer to the research question: Can early adoption of integration technologies by the organisations gain competitive advantages?

Table 6.1 Summary of Integration Technologies Adopter Categories

Adopter Typology	Adopter Categories	Case Company	Adoption Decision	Adoption Results
Initiator	• Innovators • Early adopters	• ACER Inc • MiTAC International Corporation • PRIMAX Electronics Ltd • Inventec Corporation • TATUNG Co • MicroStar Inc. (MSI) • ADI Corporation • SAMPO Technology Corporation • Compal Electronics Inc • First International Computer Inc • Arima Computer Corp • Compeq Manufacturing. Co. Ltd • Twinhead International Corporation • Delta Electronic • ASUSTeK Coputer Inc	Adopt primarily for internal IS integration and external supply chain integration	• Competitiveness strengthened • Dictating position with business partners
Facilitator	• Early majority	• AboCom Technology Ltd	Adopt in new products and services creation	• Critical to success of business • New services created
Consumer	• Late majority • Laggards	• Hi-Touch • eSynergy • Industrade	Adopt commercial packages for internal use	• End-user of innovative IS products

6.2.5 Adoption Factors

A review of the adoption literature in an organisational context indicates a considerable amount of research on the topic of integration technologies, as discussed in Sections 2.3 and 2.5. Various adoption factors for integration technologies have been analysed and reported in Section 3.4, where the researcher classified them into three categories: (1) factors for SMEs, (2) factors for large organisations, and (3) common factors. Based on the classification of the factors, together with the empirical evidence reported in Chapter 5, the researcher further analyses these factors to identify those that can be used to address the integration technologies adoption between SMEs and large organisations, as well as to confirm the research question: Do SMEs and large companies consider the different factors when taking decisions for the adoption of integration technologies? However, it is argued that the framework developed by Tornatzky & Fleischer (1990) is of significant value, and that it provides a useful starting point to consider integration technologies adoption by highlighting the specific situations for the analysis process.

There are three elements which influence the process by which innovations are adopted, as reported by Tornatzky and Fleischer (1990): (1) environmental context, (2) technological context, and (3) organisational context.

Environmental Context. Evidence shows that fierce market competition appears to stimulate the rapid diffusion of an innovation (Mansfield et al., 1997). When an organisation is facing a complex and rapidly changing environment, technology is both necessary and justified (Pfeffer & Leblebici, 1997). Furthermore, Ettlie et al. (1984) argue that the dichotomy of radical versus incremental innovation emerges in organisations. One aspect of this dimension appears to be whether or not the innovation incorporates technology that is a clear and potentially risky departure from existing practice (Hage, 1980). The impetus of rapid diffusion of innovation is proposed that if a technology is new to the adopting unit and new to the referent group of organisations, or if it requires both throughput (process) as well as output (production or service) change, then the cost required by the organisation is sufficient to warrant the designation of a radical, as opposed to incremental, innovation (Hage, 1980). In addition, requirements for participating in competition in the e-business/e-commerce marketplace also fuel the migration to integration technologies innovation adoption e.g. Web Services. The sources of environmental pressure that push the company to adopt integration technologies may therefore be noted through two strands: (1) the external environment, and (2) the internal environment.

(1) External environment of the organisation. Here, the importance of strategic alliances has been well recognised. Chau & Tam (1997) suggest such context includes the industry, competitors, regulations, and relationships with the government. In many cases, a company may adopt a technology due to influences exerted by its business partners or/and its competitors, and has nothing to do with the technology and organisation by itself. For example, Iacovou et al. (1995) reported that when US car manufacturers required all their suppliers to use EDI in their transactions with them, adopting an EDI system then become an imposition for the new entrants. Similar to this example, is the Industry Automation Programme case reported in Chapter 5

where the focal manufacturers required all their suppliers to adopt EDI over the Internet and RosettaNet standard in their transactions with them. Suppliers in this situation felt the pressure to adopt the integration technologies as their business partners requested or recommended them to. The empirical data also imply that the external pressures often related to companies like SMEs. Since SMEs are usually the weaker partners in inter-organisational relationships, small businesses are susceptible to impositions by their larger partners (Iacovou et al., 1995; Saunders & Hart, 1993). Furthermore, since the programme was financially and technically supported by the Taiwan government, this motivation drove these SMEs suppliers to adopt integration technologies to support their supply chains. In this case, such support can be seen as part of the government regulation in enhancing SMEs' e-commerce and IT capability in order to boost economic growth, since SMEs account for over 90% of operating businesses in many countries and are vital for the global economy. Additionally, as mentioned by the case companies involved in the Industry Automation Programme case and AboCom, competitive pressure is an important factor that pushes them to adopt integration technologies. This factor was also addressed by Hi-Touch as a motivation to its integration technologies adoption. Thus, competitive pressure is classified as the common factor.

(2) Internal environment of the organisation. Here, companies benefit from a rapid expansion of their business to other parts of the world, as well as strategic re-structuring through acquisitions, divestitures, and partnerships. The traditional IS architecture may no longer cope with the changes of the market uncertainty, demand of logistics, information and processes flow and economic fluctuations at a global level that may affect the coordination among their units. All these factors will demand the need for a flexible, manageable, and maintainable IT infrastructure, permitting integration of heterogeneous systems at a lower cost. For example, the case company AboCom realised its needs to become more agile and responsive, and to maximise its existing IT investments. In order to do so, AboCome understands that it needs to unlock information and functionality in individual applications and turn them into a shared, enterprise-wide resource to tackle integration problems. Thus, results in cost savings, streamlined business processes, and increased efficiency. However, as reported in Chapter 5, companies like eSynergy and Hi-Touch in this case may not be able to solve all their integration problems by adopting integration technologies due to (1) their resources constraints such as time, finance and expertises, and (2) lack of manager/Chief Executive Officer (CEO)

support, as reported in the case studies, since the manager thinks the employees are too occupied and do not have time to integrate their IS. According to the literature, the CEO is often the main decision maker and shapes the future of the business (Mudd, 1990; Rizzoni, 1991). The impact of the CEO is even stronger in small businesses (Thong & Yap, 1994). Therefore, internal pressure might not be appropriate to explain SMEs' integration technologies adoption decision-making, since SMEs do not adopt a new innovation when they feel there is a need, but rather when they have no choices (e.g. feel competitive pressure), or if there are stimulations (e.g. government support).

Technological Context. The technological context relates to the technologies available to an organisation. Its main focus is on how technology characteristics themselves can influence the adoption process (Tornatzky & Fleischer, 1990). An important group of factors affecting the degree of influence are those related to the cost-benefit/trade-off of adopting a certain innovation. Integration technologies innovation (e.g. Web Services, EAI) is a novel approach in enterprise IS infrastructure development. Thus, an evaluation of the costs and benefits related to it may lead toward perceptions of the possible gains and barriers of adoption, which may be operationalised as two 'perceived' factors, (1) benefits, and (2) barriers.

Perceived benefits are not the same as awareness, since the latter is mainly concerned with the reception of information about integration technologies. Perceived benefits therefore capture the extent of agreement with claimed benefits that are relative to the adopters' local conditions. Chau & Tam (1997) argued in their Open Systems adoption study that awareness is a pre-condition of forming a belief (i.e. perception on benefits). It is the latter that drives an adoption decision. An example of perceived benefits of integration technologies adoption is the Web Services Benefits Analysis Model (Chen, 2003). The major technological benefits as well as their derived business benefits were identified through using a similar approach taken by Shang and Seddon (2000) and Themistocleous et al. (2001). Another example is the Perception-Based model for EDI adoption in small businesses (Kuan and Chau, 2001). Integration technologies also require a substantial degree of technical competence to ensure smooth adoption processes. System security and skill shortfalls in integration technologies know-how are also proposed to be inhibitors. In order to understand the inter-relationship of each inhibitor, Attewell (1992) offers a very useful perspective on innovation adoption by emphasising the role of know-how and organisational learning, beyond the monetary cost of the innovation to higher dimensions of organisational knowledge and the role of mediating parties in facilitating the adoption process. Attewell (1992) argues that "firms delay in-house adoption of complex technology until they obtain sufficient technical know-how to implement and operate it successfully". Knowledge barriers to acquiring new innovation of Attewell's (1992) perspective could be further explained by Clark's (1992) technology management theory that "most of the companies (around 65%) in the study had a lagging-edge philosophy which was prevalent with most administrative and transaction-processing systems".

In addition, Tichy (1980) theorised that organisational changes occur in response to three major sources of organisational uncertainties: uncertainties associated with technical designs, with political allocations, and with organisational ideologies. Resolution of one uncertainty form, however, invariably increases uncertainties associated with the other two forms. Integration technologies adoption, due to the complexity of implementation and the technological uncertainties, are of the higher priority. As Arrow (1962) notes, "it takes time and expertise to incorporate complex technologies in an organisation due to the notion of learning by doing". Thus, adoption of complex technology is not a single event, but may be described as a process of knowledge accumulation. Attewell (1992) further summarised this perspective to be applicable to innovations that (1) have an abstract and demanding scientific base, (2) are fragile, in the sense that they do not always operate as expected, (3) are difficult to try in a meaningful way, and (4) are 'unpackaged', in the sense that adopters cannot treat the technology as a black box but must acquire broad tacit knowledge and procedural know-how to use it effectively.

The empirical data indicate that AboCom, Hi-Touch and case companies involved in the Industry Automation Programme have reported their perceived benefits and barriers for their integration technologies adoption. The case companies also stated that: "Perceived benefits are important, as there is no point of adopting integration technologies if adopting such technologies does not add extra value to the companies". Rogers (1995) claims that organisations adopt new technologies only when they understand that such technologies will add value to their existing IT infrastructure. Thus, perceived benefits and barriers can be seen as important common factors for the integration technologies adoption by SMEs and large organisations. In addition, as mentioned by AboCom, Hi-Touch and eSynergy, cost is always an important issue, thus perceived financial costs is another important common factor.

Organisational Context. The organisational context describes the characteristics of an organisation. Common organisation characteristics include firm size, degree of centralisation, formalisation, complexity of its managerial structure, quality of its human resources, and amount of slack resources available internally (Chau & Tam, 1997). It looks at the structure and processes of an organisation that constrain or facilitate the adoption and implementation of innovations. Initially, integration technologies were invented in order to better accommodate a complex IS infrastructure consisting of multiple platforms with different connectivity arrangement. This complexity dimension takes into account the existence of a variety of disparate operating systems, applications, interfaces, and processes. For example, ERP systems have consistently experienced periods of forming monolithic data silos. Furthermore, in the EAI approach, Web Services innovation has been proposed to unify the method of interconnectivity of heterogeneous applications across unit boundaries instead of using 'patch solutions'.

Research in organisational behaviour has suggested that task complexity will promote the ability of an organisation to innovate. The rationale is that this leads to the creation of specialised units which help to enhance successful implementation of innovations. Zmud (1982) claimed that internal liaison groups are a key element in facilitating the adoption of innovations. Zaltman et al. (1973) also reported that the diversity of expertise promotes innovativeness by conceiving and proposing more innovative ideas. Historically, the organisation's attitude towards new IS innovation has migrated from simple typewriters and calculators to what are now thought by executives as important corporate strategic technologies. The pool of diverse expertise possessed by these specialists plays a significant role in lowering knowledge barriers during the migration process, leading to lower barriers for adoption. The information systems are still viewed proprietary in many companies, e.g. like AboCom and these involved in the Industry Automation Programme. After years of piecemeal purchase, case companies reported that they have inevitably generated a disparity of systems spread throughout different units. Such systems are often from different vendors (e.g. ERP systems) which also increases the extent of complexity. Thus, the need to integrate and interlink separate data silos is perceived to be another motivation that drives companies to adopt new technological innovation. This is particularly important to large organisations, as this type of organisation has more complex IT infrastructure than SMEs.

As reported by the case companies in Chapter 5, the non-integrated infrastructure causes many problems to the organisation since it could not achieve supply chain and eProcurement integration. Although an SME like the case company Hi-Touch reported that it has 5 subsidiaries around the world, they all have different IT infrastructure and install different applications and systems. Thus, Hi-Touch found it hard to manage these systems without an integrated solution. However, due to the lack of knowledge and financial costs concerns, they have not yet adopted all the necessary integration technologies to support their systems or data integration. Industrade also claimed that due to the lack of know-how, finance resources and time, it can only able to integrate its internal IS at the moment. These indicate that IT sophistication is more important to SMEs' integration technologies adoption than IT infrastructure or IS complexity. The reason is that even though SMEs' IT infrastructure is hard to manage, and their IS are complex, their limitations for sufficient resources e.g. expertise knowledge or financial resources, etc., will still inhibit their intentions to adopt integration technologies. The knowledge here includes manager's IT/IS knowledge. As mentioned earlier that SMEs' manager is the key decision-maker, thus, its perception and knowledge on integration technologies are important motivation that drives them to integration technologies adoption. Therefore, an adopter characteristic is also perceived as an appropriate motivation that drives SMEs to adopt integration technologies. The empirical data from the Industry Automation Programme also complement this point, as the SMEs' suppliers involved in this project are from the hi-tech sector, e.g. IT manufacturing industry and their IT sophistication and managers' knowledge on IS/IT are higher than that of SMEs from other divisions. Thus, expects higher intentions to their integration technologies adoption, as these of SMEs have sophisticated IT abilities and knowledge to fulfil the integration technologies' adoption target.

Apart from the factors reported in the literature, an additional one was found to be an important in driving large firms to adopt integration technologies, according to the empirical evidence. The case companies involved in the Industry Automation Programme reported: "Adopting integrated technologies to support organisations' supply chains are an important issue, as it gives organisations a future prospect, and this is the way to success". The case companies stated that nowadays, even for the future, the competition among enterprises is about the efficiency of supply chains, which emphasises a tighter cooperation relationship of the overall supply-chain process. Thus, the perceived future prospect is found to be an additional factor affecting the integration technologies' adoption in large organisations. Although the future prospect is important, it is not the main force that drives SMEs to adopt integration technologies. The case study of eSynergy complements this viewpoint. eSynergy realised the needs and the importance of adapting to an integrated IT infrastructure; however, costs and the prior experience of the unsuccessful implementation of an ERP system have inhibited its intention to adopt any other integration technologies to support its information systems. Moreover, as stated by the managers from the case studies, the main goal for them is to survive, if they cannot manage to survive now, there will not be a future.

To better understand the factors analysed in Section 6.2, the researcher summarises these factors in Table 6.2.

Table 6.2. Summary of Integration Technologies Adoption Factors

Context	Factors for SMEs	Factors for Large Firms	Common Factors
Environment	• External pressure • Dependency on trading partners • Government regulation	• Internal pressure	• Competitive pressure
Technological		• IT infrastructure • IS complexity • Perceived future prospect	
Organisaitonal	• Adopter characteristic		• Perceived benefits • Perceived barriers • Perceived costs

The discussion in this section suggests that SMEs and large organisations often consider different factors when taking decisions for the adoption of integration technologies. Thus, the discussion and evidence here provide the answer to the research question: Do SMEs and large companies consider different factors when taking decisions for the adoption of integration technologies?

Based on the discussion in Section 6.3, Table 6.3 verifies the research questions.

Table 6.3. Verification of Research Questions

Research Questions	Dimensions	Verification
Are the nature resources of SMEs a real obstacle to the adoption of integration technologies?	Nature	6.2.1
To what extent do SMEs' integration needs differ from large companies?	Integration Needs	6.2.2
What is the relationship between integration technologies and their adoption in companies of different sizes?	Company Size	6.2.3
Can early adoption of integration technologies by the organisations gain competitive advantages?	Time	6.2.4
Do SMEs and large companies consider different factors when taking decisions for the adoption of integration technologies?	Adoption Factors	6.2.5

6.3 Revised Conceptual Model

The process of developing a revised conceptual model has been made possible only after having carried out the empirical research reported in Chapter 5. As a result, following the investigation of research issues identified in Chapter 3, the model is now presented in Figure 6.3.

As illustrated in the figure, the different adoption factors that SMEs and large organisations focus on when taking decisions on integration technologies adoption are influenced by four parameters discussed in Section 6.2: (1) nature resources, (2) integration needs, (3) time, and (4) company size. In addition, the adoption of integration technologies between SMEs and large organisations is influenced by thirteen factors: (1) adopter characteristics, (2) IT sophistication, (3) external pressure, (4) dependence on trading partners, (5) Government regulation, (6) IT infrastructure, (7) IS complexity, (8) internal pressure, (9) perceived future prospect, (10) perceived benefits, (11) perceived barriers, (12) perceived financial costs, and (13) competitive pressure. These factors are also categorised into: (1) factors for SMEs, (2) factors for large firms, and (3) common factors, as analysed in Section 6.2. In Figure 6.3, the new factor perceived future prospect derived from empirical evidence is included in a dashed box. The identified parameters are highlighted in text boxes. These text boxes consist of sub-parameters that should be considered to explain the different factors that SMEs and large firms focus on when taking adoption decisions (see to Sections 6.2.1, 6.2.2, 6.2.3 and 6.2.4).

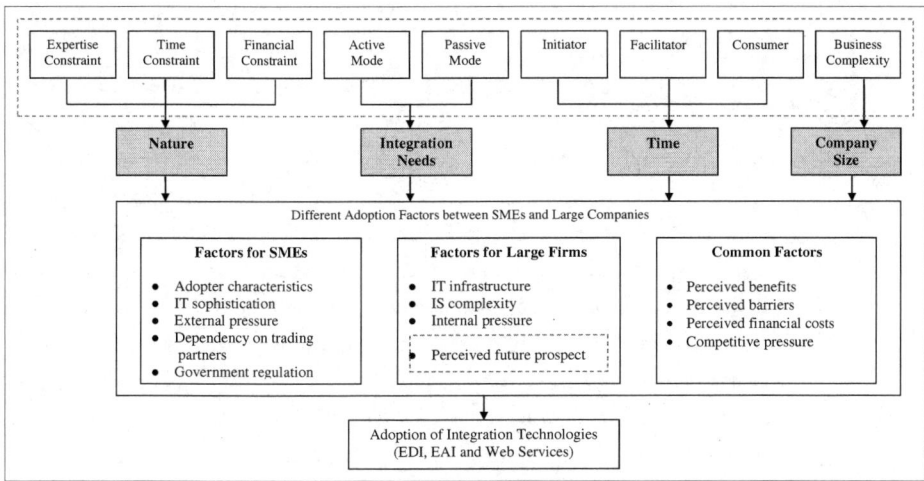

Figure 6.3 Revised Conceptual Model for Adoption of Integration Technologies between SMEs and Large Organisations

6.4 Conclusion

The case for the identification of parameters that lead to the different adoption factors that SMEs and large organisations focus on when taking decisions for integration technologies adoption, and the development of a model that is translated into a frame of reference has been argued, justified and presented. This chapter has concentrated on revising the conceptual model proposed in Figure 3.8 based on the further analysis on the empirical data and the literature review. Modifications to the conceptual model were imposed by empirical data presented and analysed in Chapter 5, as well as the further analysis reported in this chapter. Empirical evidence suggests that apart from the parameters reported in the conceptual model (see Figure 3.8), new sub-parameters should be considered to explain the different adoption factors focused on by SMEs and large organisations in relation to their adoption decision-making. One of the parameters is nature resources; it can be formed as a result of: (1) expertise, (2) financial, and (3) time constraints occurring within or outside an organisation. Another parameter is integration needs, and it was argued that these can be categorised into passive and active modes. The third parameter is time of adoption (i.e. adopter category), and the adopters (i.e. case companies) are classified into (1) initiator, (2) facilitator, and (3) consumer. These different adopters have produced different integration technologies decisions and results. Finally, last but not least, is company size. Here, the researcher found that business complexity and company size are related, and this can lead to different integration technologies adoption decisions between SMEs and large organisations.

In addition, based on the empirical evidence, the literature reported in Section 3.3, and the analysis, eleven factors were found between SMEs and large organisations for the adoption of integration technologies. These factors were then categorised into: (1) factors for SMEs: adopter characteristics, IT sophistication, external pressure, dependency on trading partners and government regulation; (2) factors for large firms: IT infrastructure, IS complexity, and internal pressure; (3) common factors: perceived benefits, perceived barriers, perceived financial costs, and competitive pressure. The empirical evidence also suggests that apart from the above-mentioned factors, a new factor should be considered when adopting integration technologies, and this is the perceived future prospect. The empirical data suggest that this factor is important in explaining the adoption of integration technologies in large organisations.

In support of the above-mentioned evidence, a revised conceptual model has been proposed in this chapter. This model proposes that thirteen factors influence the adoption of integration technologies between SMEs and large organisations, and four parameters and their sub-parameters that explain the different adoption factors focused by SMEs and large organisations when taking adoption decisions. All these sub-parameters lead to better understanding and analysis of the factors and parameters of the revised conceptual model. Thus, by contributing to better decision-making and understanding during the process of integration technologies adoption in SMEs and large organisations.

The novelty of the conceptual model presented in Figure 6.3 lies in the following:

- According to the literature review reported in Chapter 2, due to SMEs' very distinct characteristics, they use IT to support their business differently from large organisations. Thus, it is expected that SMEs may focus on different factors from large organisations when taking adoption decisions. Therefore, this model is one of the first attempts to explore and understand the adoption of integrated technologies, taking into consideration the different factors that SMEs and large organisations focus on.

- The model consists of a comprehensive set of factors that influence integrated technologies adoption, and these factors were justified and classified into three categories, namely (1) *factors for SMEs*, (2) *factors for large organisations*, and (3) *common factors*.

- The conceptual model can be used as a tool for decision-making to support organisations (SMEs and large organisations), and allow researchers to apprehend and analyse integrated technologies.

Chapter 7: Conclusions & Further Research

Summary

The purpose of this chapter is twofold: (1) to conclude the research reported in this thesis, and to present its achievements and contribution, and (2) to propose areas of further work. This chapter begins by summarising the thesis and drawing conclusions derived from both the literature and empirical research reported in this thesis. The limitations in various phases of the research undertaken are then identified, and these limitations should be taken accounted for carefully when interpreting results. Thereafter, a critical evaluation of the research process is presented. The novelty claimed in this thesis is then summarised. Finally, this last chapter concludes with the identification and discussion of further research directions, in this challenging and fast-evolving research area.

7.1 Research Overview and Findings

This thesis started with an overview of the motivation for the research and its objectives in **Chapter 1**. It has been identified in the literature and empirically confirmed that integration of enterprise application and data to simplify and automate business processes has become an important focus for many organisations. This is due to most traditional enterprise applications having been custom-built to address a specific business need. As enterprises have grown, and the need to share information across departments and business areas becomes more critical, companies are turning to integration to provide a method for interconnecting these distributed and often proprietary systems. However, the adoption of integrated technologies by SMEs has been stabilised at relatively low levels. Although integrated technologies can be beneficial for companies, SMEs seem to hesitate to invest in integrated technologies with the most frequently reported barriers being the lack of resources, know-how, and awareness. Furthermore, since small businesses possess certain unique characteristics when compared to large business, some literature thus suggested the general applicability of the studies on integration technologies adoption in large organisations and small business may be questionable. Thus, a better understanding of the ways in which SMEs adopt integration technologies is necessary because of the research in this area is proved to be limited, with SMEs requiring answers to many issues. Chapter 1 then states the aim of the research which is to investigate the adoption of integration technologies by following a comparative analysis between SMEs and large counterparts. Chapter 1 also presented an introduction to the methodology of the research, and concluded with an overview of the thesis outline.

In an attempt to meet the aim of this thesis, **Chapter 2** offered a detailed overview of the existing literature in the research areas where this research is based. It started with a literature review of the various integration technologies that can be used to assist organisations to unlock existing information assets and share them across multiple applications and business processes, providing the framework for real-time enterprises and real-time business networks. To this end, it has identified that Web Services is a relatively new area of research with the author classified their benefits and barriers to enhances knowledge on Web Services innovation. In doing so, this contributes to the body of knowledge on Web Services literature. The proposed Web Services classifications can be used to support integration technologies analysis which was also reported in Chapter 2. Thus, Chapter 2 makes further contribution to the integration technologies literature. In investigating more the adoption of integration technologies, Chapter 2 reviews the normative literature and seeks models and factors that influence integration technologies both in SMEs and large organisations. To this end, it has identified that there is an absence of theoretical models that deal with EAI and Web Services adoption, especially in SMEs, since EAI and Web Services are relatively new research areas. Chapter 2 then reviewed the theories applied in the existing literature studying integration technologies adoption in SMEs. In doing so, it shows that many of the studies on adoption of IT innovation, e.g. EDI studies, have used the Rogers (1995) diffusion of innovation theory to identify attributes of the innovation that influence its adoption. Furthermore, resource-based theory was found to be often used to explain the adoption and use of IS and technology in SMEs, since this theory emphasises understanding the internal capabilities that enable firms to secure competitive positions, and the importance of internal resources in a firm. This theory is therefore found useful in interpreting the research on the adoption of integration technologies by SMEs. Thus, to investigate the area of adoption of integration technologies between SMEs and large organisations, the resource-based theory might be used in conjunction with the diffusion theories to better interpret this research. In reviewing the relevant literature on integration technologies adoption by SMEs and large organisations, thus justifying the research, a number of important research issues have emerged, which indicated that: (1) there is an absence of a theoretical model that explains the ways in which SMEs adopt integration technologies, (2) since EAI and Web Services are relatively new areas, only a few studies have been carried out, and there are thus limited studies focusing on their adoption by SMEs, and (3) existing works point out that small organisations have been shown to have different technology adoption patterns from large ones. However, it is unclear whether SMEs and large organisations take decisions for the adoption of integration technologies focusing on different factors.

Chapter 3 has concentrated on investigating the research issues derived from Chapter 2. In doing so, a number of research questions were raised, and based on these, the following parameters were identified by the researcher that influence the different adoption factors focused on by SMEs and large firms when taking decisions for their integration technologies adoption: (1) nature resources, (2) time, (3) integration needs, and (4) company size. Additionally, results from a small survey undertaken in parallel with the literature review were used to support the analysis. Thereafter, the adoption factors were then classified into three categorises: common factors, factors for SMEs and factors for large organisations. Based on the identified parameters and the factors classification, a novel conceptual model was introduced, and aimed to support decision-making process. The model takes into consideration the parameters identified in normative literature as influencing factors for the integration technologies adoption between SMEs and large organisations. The proposed model also takes into account the different factors that SMEs and large organisations focus on when taking decisions for their integration technologies adoption. This model meets the aim of this thesis reported in Chapter 1. The conceptual model was then empirically examined and modified in Chapters 5 and 6.

To undertake the research focusing on the issues identified in Chapters 2 and 3, a research methodology was developed and adopted. The justification for the selection of the particular methodological stand was presented in **Chapter 4,** together with the reasons for selecting a qualitative research approach within a case study strategy. The chapter also presented the research design and process. Particular emphasis was given to the techniques for the collection of the empirical material, such as interviews and unofficial meetings with the organisers, which were supported by a variety of relevant resources. Finally, the chapter discussed the issue of generalisation from interpretive case studies, focusing on issues related to the justification, the validity, reliability and triangulation of the results of this research.

Chapter 5 serves the principle of contextualisation of an interpretive research, and gives a detailed description of the empirical context of this research. In doing so, the Industry Automation Programme project that served as the empirical base and the initial investigation for this research was first described. The project aimed to push 15 case companies' suppliers to adopt integration technologies to support their supply chains. This project thus well justifies the purpose of this research. It is also explained how this research has emerged working along with the Industry Automation Programme by presenting the setting of the multiple case studies, reasons for their selection, and the conditions under which they have been performed. In addition, three more case studies took place (one large organisation, and three SMEs – adopter and non-adopters) in the second stage case study, where a more in-depth analysis of the issues under investigation is performed. Empirical evidence derived from the cases of Industry Automation Programme, Hi-Touch, eSynergy, Industrade, and AboCom also confirmed many of the issues identified in Chapters 2 and 3.

Chapter 6 presents the empirical data analysis and the modifications to the proposed conceptual model. The empirical evidences that derived from the case studies reported in

Chapter 5 have indicated a number of modifications to the conceptual model and these findings have been considered in Chapter 6 as novel contribution and resulted in the revision of the conceptual model (see Figure 6.3). A further analysis also took place in Chapter 6, based on the empirical evidence derived from the case studies reported in Chapter 5 and the literature reported in Chapter 2, to validate the research questions identified in Chapter 3. In doing so, modifications were made to the conceptual model by adding factors derived from empirical research. These factors deal with:

- **Factors explicitly for SMEs:** IT sophistication, external pressure, adopter characteristics, dependence on trading partners, and government regulation;

- **Factors explicitly for large firms:** IT infrastructure, IS complexity, internal pressure, and perceived future prospect;

- **Common factors:** perceived benefits, perceived barriers, perceived financial costs, and competitive pressure.

Empirical evidence also suggests that apart from the parameters reported in the conceptual model (see Figure 3.8), new sub-parameters should be considered to explain the different adoption factors focused on between SMEs and large organisations in relation to their integration technologies adoption decision-making. These sub-parameters are as follows:

- **Nature resources:** time, financial and expertise constraints

- **Integration needs:** passive and active modes

- **Company size:** business complexity

- **Time:** initiator, facilitator and consumer

The conceptual model can therefore be used as a frame of reference when organisations are taking their decisions for integration technologies. In doing so, the researcher has achieved the aim of this thesis as identified in Section 1.7.

7.1.1 Main Findings

The main findings derived from the work presented in this thesis as follows:

1. A review of normative literature suggests that there is an absence of theoretical models that describe the adoption of integration technologies by SMEs. The reason for this is attributed to EAI and Web Services being new research areas with many topics remaining under investigation.

2. The literature reveals that SMEs have very different characteristics from large organisations, thus it is expected that both might approach integration technologies adoption differently. However, the existing literature does not specify whether they focus on different factors when taking adoption decisions. Therefore, this forms another research gap which needs further investigation.

3. To address these voids in the literature parameters identified as (1) *nature resources*, (2) *integration needs*, (3) *time*, and (4) *company size* can be used to explain the different factors focused on when taking decisions for integration technologies adoption. Furthermore, the analysis of the literature and the empirical data suggests that new sub-parameters should also be considered to explain these different factors. These sub-parameters are (1) nature resources: *time, finance* and *expertise constraints*, (2) integration needs: *passive* and *active modes*, (3) time: *initiator*, *facilitator* and *consumer*, and (4) company size: business complexity.

4. From the empirical data and the theoretical analysis, a number of adoption factors were found, which were then classified into three categories: (1) *factors explicitly for SMEs*: adopter characteristics, external pressure, dependency on trading partners, and government regulation, (2) *factors explicitly for large organisations*: IT infrastructure, IS complexity, perceived future prospect, and internal pressure, and (3) *common factors:* perceived benefits, perceived barriers, perceived financial costs, and competitive pressure.

5. The research model was developed based on the prior theoretical background discussion, as reported in Chapter 3. By adopting the resource-based view, together with the theoretical diffusion theories proposed by Welsh & White (1981), Rogers (1995) and Attewell (1992), and taking into account the distinctive characteristics of small businesses, the integration technologies adoption in SMEs and large organisations is conceptualised in terms of the identified parameters, sub-parameters, adoption factors for SMEs, adoption factors for large organisations, and common factors.

6. The conceptual model can be used as a tool for decision-making to support organisations, and to allow researchers to apprehend and analyse integration technologies adoption between SMEs and large organisations. The concepts of the proposed model can be used for the adoption of inter-organisational information systems, EDI, Middleware, EAI and Web Services by SMEs and large organisations since this research focuses on integrated technologies in both of them.

7. The researcher classifies Web Services benefits using the model proposed by Shang and Seddon (2000). This model divides benefits derived from integrated IT infrastructures into: (1) operational, (2) managerial, (3) technical, (4) strategic, and (5) organisational. The researcher claims and empirically verifies that the same model can be used for the classification of Web Services barriers. In addition, the benefits and barriers of EAI, EDI and Web Services are also comparatively analysed to provide a better view on each integrated technology.

7.2 Research Contributions

This research set out to meet a number of objectives described in Chapter 1, which have been accomplished as follows.

● To conduct a literature review in the area of integration technologies and the issues related to its adoption in SMEs and large organisations. In doing so, research issues will be identified regarding the adoption of integration technologies for further investigation.

Based on the literature review, a number of research gaps have been identified and have been further examined and investigated by the researcher.

● To analyse and assess the relevant information, theories and characteristics of SMEs. In doing so, useful criteria related to SMEs' characteristics and the relevant theories that are often used to study the adoption of integration by SMEs will be identified.

The analysis of characteristics of SMEs made it obvious that SMEs have different characteristics from larger corporations, thus they might approach integration technologies adoption differently. This viewpoint has been analysed and interpreted through theoretical diffusions theories and resource-based theory, which focus on internal and external resources of organisations.

- To investigate the issues and approaches associated with the adoption of integration technologies between SMEs and large organisations. In doing so, how, why and in what ways the integration technologies have been adopted by SMEs and large organisations will be identified.

Resource-based analysis and the support of the diffusion innovation literature have led to the identification of the parameters and sub-parameters that explain the different adoption factors that SMEs and large organisations focused on when taking decisions on their integration technologies adoption.

- To study the relevant existing models and frameworks for the adoption of integration technologies by SMEs and large organisations. In doing so, a framework will be developed for the adoption of integration technologies based on a comparative analysis between SMEs and large organisations that might be used as a decision-making tool.

The studies of the existing adoption models and the empirical evidence have led to the proposition of a number of factors that can be used to explain the integration technologies adoption in SMEs and large organisations.

The accomplishment of the above objectives has been made possible after the synthesis of the identified parameters with the identified adoption factors (i.e. theoretical background), developing a novel conceptual model for the examination of issues related to the adoption of integration technologies innovation, taking into account the different factors that SMEs and large organisations focused on when taking adoption decisions. This was demonstrated by their applications in the adoption of integrated technologies aiming to overcome limitations in the literature of innovations adoption and address open issues in the practice of integration technologies adoption. Thus, this research has contributed to both theory and practice. The individual elements of the contribution made by this work stem from different components in this thesis: from the contextual information provided in Chapters 1, 2 and 3, to the research methodology reported in Chapter 4, through the design and the conduct of the case studies reported in Chapters 4 and 5, and finally, the empirical analysis of the cases and the development of conceptual model presented in Chapters 5 and 6.

An important issue related to the contribution of any research is how the results of a particular study can be generalised and prove useful in other research contexts. In other words, it is important for future researchers to be able to use the conclusions of a

---

particular piece of research to study a similar subject in a different geographical, political or social setting. For this research, it is interesting to examine the relevance of its conclusions to other innovations, rather than integration technologies or other geographical areas. This research has developed a theoretical framework that can guide future studies in the same research areas. More specifically, the research model developed in this study can be used as a guide for the examination of other innovations such as electronic commerce, supply chain integration, and ubiquitous computing.

Additionally, the results of this research can prove useful for researchers studying or stakeholders involved in the adoption of integration technologies outside Asia geographical region. The experience of countries where integrated technologies have been introduced earlier can guide SMEs in less technologically advanced countries in their adoption strategy formulation. Furthermore, the results can also prove useful for SMEs from other industries, since this research was based on hi-tech and IT manufacturing industries.

The following is a review of what is claimed to be the main contribution and research novelty of the thesis.

7.2.1   Contribution to Theory

The most important contribution of this thesis is the development of a comprehensive novel conceptual model for integration technologies adoption by comparatively analysing the issues between SMEs and large organisations (see Figure 6.3). The model makes a contribution at two levels. Firstly, at the conceptual level, it incorporates factors identified in previous studies as influencing the adoption of integration technologies by SMEs and large organisations. The researcher extends and analyses this work by classifying them into three categories, namely (1) factors explicit to SMEs, (2) factors explicit to large firms, and (3) common factors. The factors representing each category were later examined through empirical data. In addition, based on the theoretical background analysis, a number of research questions were presented which helped the researcher to identify the parameters that can be used to explain the different factors focused on when taking decisions for integration technologies adoption. The identified parameters were then incorporated in the proposed research model, and this results in the development of a consistent model for the adoption of integration technologies in SMEs and large organisations. Secondly, at the theoretical level, the empirical data were interpreted and analysed through theoretical diffusion and resource-based theories, resulting in the identification of sub-parameters which were also incorporated in the proposed research model. The proposed conceptual model supports better understanding in the research area and better decision-making.

Another contribution deals with the proposition of classifications of Web Services barriers and benefits. In Chapter 2, barriers and benefits classifications were based on the model proposed by Shang & Seddon (2000), which was proposed for the categorisation of ERP benefits. The novelty claimed is that such classifications can be adapted and followed in the case of Web Services. In doing so, the researcher expands existing knowledge on Web Services, since there is an absence of classification of Web Services benefits and barriers. This contribution thus supports decision-makers and researchers to better understand the impact of such technology, and therefore supporting robust evaluation.

7.2.2 Contribution to Methodology

The main methodological contribution of this research has been the use of the case study strategy in a multi-organisational context. As analysed in Chapter 2, the majority of studies for integration technologies adoption are limited to a single organisation, a single type of organisation (either small or large), or an industry sector. This research, by investigating adoption in SMEs and large organisations, which inherently includes different types of organisations (SMEs and large firms) and a large number of organisations (a project with 15 case companies and a number of SMEs suppliers), offered a higher level approach to the case study strategy. In line with that, the unit of analysis was adoption activities with the participation of a number of organisations and individuals as well as different types of organisations, which gives a new dimension to typical case studies where the focus is either on individuals or groups or a single organisation.

Additionally, a quantitative approach is used in this work as an additional research technique (pilot study) to support research questions' identification and refinement, as reported in Chapter 3, which is another contribution to methodology. This kind of methodology is called the dominant less-dominant method in the literature, as reported by Lessing & Schulze (2002). who state that in a dominant less-dominant research model, the researcher conducts the study within a single, dominant paradigm. Only a small component of the study is undertaken from the alternative paradigm. In this thesis, a quantitative approach was used as an exploratory case investigation to support the theoretical analysis. A number of major IS journals and conference proceedings also report that combining the qualitative and quantitative techniques can result in an enriched research process and results (Benbasat, Goldstein, & Mead, 1987). It is argued that running qualitative research alongside quantitative research offers a synergy whereby objective quantitative data can provide a structure to analysis of subjective qualitative data (Siber, 1973).

7.2.3 Contribution to Practice

The most obvious practical contribution of this research is the rich insight it provides to the context of integration technologies adoption, offering recommendations to integration technologies providers, adopters and non-adopters. Consequently, SMEs can also gain some practical advantages when receiving advice from better adoption practices. The identification of the parameters and research questions in this research can be proved useful to clarify the queries that researchers or organisations might have regarding the different factors focused on by SMEs and large firms when taking adoption decisions as presented in Chapter 6. As investigating the adoption of integration technologies is a relatively new subject, any scientific investigation on the matter can be a useful guidance for researchers or organisations. It is also believed that the research reported in this thesis and the main findings reported in Chapter 6 have gone some way to identifying the means to address many aspects of the complex issues associated with the adoption in SMEs and large organisations. This thus leads to a better decision-making process for researchers and organisations.

7.3 Limitations of the Research Approach

As described in Chapter 4, the use of qualitative methods was justified for gathering the necessary data. The reason is that such methods allow generalisation of soft and rich contextual data, which are associated with human and organisational issues. The analysis in Chapter 4 showed that interpretive research is often criticised for the subjective influence the researcher's interpretation might have on the findings. This possible pitfall has been acknowledged in this research by using material from multiple case studies, various resources, and interviewees' views. The main limitation in such research analysis is that the collection of the data, and consequently the empirical results, will depend heavily on the extent of access to interviewees given to the researcher. However, if the interviewees participating in the research do not see the research process as legitimate, they can either hide important information or even decide not to provide any information at all. The acquaintance of the researcher with the interviewees participating in the Industry Automation Programme case study, and the strong interest of interviewees from Hi-Touch, Industrade, and AboCom in the research findings proved very positive factors in the minimisation of problem

Moreover, the researcher has acknowledged a number of additional issues regarding the use of qualitative research methods. Firstly, the inability of the researcher to interpret events from a subjective point of view without some degree of bias. However, to address this, this researcher does consider that there will always be elements of bias inherent in qualitative data analysis, from its subjective nature. Secondly, the relationship between theory and research might be considered weak and unstructured, as qualitative approaches may be criticised for not instilling theoretical elements. However, in the case of this research, the author sought to partially address this concern through developing a conceptual model proposing factors that influence integration technologies adoption. To minimise the above problem, resource-based and theoretical diffusion theories were used to interpret and analyse the different factors focused on when taking decisions for integration technologies adoption, thus resulting in the identification of the parameters and sub-parameters.

Finally, there is much concern regarding the extent that qualitative research can be generalised beyond the confines of the inquiry, as the sample of companies is often relatively small. Indeed, qualitative case study research does not offer the pretence of replication, as controlling the research setting destroys the interaction of variables, and therefore affects the underlying philosophy of interpretivism. In re-assuring sceptics of interpretivism, the four companies taking part in this study, plus an additional Industry Automation Programme case study which involved 15 large companies and a number of SMEs suppliers, would have increased its external validity. The study was also conducted within a structured methodology, and guided by theoretical concepts and models, with a number of data gathering methods and processes being used. However, the methodology presented in Chapter 4 was developed, as it was considered safer to identify and investigate independent variables, following a review of literature. Having now increased the external validity and evaluated the research process, the concern addressed in this section does not need to be considered important.

7.4 Recommendations for Further Research

The following recommendations are made for further research:

1. The identification and development of a conceptual model for integration technologies adoption in SMEs and large organisations have established those issues that appear crucial within one large organisation, two SMEs (adopter and non-adopter), and a project case which involved 15 multinational organisations and a number of SMEs suppliers. Refinement of the proposed model may be considered to further substantiate and verify the research questions presented. Therefore the researcher suggests validating the identified research questions through a large-scale survey questionnaire, rather than continuing with an interpretivist epistemology. Although a small exploratory survey questionnaire was designed in this thesis to support the analysing of the research questions reported in Chapter 3, the researcher suggests it will be useful to have the identified research questions validated in such a way too. A large-scale survey will offer the opportunity to establish generic significance of the issues related to the proposed model. In surveying a representative sample of large and small organisations, the factors and the presented research questions related to the proposed research model can be better verified and understood.

2. Another important point which needs to be addressed here is that in an effort to investigate important factors affecting the adoption of innovations, such as integration technologies, theoretical diffusion theories, resource-based theory and empirical observations were considered. Baskerville & Pries-Heje (2001) have claimed that, in applying a multi-theory approach to IS diffusion, multiple valid innovation theories coexist, that each applies under different conditions, and that researchers should therefore focus on identifying the contingencies that indicate when an innovation theory is appropriate.

3. Another recommendation is that the parameters identified by this research in the field of integrated technologies adoption in SMEs and large organisations can be divided further by taking into consideration more issues related to the differences between SMEs and large organisations. For example, IS management, economy scales, etc.. Other technology innovations with common integrated technologies characteristics, such as inter-organisational system and supply chain integration,

etc., would also be studied, following a similar comparative analysis approach between small and large organisations.

4. Furthermore, the examination of integration technologies adoption in other sectors and other developing countries, where their technological capabilities are relatively low, could also be interesting. This is because that, although these companies seem to face more problems in adopting integration technologies, these problems might prove useful for software vendors, developer and researchers to better understand the market demands. Finally, the development of a framework for the evaluation of adoption activities based on SMEs' and large organisations' views and requirements can be a practical tool that can contribute to better decision-making.

7.5 Closing Statement

The experience from Ph.D. research is unique, and is a very individualistic venture. Upon the completion of this thesis, the researcher has learnt how to nail down thing which relies on insight, lateral thinking, inspiration, and a lot of hard work. Moreover, the researcher has improved her problem-solving skill by realising that to solve a problem, the most important thing is to understand the problem If the problem is fully understood, it is easier to find a way to solve it. If the problem is not fully understood, the problem solved may not be the problem the researcher expected to solve. The researcher also realised that how to communicate with people is a hard task from doing case studies. Case study is based on people, and everyone has different ways of thinking. It is impossible to control people' minds, thus communication skill is very important in this case, and is the key to a successful interview. Therefore, after completing this thesis, the researcher has more confidence in her research ability, and look at things differently than people who did not go through this process.

References

Abreu, E. (2001). 'XML is Now the Standard Language for the Internet', *IDG.Net*, (http://www.thestandard.com/article/0,1902,24180,00.html), [accessed Nov 2001].

Ajzen, I. (1985). *From Intentions to Action: A Theory of Planned Behaviour. in Action Control: From Cognition to Behaviour*, J. Kuhl and J. Beckmanin Eds., Springer, Heidelberg.

Angeles, R. (2000). 'Revisiting the Role of Internet-EDI in the Current Electronic Commerce Science', *Logistics Information Management*, 13(1), 45-57.

Anthony, R. N. (1965). *Planning and Control Systems: A Framework for Analysis*, Graduate School of Business Administration, Harvard University, Boston.

Aponovich, D. (2002). 'Five Barriers to Implementing Web Services', (http://itmanagement.earthweb.com/erp/article.php/965371), [accessed March 2003].

Arrow, K. (1962). 'The Economic Implications of Learning by Doing', *Review of Economic Studies*, 29, 155-173.

Atkinson, B. and Libera, D. G. (2002). 'Specification: Web Services Security', Microsoft, (http://www-106.ibm.com/developerworks/webservices/library/ws-secure/) [accessed March 2003].

Atkinson, J. and Storey, D.J. (1993). *Employment, the Small Firm, and the Labour Market*, Routledge, London.

Attewell, P. (1992). 'Technology Diffusion and Organizational Learning: the Case of Business Computing', *Organisation Science*, 3, 1-19.

Banerjee, S. and Golhar, D. Y. (1994). 'Electronic Data Interchange: Characteristics of Users and Nonusers', *Information and Management*, 26(2), 65-74.

Banks, M. (2003). 'Web Services Await Standards', *IT Week*, (http://www.vnunet.com/Analysis/1138661).

Bannock, G. and Daly, M. (1994). *Small Business Statistics*, Chapman, London.

Barney, J. (1991). 'Firm Resources and Sustainable Competitive Advantage', *Journal of Management*, 17(1), 99-120.

Baron, J. P., Shaw, M. J. and Bailey, A. D. (2000). 'Web Based e-Catalog Systems in B2B Procurement', *Communications of the ACM*, 43(5), 93-1000.

Barua, A. and Lee, B. (1997). 'An Economic Analysis of the Introduction of an Electronic

Data Interchange System', *Information Systems Research,* 8(4), 398-422.

Baskerville, R., and Pries-Heje, J. (2001) 'A Multiple-Theory Analysis of a Diffusion of Information Technology Case,' *Information Systems Journal,* 11, 181-212.

Benbasat, I., Goldstein, D. K. and Mead, M. (1987). 'The Case Research Strategy in Studies of Information Systems', *MIS Quarterly,* 11(3), 369-386.

Benbasat, I. and Zmud, R. W. (1999). 'Empirical Research in Information Systems: The Practice of Relevance', *MIS Quarterly,* 23(1), 3-17.

Beretta, S. (2002). 'Unleashing the Integration Potential of ERP Systems: The Role of Process-Based Performance Measurement Systems', *Business Process Management Journal,* 8(3), 254-277.

Berlind, D. (2002). 'IBM, Microsoft Patents Pose Dangers', *CNET Networks, Inc.,* (http://techupdate.zdnet.com/techupdate/stories/main/0,14179,2861123,00.html), [accessed March 2003].

Bernstein, R. J. (1983). *Beyond Objectivism and Relativism: Science, Hermeneutics, and Praxis,* University of Pennsylvania Press, Philadelphia.

Bharadwaj, A. (2000). 'A Resource-Based Perspective on Information Technology Capability and Firm Performance: An Empirical Investigation', *MIS Quarterly,* 24 (1), 169-196.

Bolton, J. E. (1971). *Report of the Committee of Inquiry on Small Firms,* HMSO, London.

Bonoma, T. V. (1983). *A Case Study in Case Research: Marketing Implementation,* Working Paper 9-585-142, Harvard University Graduate School of Business Administration, Boston, Massachusetts.

Borch, O. J. and Arthur, M. B. (1995). 'Strategic Networks Among Small Firms: Implications for Strategy Research Methodology', *Journal of Management Studies,* 32(4), 18-32.

Bradford, M. and Florin, J. (2003). 'Examining the Role of Innovation Diffusion Factors on the Implementation Success of Enterprise Resource Planning Systems', *International Journal of Accounting Information Systems,* 4(3), 205-225.

Brancheau, J. C. and Wetherbe, J. C. (1990). 'The Adoption of Spreadsheet Software: Testing Innovation Diffusion Theory in the Context of End-User Computing', *Information Systems Journal,* 1(2), 115-143.

Bridge, S., O'Neill, K. and Cromie, S. (1998). *Understanding Enterprise, Entrepreneurship & Small Business,* Macmillan Press, Hampshire, London.

Brousseau, E. (1994). 'EDI and Inter-Firm Relationships: Toward a Standardisation of Coordination Processes?', *Information Economics and Policy,* 6, 319-347.

Brouthers, K. D., Andriessen, F. and Nicolaes, I. (1998). 'Driving Blind: Strategic Decision-Making in Small Companies', *Long Range Planning,* 31(1), 130-138.

Brown, B. and Butler, J. E. (1995). 'Competitors as Allies: a Study of the Entrepreneurial Networks in the US Wine Industry', *Journal of Small Business Management,* 33 (3), 57-66.

Brown, C., Hamilton, J. and Medoff, J. (1990). *Employees Large and Small,* Harvard University Press, Cambridge, Mass.

Burns, P. (2001). *Entrepreneurship and Small Business,* Palgrave, New York.

Caldeira, M. M. and Ward, M. J. (2003). 'Using Resource-Based Theory to Interpret the Successful Adoption and Use of Information Systems and Technology in Manufacturing Small and Medium-Sized Enterprises', *European Journal of Information Research,* 12, 127-141.

Cambridge Small Business Research Centre (CSBRC) (1992). *The State of British Enterprise,* Department of Applied Economics, University of Cambridge, Cambridge.

CapeClear (2002a). 'British Telecom and Web Services', *Cape Clear Software Inc.,* (http://www.capeclear.com/customers/), [accessed March 2003].

CapeClear (2002b). 'WinVision, Inc. Embeds Cape Clear ISV Edition in WebTrans Java Web Services', *Cape Clear Software Inc.,* (http://www,capeclear.com), [accessed March 2003].

CapeClear (2002c). 'MoneyMate Delivers European Financial Information with Web Services and Cape Clear Software Inc.' *Cape Clear Software Inc.,* (http://www.capeclear.com), [accessed March 2003].

CapeClear (2003). 'Simplified Integration with Web Services', *A White Paper from Cape Clear Software Inc.,* (http://whitepaper.tpj.com/cmptpj/search/tabsortbrowse /research/1717/26/2/index.jsp), [accessed March 2003].

Carter, S. and Evan, J. D. (2000). *Enterprise and Small Business: Principles, Practice and Policy,* Pearson Education, Essex, U.K.

Cavaye, A. (1996). 'Case Study Research: a Multi-Faceted Research Approach for IS', *Information Systems Journal,* 6(3), 227-242.

Cerami, E. (2002). *Web Services Essentials,* O'Reilly & Associates, Inc., Sebastopol.

Chang, L. and Powell, P. (1998). 'Towards a Framework for Business Process Re-engineering in Small and Medium-Sized Enterprises', *Information Systems Journal,* 8(3), 199-215.

Charlesworth, I. and Jones, T. (2003). 'The EAI and Web Services Report', *EAI Journal,* (http://www.sybase.com/content/1024767/eAIJournalReport.pdf), [accessed Jan 2004].

Charlesworth, I., Hamilton, J., Holden, M., Holt, E., Jagger, T., Jennings, T. and Jones, T. (2002). 'EAI and Web Services: Cutting the Cost of Enterprise Integration', In Technology Evaluation and Comparison Report, Butler Group Limited, Hull, Yorkshire, UK.

Chau, P. Y. K. and Tam, Y. K. (1997). 'Factors Affecting the Adoption of Open Systems: An Exploratory Study', *MIS Quarterly,* March, 1-24.

Chau, P. Y. K. and Hui, K. L. (2001). 'Determinants of Small Business EDI Adoption: An Empirical Investigation', *Journal of Organisational Computing and Electronic Commerce,* 11(4), 229-252.

Chau, W. F. (1986). 'Radical Developments in Accounting Thought', *The Accounting Review,* 61, 601-632.

Chen, H. and Themistocleous, M. (2004). 'Understanding Web Services Benefits and Barriers through Classification and Case Studies', In *Proceedings of the European Mediterranean Conference on Information Systems (EMCIS)*, July 25-27, Tunis, Tunisia, CD-ROM.

Chen, H., Themistocleous, M. and Chiu, K. H. (2003). 'Inter-Organisational Application Integration: the Case of 15 Taiwan's SMEs', In *Proceedings of the ISOneWorld Conference*, April 23-25, Las Vegas, Nevada, USA, CD-ROM.

Chen, H., Themistocleous, M. and Chiu, K. H. (2004). 'Approach to Supply Chain Integration Followed by SMEs: an Exploratory Case Study', In *Proceedings of the Americas Conference on Information Systems (AMCIS)*, Aug 6-8, New York, USA, CD-ROM.

Chen, J. and Williams, B. C. (1998). 'The Impact of Electronic Data Interchange (EDI) on SMEs: Summary of Eight British Case Studies', *Journal of Small Business Management,* 36(3), 68-72.

Chen, M. 2003. 'An Analysis of the Driving Forces for the Adoption of Web Services', In *Proceedings* of *the Second Workshop on e-Business*, Dec 13-14, Seattle, USA, 173-184.

Chen, M. (2003) 'Factors Affecting the Adoption and Diffusion of XML and Web services Standards for E-business Systems,' *International Journal of Human-Computer Studies,* 58, 259-279.

Chung, S. H. and Snyder, C. A. (2000). 'ERP Adoption: a Technological Evolution Approach', *International Journal of Agile Management Systems,* 2(1), 24-32.

Chwelos, P., Benbasat, I. and Dexter, A. S. (2001). 'Research Report: Empirical Test of an EDI Adoption Model', *Information Systems Research,* 12(3), 304-321.

Clark, J., T. D. (1992). 'Corporate Systems Management: An Overview and Research Perspective,' *Communications of the ACM,* 35(2), 61-75.

Clarke, R. (1998). 'Electronic Data Interchange (EDI): An Introduction', *Business Credit,* (http://www.anu.edu.au/people/Roger.Clarke/EC/EDIIntro.html), [accessed Jan 2002].

Cohn, T. and Lindberg, R. A. (1972). *How Management is Different in Small Companies*, American Management Association, New York.

Conner, K. (1991). 'A Historical Comparison of Resource-Based Theory and Five Schools of Thought within Industrial Organisation Economics: Do We Have a New Theory of the Firm?' *Journal of Management*, 17(1), 121-154.

Conner, K. and Prahalad, C. (1996). 'A Resource-Based Theory of the Firm: Knowledge versus Opportunism', *Organisation Science*, 7(5), 477-501.

Cordeiro, M. I. and Carvalho, J. (2002). 'Web Services: What they are and their Importance for Libraries', *VINE*, 32(4), 129-157.

Coyle, F. (2002). 'XML, Web Services and the Changing Face of Distributed Computing', *ACM IT Magazine and Forum*, (http://www.acm.org/ubiquity/views/f_coyle_1.H tml), [accessed April 2003].

Cragg, P. B. and King, M. (1993). 'Small-Firm Computing: Motivators and Inhibitors', *MIS Quarterly* 17(1), 47-60.

Cragg, P. B. and Zinatelli, N. (1995). 'The Evolution of Information in Small Businesses', *Information and Management*, 29(1), 1-8.

Creedy, J. and Whitfield, K. (1988). 'The Economic Analysis of Internal Labour Markets', *Bulletin of Economic Research*, 4(4), 247-267.

Curbera, F., William, A., Weerawarana, N. and Weerawarana, S. (2001). 'Web Services: Why and How', IBM T.J. Watson Research Center, (http://www.research.ibm.com /people/b/bth/OOWS2001/nagy.pdf), [accessed March 2003].

Curran, J., Stanworth, J. and Watkins, D. (1986). *The Survival of the Small Firm: Employment, Growth, Technology and Politics, Volume 2*, Gower Publishing, Hants, U.K.

Currie, W., Wang, X. and Weerakkod, Y. V. (2004). 'Developing Web Services Using the Microsoft.Net Platform: Technical and Business Challenges', *Journal of Enterprise Information Management*, 17(5), 335-350.

Damanpour, F. (1991). 'Organisational Innovation: A Meta-Analysis of Effects of Determinants and Moderators', *Academy of Management Journal*, 34, 555-590.

Damiani, E., Di Capitani, D. S. and Samarati, P. (2002). 'Towards Securing XML Web Services', In *Proceedings of the ACM Workshop on XML Security*, Nov 22, Fairfax VA, USA, 90-96.

Daniel, E. (2003). 'An Exploration of the Inside-Out Model: E-commerce Integration in UK SMEs', *Journal of Small Business and Enterprise Development*, 10(3), 233-249.

Darin, P. (2002). 'Using Web Services for Integration', *Darin Partners and Zap Think*, (http://www.xml.org/xml/wsi.pdf), [accessed March 2003].

Davenport, T. (1998). 'Putting the Enterprise into the Enterprise System', *Harvard Business Review*, (July-August), 121-131.

Davery, N. (2003). 'Bigger then the Browser', Information Technology', *Asia Pacific*

Development, (http://www.gdsinternational.com/infocentre/pdf/apdit/webs.pdf), [accessed April 2004].

Davis, F. D. (1989). 'Perceived Usefulness, Perceived Ease of Use, and User Acceptance of Information Technology', *MIS Quarterly,* 13, 319-340.

Deakins, D. and Freel, M. (2003). *Entrepreneurship and Small Firms,* Third Edition, McGraw-Hill Education, Berkshire, U.K.

Deitel, H. M., Deitel, P. J., DuWaldt, B. and Trees, L. K. (2003). *Web Services: A Technical Introduction,* Pearson Education Inc., New Jersey.

Delamont S. (1992) *Fieldwork in Educational Setting: Methods, Pitfalls and Perspectives*, Flamer Press, London.

DeLone, W. H. (1981). 'Firm Size and the Characteristics of Computer Use', *MIS Quarterly,* December, 65-77.

DeLone, W. H. (1988). 'Determinants of Success for Computer Usage in Small Business', *MIS Quarterly,* March, 51-61.

Delone, W. H. and Mclean, E. R. (2003). 'The Delone and Mclean Model of Information Systems Success: A Ten-Year Update', *Journal of Management Information Systems*, 19(4), 9-30.

Denzin, N. Y. K. (1978). *The Research Act: A Theoretical Introduction to Sociological Methods',* McGraw, New York.

Denzin, N. and Lincoln, Y. (1994). *Handbook of Qualitative Research*, Sage, Thousand Oaks.

Denzin, N. Y. K. and Lincoln, Y. S. (1998). *Major Paradigms and Perspectives,* In *Strategies of Qualitative Inquiry,* Sage, Thousand Oaks.

Doukidis, G., Themistocleous, M., Drakos, W. and Papazafeiropoulou, A. (1998). *Electronic Commerce,* New Technology Publications, Athens, Greece.

Duke, S., Makey, P. and Kiras, N. (1999). *Application Integration Management Guide: Strategies and Technologies,* Butler Group, Hull, U.K.

European Commission (2003). 'Enterprise Policy', *European Commission*, (http://europa.eu.int/comm/index_en.htm), [accessed Jan 2003].

Dyer, W. G., Wilkins, A. L. and Eisenhardt, K. M. (1991). 'Better Stories, not Better Constructs, to Generate Better Theory', *Academy of Management Review,* 16(3), 613-627.

Edwards, P. and Newing, R. (2000). *Application Integration for e-Business,* Business Intelligence 2000, London, U.K.

Ein-Dor, P. and Segev, E. (1978). 'Organisational Context and the Success of Management Information Systems', *Management Science,* 24(6), 1067-1077.

Elite. 2002. 'Case Study', *Elite Information Systems,* (http://www.elite.com), [accessed

March 2003].

Ettlie, J. E., Bridges, W. P., and O'Keefe, R. D. (1984). 'Organisation Strategy and Structural Differences for Radical versus Incremental Innovation', *Management Science*, 30(6), 682-695.

EuroControl (2001). 'KPI Measurement, Monitoring and Analysis Guide', *EuroControl*, (http://www.eurocontrol.int/ais/ahead/s_level/kpi-measurementguide-s-lev-0008. pdf), [accessed Jan 2002].

Fishbein, M. and Ajzen, I. (1975). *Belief, Attitude, Intention, and Behaviour: An Introduction to Theory and Research*, Addison-Wesley, Reading, U.K.

Fletcher, P. and Waterhouse, M. (2002). *Web Services Business Strategies and Architectures*, Expert Press, Birmingham, U.K.

Flick, U. (1998). *An Introduction to Qualitative Research: Theory, Method and Applications*, Sage, London, U.K.

Frey, J. H. and Fontana, A. (1991). 'The Group Interview in Social Research', *Social Science Journal*, 28, 175-187.

French, B. (2002). 'Enterprise Integration Modelling', *ActionLine*, (http://www.contivo.com/news/articles/EIM_ActionLine.pdf), [accessed March 2003].

Fuller, P. B. (1994). 'Assessing Marketing in Small and Medium-Sized Enterprises', *European Journal of Marketing*, 28(12), 34-49.

Gadamer, H. G. (1989). *Truth and Method*, Sheed and Ward, London.

Galliers, R. (1991). '*Choosing Appropriate Information Systems Research Approaches: A Revised Taxonomy*', In Information Systems Research: Contemporary Approaches & Emergent Traditions, H. E. Nissen, H. K. Klein, and R. Hirschheim Eds., Elsevier Science Publishers, Amsterdam, North-Holland.

Galliers, R. D. (1992). *Information Systems Research: Issues, Methods and Practical Guidelines*, Blackwell Scientific, Oxford.

Garfinkel, H. (1967). *Studies in Ethnomethodology*, Prentice Hall, Englewood Cliffs, NJ.

Gaugler, T., Seffinga, J., Stadler, V. and Teufel, S. (1996). 'An Empirical Examination of the Benefits of EDI Depending on its Technical and Organisational Integration - a Hypothesis Based Study', Swiss National Science Foundation, (http://www.ifi.unizh.ch/ikm/OBI/edi.pdf), [accessed March 2002].

Gaynor, M., Wyner, G., Iyer, B. and Freeman, J. (2003). 'Web Services', *In Proceedings of the Ninth Americas Conference on Information Systems (AMCIS)*, August 4-5, Tampa, Florida, U.S.A, 3171-3177.

Geertz, C. (1979). *From the Native's Point of View: on the Nature of Anthropological Understanding*, University of California press, *In Interpretive Social Science: A Reader*, P. Rabinow and W. M. Sullivan Eds., Berkeley, U.S.A.

Gibson, N., Holland, C. and Light, B. (1999). 'Enterprise Resource Planning: A Business Approach to Systems Development', *In Proceedings of the 32nd Hawaii International Conference on System Sciences (HCISS)*, Jan 5-8, Hawaii, U.S.A, 1-9.

Gibson, T. (2001). 'The Importance of SMEs to Central Asia and the Importance of Equity for SMEs', *Institute for SME Finance*, (http://www.smeinstitute.org/seminars/asia /english/importance.pdf), [accessed Dec 2002].

Gill, J. and Johnson, P. (1991). *Research Methods for Managers,* Paul Chapman Publishing, London.

Glass, R. and Vessey, I. (1999). 'Enterprise Resource Planning Systems: can they Handle the Enhancement Changes most Enterprises Require?', In *Proceedings of the First International Workshop on Enterprise Management and Enterprise Resource Planning Systems: Methods Tools and Architectures (EMRPS)*, Nov 25-27, Venice, Italy.

Goss, D. (1991). *Small Business and Society,* Routledge, London.

Gruman, G. (2003). 'Getting Ready for Web Services - Case Study Early Adopter', *CIO Magazine, Emerging Technology*, (http://www.cio.com/archive/030103/et_article .Html), [accessed June 2003].

Gubrium, J. F. and Holstein, J. A. (2000). *'Analysing Interpretive Practice'*, In *Handbook of Qualitative Research*, N. Y. K. Denzin and Y.S.Lincoln Eds., Sage, Thousand Oaks, CA, 487-508.

Gupta, A. (2000). 'Enterprise Resource Planning: the Emerging Organisational Value Systems', *Industrial Management & Data Systems,* 100(3), 114-118.

Hakim, C. (1987). *Research Design: Strategies and Choices in the Design of Social Research,* Allen & Unwin, London, UK.

Hage, J. (1980). *Theories and Organisations*, Wiley, New York, USA.

Hagel, J. and Brown, J. (2001). 'Your Next IT Strategy', *Harvard Business Review,* Oct, 105-113.

Hailstone, R. and Perry, R. (2002). *IBM and the Strategic Potential of Web Services: Assessing the Customer Experience,* An IDC White Paper, IBM, USA.

Harreld, H. (2002). 'Vitria Marries Web services and Business Process Management', *InfoWorld News*, (http://www.infoworld.com/article/02/05/17/02051hnvitria_1.h tml), [accessed March 2003].

Hart, P. J. and Saunders, C. S. (1998). 'Emerging Electronic Partnerships: Antecedents and Dimensions of EDI Use from the Supplier's Perspective', *Journal of Management Information System,* 14(4), 87-111.

Heck, E. and Ribbers, P. (1999). 'The Adoption and Impact of EDI in Dutch SMEs', In *Proceedings of the 32nd Hawaii International Conference on System Sciences*

(HCISS), Jan 5-8, Maui, Hawaii.

Herriott, R. E. and Firestone, W. A. (1983). 'Multi-Site Qualitative Policy Research: Optimising Description and Generalisability', *Educational Researcher,* 12, 14-19.

Hicks, J. O. (1997). *Management Information Systems: A User Perspective,* West Publications, Minneapolis/St Paul.

Hill, J. and McGowan, P. (1999). 'Small Business and Enterprise Development: Questions about Research Methodology', *International Journal of Entrepreneurial Behaviour and Research,* 5(1), 5-18.

Hirschheim, R. and Klein, H. K. (1994). 'Realising Emancipatory Principles in Information Systems Development: The Case for ETHICS', *MIS Quarterly,* 18(1), 83-109.

Holland, C. and Light, B. (1999). 'Global Enterprise Resource Planning Implementation', In *Proceedings of the 32nd Hawaii International Conference on System Sciences (HICSS),* Jan 5-8, Maui, Hawaii.

Holland, C., Light, B. and Kawalek, P. (1999). 'Beyond Enterprise Resource Planning Projects: Innovative Strategies for Competitive Advantage', In *Proceedings of the 7th European Conference on Information Systems (ECIS),* June 23-25, Copenhagen, Denmark, 288-301.

Holmes, S. and Gibson, B. (2001). *Definition of Small Business, Final Report,* University of Newcastle, Newcastle, U.K.

Howard, D. and Hine, D. (1997). 'The Population of Organisations Life Cycle (POLC): Implications for Small Business Assistance Program', *International Small Business Journal,* 15(3), 30-41.

Hu, P. J., Chau, P. Y. K., Sheng, O. R. L. and Tam, Y. K. (1999). 'Examining the Technology Acceptance Model Using Physician Acceptance of Telemedicine Technology', *Journal of Management Information Systems,* 16(2), 91-112.

Hughes, M., Golden, W. and Powell, P. (2003). 'Inter-Organisational ICT Systems: the Way to Innovative Practice for SMEs', *Journal of Small Business and Enterprise Development,* 10(3), 277-286.

HurwitzGroup. (2002). 'Case Study: T-Motion Powered by Systinet - T-Motion Uses Web Services to Deliver Content to Wireless Phone Subscribers', Hurwitz Group, Inc, (http://www.hurwitz.com), [accessed March 2003].

Iacovou, C., Benbasat, I. and Dexter, A. (1995). 'Electronic Data Interchange and Small Organisations: Adoption and Impact of Technology', *MIS Quarterly,* 19(4), 465-485.

IBM. (2003a). 'Case Studies: Web Services', *IBM,* (http://www.3.ibm.com/software/ebusi ness/jstart/casestudies/dmc.shtml), [accessed Jan 2004].

IBM. (2003b). 'Case Studies: Web Services', *IBM,* (http://www-3.ibm.com/software/ebusi Ness/jstart/casestudies/ford.shtml), [accessed Jan 2004].

IBM. (2003c). 'Case Studies: Web Services', *IBM*, (http://www-3.ibm.com/software/ebusi Ness/jstart/casestudies/alico.shtml), [accessed Jan 2004].

IDC (1999). 'India: Corporate Growth Driving ERP Adoption', *Business Line*, (http://www.ebizframe.com/credhome%5B1%5D.htm), [accessed March 2002].

Intrinsyc (2003). 'Case Study: Panasonic Security & Digital Imaging', *Intrinsyc Software Inc*, (http://www.intrinsyc.com), [accessed Jan 2004].

Iyer, B., Freedman, J., Gaynor, M. and Wyner, G. (2003). 'Web Services: Enabling Dynamic Business Networks', *Communications of the Association for Information Systems,* 11, 525-554.

Janesick, V. (2000). 'The Choreography of Qualitative Research Design', In *Handbook of Qualitative Research*, Sage, Thousand Oaks, CA.

JSBRI (2002). *White Paper on Small and Medium Enterprises in Japan: The Age of the Local Entrepreneur-Birth, Growth and Revitalization of the National Economy,* Japan Small Business Research Institute, Japan.

Kagan, A., Lau, K. and Nusgart, K. R. (1990). 'Information System Usage within Small Business Firms', *Entrepreneurship: Theory and Practice,* 14(3), 25-37.

Kalakota, R. and Whinston, B. (1996). *Frontiers of Electronic Commerce,* Addison-Wesley, Boston, Massachusetts ,USA.

Kalakota, R. and Robinson, M. (2001). *e-Business: Roadmap for Success,* Addison-Wesley, Boston, Massachusetts, USA.

Kappelman, L. A., Richards, T. C. and Tsai, R. J. (1996). 'A Manager's Guide to Electronic Data Interchange: Doing Business on the Information Superhighway', *Logistics Information Management,* 9(1), 12-17.

Kaye, D. (2003). *Loosely Coupled: the Missing Pieces of Web Services,* RDS Press, Marin County, California.

Kelly, S., Holland, C. and Light, B. (1999). 'Enterprise Resource Planning: A Business Approach to Systems Development', In *Proceedings of the 5th Conference on Information Systems (AMCIS)*, Aug 13-15, Milwaukee, Wisconsin, USA, 785-787.

Kendall, J., Tung, L. L., Chua, K. H., Ng, C. H. D. and Tan, S. M. (2001). 'Electronic Commerce Adoption by SMEs in Singapore', In *Proceedings of the 34th Hawaii International Conference on System Sciences*, Jan 3-6, Outrigger Wailea Resort, Island of Maui.

Kirby, A. D. (2003). *Entrepreneurship,* McGraw-Hill Education, Glasgow, U.K.

Kirzner, R. (2001). 'Large Financial Institution Creates Successful Web Services with Tools from Sun', *IDC*, (http://www.idc.com), [accessed March 2002].

Klandt, H. (1993). *Entrepreneurship and Business Development,* Avebury Ashgate

Publishing, Hants, U.K.

Klein, K. K. and Myers, M. D. (1999). 'A Set of Principles for Conducting and Evaluating Interpretive Field Studies in Information Systems', *MIS Quarterly,* 23(1), 67-94.

Krill, P. (2003). 'Web Services Still Challenged by Standards', *InfoWorld News,* (http://www.infoworld.com/article/03/10/02/HNwspanel_1.html), [accessed April 2004].

Kuan, K. K. Y. and Chau, P. Y. K. (2001). 'A Perception-Based Model for EDI Adoption in Small Businesses Using a Technology-Organisation-Environment Framework', *Information and Management,* 38(8), 507-521.

Land, F. (1992). 'The Information Systems Domain', In *Information Systems Research: Issues, Methods, and Practical Guidelines*, R. Galliers Ed., Blackwell Scientific, Oxford.

Lee, A. A. (1991). 'Integrating Positivist and Interpretive Approaches to Organisational Research', *Organisation Science,* 2(4), 342-265.

Lessing, A. C. and Schulze, S. (2002). 'Postgraduate Supervision and Academic Support: Students' Perceptions,' *South African Journal of Higher Education,* 16(2), 139-149.

Levy, M., Powell, P. and Yetton, P. (2001), 'SMEs: Aligning IS and the Strategic Context', *Journal of Information Technology*, 16, 133-144.

Levy, M., Powell, P. and Yetton, P. (2003). 'IS Alignment in Small Firms: New Paths through the Maze', In *Proceedings of the European Conference on Information Systems (ECIS)*, June 19-21, Naples, Italy, CD-ROM.

Lin, B., Vassar, J. and Clark, L. (1993). 'Information Technology Strategies for Small Business', *Journal of Applied Business Research,* 9(2), 25-29.

Ling, C. Y. (2001). 'Model of Factor Influences on Electronic Commerce Adoption and Diffusion in Small and Medium Sized Enterprises', In *Proceedings of the European Conference on Information Systems (ECIS)*, June 27-29, Bled, Slovenia, PhD Consortium.

Lin, Z., Zhao, H. and Ramanathan, S. (2003). 'Pricing Web Services for Optimising Resource Allocation - An Implementation Scheme', *In Proceedings of the Second Workshop on e-Business*, Dec 13-14, Seattle, USA, 185-191.

Lincoln, Y. S. and Guba, E. G. (2000). 'Paradigmatic Controversies, Contradictions, and Emerging Confluence', In *Handbook of Qualitative Research*, N.Y.K. Denzin and Y. S. Lincoln Eds., Sage, Thousand Oaks, CA.

Linthicum, D. (1999). *Enterprise Application Integration,* Addison-Wesley, Massachusetts.

Linthicum, D. S. (2001). 'Next-Generation EAI: Eight Prophecies for 2001', *EBIZ,* (http://eai.ebizq.net/str/linthicum_1.html), [accessed March 2003].

Linthicum, D. S. (2004). *Next Generation Application Integration: From Simple Information to Web Services,* Pearson Education, Boston.

Lublinsky, B. and Farrell, M. (2002). 'Web Services', *EAI Journal,* (http://www.eaijournal.com/PDF/WebServicesLublinsky.pdf), [accessed March 2003].

Macehiter, N. (2002). 'Viewpoint: Barriers slow Web Services Adoption', VNU Business Publications Ltd 18 March 2002, (http://www.webactivemagazine.co.uk/Analysis /1130344), [accessed March 2003].

Manes, A. T. (2003). *Web Services: A Manager's Guide,* Addison Wesley, Boston.

Mansfield, E., Rapoport, J., Romeo, A., Villani, E., Wagner, S. and Husic, F. (1997). *The Production and Application of New Industrial Technology*, Norton, New York.

Markus, L., Tanis, C. and Van Fenema, P. (2000). 'Multisite ERP Implementations', *Communications of the ACM,* 43(4), 42-46.

Markus, M. and Tanis, C. (1999). *In Framing the Domain of IT Management: Projecting the Future through the Past,* Pinnaflex Educational Resources, Oklahoma, USA.

Marshall, C. and Rossman, G. B. (1999). *Designing Qualitative Research,* Sage, London.

Marlow, S. (2000). 'Investigating the Use of Emergent Strategic Human Resource Management Activity in the Small Firm', *Journal of Small Business and Enterprise Development,* 7(2), 135-148.

Martin, M. (1998). 'An ERP Strategy', *Fortune,* 127(2), 149-151.

Microsoft (2001). 'Software Provider, Insurance Community Gain Unprecedented Integration with .NET Platform and XML Web Services', *Microsoft Corp.,* (http://www.microsoft.com), [accessed March 2003].

Microsoft (2001). 'Case Study: Converting to Web Services Simplifies Everything for ISV', *Microsoft Corp.,* (http://www.devx.com/SummitDays/Article/6694), [accessed March 2003].

Miles, M. B. and Huberman, A. M. (1994). *Qualitative Data Analysis: An Expanded Sourcebook,* Sage, Newbury Park, California, USA.

Miller, G. (2003). '.Net vs. J2EE', *Communications of the ACM,* 46(6), 64-67.

Milroy, A. and Doyle, A. (2002). *The Benefits of Web Services: Australia,* An IDC White Paper, Australia.

Mirani, R. and Lederer, A. L. (1998). 'An Instrument for Assessing the Organisational Benefits of IS Project', *Decision Sciences,* 29, 803-838.

Mishler E.G. (1986). *Research Interviewing: Context and Narrative*, Harvard University Press, Cambridge, M.A.

MOEATD (2001). *RosettaNet Standard and B2B E-business,* Ministry of Economic

Affairs, Technology Department Taiwan.

Moore, G. C. and Benbasat, I. (1991). 'Development of an Instrument to Measure the Perceptions of Adopting an Information Technology Innovation', *Information Systems Research,* 2(3), 193-222.

Morgan, G. (1980). 'Paradigms, Metaphors and Puzzle Solving in Organisation Theory', *Administrative Science Quarterly,* 25, 605-622.

Morgenthal, J. and La Forge, B. (2000). *Enterprise Application Integration with XML and Java,* Prentice-Hall, Inc, New Jersey, USA.

Morphy, E. (2003). 'New NetLedger App Links Front, Back Offices', *CRMDaily.com*, (http://www.crmdaily.com/perl/printer/21996/), [accessed Dec 2003].

Morrell, M. and Ezingeard, F. N. (2002). 'Revisiting Adoption Factors of Inter-Organisational Information Systems in SMEs', *Logistics Information Management,* 15(1), 46-57.

Mozhdehi, B. (2001). 'Approaches to B2B Data Integration', *EBIZ*, (http://b2b.ebizq.net/scm/mozhdehi_1a.html), [accessed March 2003].

Mudd, S. (1990). 'The Place of Innovativeness in Models of the Adoption Process: An Integrative Review,' *Technovation,* 10, 19-136.

Murray, C. A. (2003a). 'Web Services Security Specifications', *CMP United Business Media*, (http://www.commweb.com/article/NMG20021223S0014), [accessed Dec 2003].

Murray, M. C. (2003b). 'An Initial Investigation of Web Services in Healthcare', In *Proceedings of the Ninth Americas Conference on Information Systems (AMCIS),* Aug 4-6, Tampa, Florida, USA, 901-905.

Myers, M. D. (1997). 'Qualitative Research in Information Systems', *MIS Quarterly,* 21(2), 241-242.

Nayak, A. and Greenfield, S. (1994). *The Use of Management Accounting Information for Managing Micro Businesses,* Routledge, London.

Neel, D. (2002). 'IDF: Experts Wrangle with Web Services Barriers', *InfoWorld,* (http://infoworld.com/article/02/02/27/020227hnwebbarriers_1.html), [accessed Jan 2003].

Newcomer, E. (2002). *Understanding Web Services: XML, WSDL, SOAP, and UDDI,* Addison Wesley, Boston.

Nilakanta, S. and Scamell, R. (1990). 'The Effect of Information Sources and Communication Channels on the Diffusion of Innovation in a Data Base Development Environment', *Management Science,* 36(1), 24-40.

Orlikowski, W. and Baroudi, J. (1991). 'Studying Information Technology in Organisations: Research Approaches and Assumptions', *Information Systems Research,* 2(1), 1-28.

Papazafeiropoulou, A. (2002). *A Stakeholder Approach to Electronic Commerce Diffusion'*, PhD Thesis, Information Systems and Computing Department, Brunel University, London.

Patankar, A. (2003). 'Web Services Enabled Architecture for Interorganizational Business Process Management', In *Proceedings of the Ninth Americas Conference on Information Systems (AMCIS)*, Aug 4-6, Tampa, Florida, USA, 1950-1959.

Pawar, K. and Driva, H. (2000). 'Electronic Trading In a Supply Chain: a Holistic Implementation', *Logistics Information Management,* 13(1), 21-32.

Pearce, J. A., Chapman, B. L. and David, F. R. (1982). 'Environmental scanning for small and Growing Firms', *Journal of Small Business Management,* July, 27-34.

Pender, L. (2000). 'Will Integration Tools Patch the Holes Left by an Unsatisfactory ERP Implementation?', *CIO Magazine*, (http://www.cio.com/archive/091500/erp_cont Ent.html), [accessed Feb 2002].

Pettiigrew, A., Whipp, R. and Rosenfeld, R. (1989). 'Competitiveness and the Management of Strategic Change Processes', *In the Competitiveness of the European Industry,* A, Francis and P, Tharakan. Eds., Routledge, London.

Pfeffer, J., and Leblebici, H. (1997). 'Information Technology and Organisation Structure,' *Pacific Sociological Review,* 20(2), 241-261.

Polkinghorne, D. (1983). *Methodology for the Human Sciences: Systems of Inquiry,* University of Chicago Press, Chicago.

Pollard, C. E. and Hayne, S. C. (1998). 'The Changing Face of Information Systems Issues in Small Firms', *International Small Business Journal,* 16(3), 70-87.

Pollock, T. J. (2001). 'The Big Issue: Interoperability vs. Integration', *EAI Journal,* (http://eai.ittoolbox.com/documents/document.asp?i=1597).

Poon, S. and Jevons, C. (1999). 'Internet-Enabled International Marketing: a Small Business Network Perspective', *Journal of Marketing Management,* 13, 29-41.

Poon, S. and Swatman, P. M. C. (1999). 'An Exploratory Study of Small Business Internet Commerce Issues', *Information and Management,* 35, 9-18.

Porter, M. and Millar, V. E. (1985). 'How Information gives you Competitive Advantage', *Harvard Business Review,* 63(4), 149-169.

Premkumar, G. and Potter, M. (1995). 'Adoption of Computer Aided Software Engineering (CASE) Technology: An Innovation Adoption Perspective', *Database Advances,* 26(2-3), 105-123.

Premkumar, G. and Ramamurth, K. (1995). 'The Role of Inter-Organisational and Organisational Factors on the Decision Mode for Adoption of Inter-Organisational Systems', *Decision Sciences,* 26(3), 303-336.

Premkumar, G., Ramamurth, K. and Nilakanta, S. (1994). 'Implementation of Electronic Data Interchange: An Innovation Diffusion Perspective', *Journal of Management Information System,* 11(2), 157-179.

Putney, L. and Green, J. (1999). 'Evolution of Qualitative Research Methodology: Looking Beyond Defense to Possibilities', *Reading Research Quarterly,* 34, 368-277.

Radeka, K. (2002). *Designing a Web Services Project for Maximum Value: The 90 Day Challenge,* Hewlett-Packard Company, Vancouver.

Raghunathan, S. and Yeh, A. B. (2001). 'Beyond EDI: Impact of Continuous Replenishment Program (CRP) between a Manufacturer and its Retailers', *Information Systems Research,* 12(4), 406-419.

Rai, A. and Howard, G. S. (1993). 'An Organisational Context for CASE Innovation', *Information Resources Management Journal,* 6(3), 2-34.

Ratnasingam, P. (1998). 'Internet-Based EDI Trust and Security', *Information Management and Computer Security,* 6(1), 33-39.

Ratnasingam, P. and Pavlou, P. A. (2002). 'The Role of Web Services in Business to Business Electronic Commerce', In *Proceedings of the Eighth Americas Conference on Information Systems (AMCIS),* August 4-6, Tampa, Florida, USA, 2239-2243.

Ratnasingam, P. (2004). 'The Impact of Collaborative Commerce and Trust in Web Services. *Journal of Enterprise Information Management* 17(4), 382-387.

Ravarini, A., Tagliavini, M., Pigni, F. and Sciuto, D. (2000). 'A Framework for Evaluating ERP Acquisition within SMEs', In *Proceedings of AIM International Conference,* Nov 8-10, Montpellier, France, 1-11.

Raymond, L. (1985). 'Organisational Characteristics and MIS Success in the Context of Small Business', *MIS Quarterly,* March, 37-52.

Raymond, L. and Bergeron, F. (1996). 'EDI success in small and medium-sized enterprises: a field study', *Journal of Organisational Computing and Electronic Commerce,* 6(2), 161-172.

Ring, K. and Ward, D. N. (1999). *Enterprise Application Integration: Making the Right Connections,* Ovum Ltd, London, UK.

RIS (2002). 'Key Performance Indicator Management and Review', Resolution Integration Solution, Inc, (http://www.ris-resolution.com/kpi.shtml), [accessed March 2003].

Rizzoni, A. (1991). 'Technological Innovation and Small Firms: a Taxonomy', *International Small Business Journal,* 9(3), 31-42.

RNT (2001). 'RosettaNet in Taiwan', RosettaNet, (http://www.rosettanettaiwan.org.tw/), [accessed June 2002].

Robson, L. (1994). 'EDI - Changing Business Practice', *Logistics Information Management,* 7(4), 35-40.

Rodgers, K. (2003). 'Getting to Grips with Web Services', Procullux Media Ltd., (http://www.looselycoupled.com/stories/2003/grips-ws-infr0724.html), [accessed

Jan 2004].

Rogers, M. E. (1995). *Diffusion of Innovations* (Fourth eds.), The Free Press, New York, NY.

Roethlisbeger, F. J. (1977). 'The Elusive Phenomena', *Harvard Business Review*, Boston, Massachusetts, USA.

Rosenberg, J. (2003). *Web Services Security Today with SSL: Simple Strategies for Securing and Monitoring Web Services,* Service Integrity Incorporated, Newton.

Rosenberg, J. and Mateos, A. (2003). *Production Web Services: The Critical Need for Monitoring and Analysis,* Service Integrity Inc., Newton.

Rothwell, R. and Zegveld, W. (1982). *Innovation and the Small and Medium Sized Firm,* Frances Pinter, London, UK.

Ruh, W., Maginnis, F. and Brown, W. (2000). *Enterprise Application Integration: A Wiley Tech Brief,* Wiley, New York, USA.

Stake, R. E. (2000). 'Case Studies', In *Handbook of Qualitative Research*, N.Y. K. Denzin and Y.S. Lincoln Eds., Sage, Thousand Oaks, 435-454.

Samtani, G. and Sadhwani, D. (2002). 'EAI and Web Services: Easier Enterprise Application Integration?', *Web Services Architect,* (http://www.webservicesarchit ect.com/content/articles/samtani01.asp).

Sanchez, E., Beery, D. and Shehab, J. (2002). 'Review: EAI Systems Bring IT Together', *CMP,* (http://www.networkcomputing.com/1302/1302f5.html), [accessed March 2003].

Saunders, C. and Hart, P. (1993). 'Electronic Data Interchange Across Organisational Boundaries: Building a Theory of Motivation and Implementation', In *Proceedings of the Administrative Sciences Association of Canada Twenty-First Annual Conference*, May 1993, Lake Louise, Alberta, Canada.

Schonefeld, M. and Vering, O. (2000). 'Enhancing ERP-Efficiency through Workflow-Services', In *Proceedings of the Americas Conference on Information Systems (AMCIS)*, Aug 10-13, Long Island, California, USA, 640-645.

Scott, M., Roberts, I., Holroyd, G. and Sawbridge, G. (1989). *Management and Industrial Relations in Small Firms,* Research Paper No. 70, Department of Employment, London.

Scheurich J. (1997). *Research Method in the Post-modern.*, The Falmer Press, London.

Schutz, A. (1967). *The Phenomenology of the Social World*, Northwestern University Press, New York.

Schwandt, T. A. (2000). 'Three Epistemological Stances for Qualitative Inquiry: Interpretivism, Hermeneutics, and Social Constructionism', In *handbook of Qualitative Research*, N.Y. K. Denzin and Y. S. Lincoln Eds., Sage, Thousand Oaks, CA.

Shang, S. and Seddon, P. (2000). 'A Comprehensive Framework for Classifying the Benefits of ERP Systems', In *Proceedings of the Americas Conference on Information Systems (AMCIS)*, August 11-13, Long Beach, California, USA, 1005-1114.

Shang, S. and Seddon, P. B. (2002). 'Assessing and Managing the Benefits of Enterprise Systems: the Business Manager's Perspective', *Information Systems Journal*, 12, 271-299.

Shaw, E. (1999). 'A Guide to the Qualitative Research Process: Evidence from a Small Firm Study', *Qualitative Market Research: An International Journal*, 2(2), 59-70.

Siber, S. D. (1973). 'The Integration of Fieldwork and Survey Methods', *American Journal of Sociology*, 78(6), 1335-1359.

Smith, J. (1999). 'Information Technology in the Small Business: Establishing the Basis for a Management Information System', *Journal of Small Business and Enterprise Development*, 6(4), 326-340.

Smithson, S. and Cornford, T. (1996). *Project Research in Information Systems: A Student's Guide*, Antony Rowe, Wiltshire, U.K.

Sommer, R. A. (2003). 'Business Process Flexibility: a Driver for Outsourcing', *Industrial Management & Data Systems*, 103(3), 177-183.

StencilGroup (2001). 'Defining Web Services', *Stencil Group*, (http://www.stencilgroup.com/ideas_scope_200106wsdefined.pdf), [accessed Jan 2003].

Storey, D. J. (1994). *Understanding the Small Business Sector*, Routledge, London, U.K.

Storey, D. J and Cressy, R. (1995). *Small Business Risk: a Firm and Bank Perspective*, Working Paper, SME Centre, Warwick Business School.

Sullivan, T. and Lamonica, M. (2001). 'Web Services Standards Take Center Stage', InfoWorld News April 13, (http://archive.infoworld.com/articles/hn/xml/01/04/16 /010416hnwebserve.xml).

Sumner, M. (1999). 'Critical Success Factors in Enterprise Wide Information Management Systems Projects', In *Proceedings of the Special Interest Group on Computer Personnel Research Annual Conference (SIGCPR)*, April 8-10, New Orleans, LA, USA, 297-303.

Systinet. (2002a). 'Case Study: Entergy Powered by Systinet WASP', *Systinet Corp.*, (http://www.systinet.com/resources/case_studies), [accessed March 2003].

Systinet. (2002b). 'Case Study: Interwoven Embeds Systinet WASP for Web Services Functionality', *Systinet Corp.*, (http://www.systinet.com/resources/case_studies), [accessed March 2003].

Systinet. (2002c). 'Case Study: Retail Decisions Embeds Secure Web Services for Fraud Detection', *Systinet Corp.*, (http://www.systinet.com/resources/case_studies), [accessed March 2003].

Tagliavini, M., Faverio, P., Ravarini, A., Pigni, F. and Buonanno, G. (2002). 'Exploring the

Use of ERP systems by SMEs', In *Proceedings of the 6th World Multi Conference on Systematics Cybernetics and Informatics*, March 24-28, Orlando, Florida, USA, 14-18.

Themistocleous, M. and Chen, H. (2004). 'Investigating the Integration of SMEs' Information Systems: an Exploratory Case Study', *International Journal of Information Technology and Management*, 3(2, 3, 4), 208-234.

Themistocleous, M. (2002). *Evaluating the Adoption of Enterprise Application Integration in Multinational Organisations*, PhD Thesis, Department of Information Systems and Computing, Brunel University.

Themistocleous, M. and Irani, Z. (2001). 'Benchmarking the Benefits and Barriers of Application Integration', *Benchmarking: An International Journal*, 8(4), 317-331.

Themistocleous, M., Irani, Z. and O'Keefe, R. (2001a). 'ERP and Application Integration Exploratory Survey', *Business Process Management Journal*, 7(3), 195-204.

Themistocleous, M., Irani, Z., Okeefe, R. M. and Paul, R. (2001b). 'ERP Problems and Application Integration Issues: An Empirical Survey', In *Proceedings of the 34th Hawaii International Conference on System Sciences (HICSS)*, Jan 3-6, Hawaii, U.S.A, CD-ROM.

Themistocleous, M., Irani, Z., Psannis, K. and Vrehopoulos, A. (2001c). 'Application Integration of Information Technology: Classification of Benefits and Barriers', In *Proceedings of the International Workshop on New Models of Business: Managerial Aspects and Enabling Technology*, June 28-29, St. Petersburg, Russia, 153-161.

Thong, J. Y. L. (1999). 'An Integrated Model of Information Systems Adoption in Small Business', *Journal of Management Information Systems*, 15, 187-214.

Thong, J. Y. L. (2001). 'Resource Constraints and Information Systems Implementation in Singaporean Small Businesses', *Omega: The International Journal of Management Science*, 29(2), 143-156.

Thong, J. Y. L. and Yap, C. S. (1994). 'CEO Characteristics, Organisational Characteristics and Information Technology Adoption in Small Business', *Omega*, 23, 429-442.

Thong, J. Y. L., Yap, C. S. and Raman, K. S. (1996). 'Top Management Support, External Expertise and Information Systems Implementation in Small Businesses', *Information Systems Research*, 7(2), 248-267.

Tichy, N. M. (1980). 'Problem Cycles in Organisations and the Management of Changes', In Kimberly, J. R. and Miles, R. H. Eds, *The Organisational Life Cycle*, Jossey-Bass, San Francisco.

Townroe, P. and Mallalieu, K. (1993). 'Founding a New Business in the Countryside', In D.J.Storey, *Understanding the Small Business Sector*, Routledge, London.

Tornatzky, L. G. and Fleischer, M. (1990). *The Processes of Technological Innovation*, Lexington Books, Lexington, MA.

Tuunainen, V. K. (1998). 'Opportunities of Effective Integration of EDI for Small Businesses in the Automotive Industry', *Information and Management*, 34(6), 361-375.

Van, M. J. (1983). *Qualitative Methodology*, Sage, London.

Vega, L., Salvador, R. and Guerra, L. (1997). 'Determinants and Outcomes of Electronic Data Interchange Integration', In *Proceedings of the International Conference on Business Informatics*, July 5-6, Berlin, Germany.

Venkatraman, N. (1994), 'IT-Induced Business Transformation: From Automation to Business Scope Redefinition', *Sloan Management Review, Winter*, 73-87.

Vidgen, R., Francis, D., Powell, P. and Woerndl, M. (2004). 'Web Service Business Transformation: Collaborative Commerce Opportunities in SMEs', *Journal of Enterprise Information Management*, 17(5), 372-381.

Viswanadham, N. and Gaonkar, R. (2001). 'Recent Trends in Enterprise Computing', *Industrial Automation Asia Journal December*, (http://www.messe-duesseldorf.de /MDA/2001/icamasia/_media_/_docs_/show_preview.pdf).

Waarts, E., Everdingen, Y. and Hillegersberg, J. (2002). 'The Dynamics of Factors Affecting the Adoption of Innovations', *The Journal of Product Innovation Management*, 19(6), 412-423.

Walczuch, R., Braven, D. G. and Lundgren, H. (2000). 'Internet Adoption Barriers for Small Firms in the Netherlands', In *Proceedings of the Americas' Conference on Information Systems (AMCIS)*, Aug 10-13, Long Beach, California.

Walsham, G. (1995a). 'Interpretive Case Studies in IS Research: Nature and Method', *European Journal of Information Systems*, 4, 4-81.

Walsham, G. (1993). *Interpreting Information Systems in Organisations*, Wiley Series in Information Systems, Wiley, Chichester.

Walsham, G. (1995b). 'The Emergence of Interpretivism in IS Research', *Information Systems Research*, 4, 74-81.

Wang, X. W., Teo, H. H., Wei, K. K., Sia, C. L. and Lee, M. (2003). 'Effects of Learning Capacity and Knowledge Base on Executive Decision Formation for IT Adoption: an Empirical Study of Small and Medium-Sized Organisations', In *Proceedings of the European Conference on Information Systems (ECIS)*, June 19-21, Naples, Italy, CD-ROM.

Watch, J. (2002). 'WS-I: Another Standards Battle Begins', *Software Development Times 15 May 2002*, (http://www.sdtimes.com/cols/javawatch_054.htm), [accessed March 2003].

WebCollage (2001). *Interactive Web Services: Architecture Whitepaper*, WebCollage Inc., United States.

Welsh, J. A. and White, J. F. (1981). 'A Small Business is not a Little Big Business', *Harvard Business Review*, 59(4), 18-32.

Willcocks, L. (1994). *Information Management: Evaluation of Information Systems Investments,* Chapman & Hall, London.

Willis, T. H. and Willis-Brown, A. H. (2002). 'Extending the Value of ERP', *Industrial Management & Data Systems,* 102(1), 35-38.

Winefield, I. (1991). *Organisations and Information Technology: Systems, Power and Job Design,* Blackwell Scientific, Oxford.

Wong, S. (2001). 'Web Services: The Next Evolution of Application Integration', *EBIZ,* (http://e-serv.ebizq.net/wbs/wong_1.html), [accessed March 2003].

Wong, W. 2002. 'Why Web Services Make Business Sense', *CNET News,* (http://news.com.com/2009-1017-275442.html?legacy=cnet), [accessed March 2003].

Wu, C. H. and Sawy, O. A. 2003. 'Web Services Innovation Characteristics: a Preliminary Research Study', In *Proceedings of the IsOneWorld Conference,* April 14-16, Las Vegas, Nevada, USA, CD-ROM.

W3C (2002). 'Extensible Markup Language (XML)', *W3C,* (http://www.w3.org/XML/), [accessed March 2003].

Xu, H., Seltsikas, P. and O'Keefe, B. (2003). 'The Implications of Web Services Innovation for General Adopters: Findings and Recommendations', In *Proceedings of the Second Workshop on e-Business,* Dec 13-14, Seattle, USA, 160-172.

Yasai-Ardekani, M. and Haung, R. S. (1997). 'Contextual Determinants of Strategic Planning Processes', *Academy of Management Studies,* 34(5), 729-768.

Yasin, B. (2001). 'XML Standard to Keep Web Services Secure', *InternetWeek 30 July 2001,* (http://www.dewpoint.com/pdf/InternetWeek.pdf), [accessed March 2003].

Yin, R. K. (1994). *Case Study Research, Design and Methods,* Sage, Newbury Park, CA.

Yin, Y. K. (2001). 'Legacy Integration Problems in Enterprise Application Integration (EAI)', *EAI Journal,* (http://www.cs.ust.hk/~scc/comp610e/assignment/ykwok.pdf), [accessed Jan 2003].

Yu, S. C. and Chen, R. S. (2003). 'Web Services: XML-based System Integrated Techniques', *The Electronic Library from Emerald,* 21(4), 358-366.

Yuan, E. (2000). *Electronic Business White Paper Taiwan: In the Age of Electronic Business and the Digital Economy,* Compiled and Printed by iAeB Program Office, Taipei, Taiwan.

Zahavi, R. (1999). *Enterprise Application Integration with CORBA,* Wiley, New York, USA.

Zaltman, G. D. R. and Holberk, J. (1973). *Innovations and Organisations,* Wiley, London.

Zeng, Y., Chiang, R. H. L. and Yen, D. C. (2003). 'Enterprise Integration With Advanced

Information Technologies: ERP and Data Warehousing', *Information Management & Computer Security,* 11(3), 115-122.

Zhang, X. and Huang, A. (2004). 'An Exploratory Study of Web Service Adoption', In *Proceedings of the Tenth Americas' Conference on Information Systems (AMCIS),* Aug 5-8, New York, USA, CD-ROM.

Zinner, H. (1999). *Diffusion of Information Systems: Barriers and Drivers for Magnifying EDI in Danish Enterprises,* PhD Thesis, Centre for Electronic Commerce, Copenhagen Business School, Copenhagen, Demark.

Zmud, R. W. (1982). 'Diffusion of Modern Software Practices: Influence of Centralisation and Formalisation', *Management Science*, 28(12), 1421-1431.

Summary

To better understand the parameters that influence the adoption of integration technologies in SMEs and large organisations, a questionnaire was designed to support the analysis reported in Chapter 3. According to Rossman and Wilson (1991), there are suggest three broad reasons for linking qualitative and quantitative data: (1) to enable confirmation or corroboration of each other through triangulation, (2) to elaborate or develop analysis, providing richer detail, and (3) to initiate new lines of thinking through attention to surprises or paradoxes, turning ideas around, providing fresh insight. Therefore, bearing this in mind, this appendix reports an additional investigation to assist the researcher to analyse the identified parameters (as introduced in Chapter 3, Figure 3.2) for the adoption of integration technologies in SMEs and large firms. As it serves as an additional investigation, not a formal quantitative research, the survey data are not tested by various quantitative statistical methods.

A.1 Introduction

The questionnaire contained two sections regarding: (1) general company information, and (2) integration technologies adoption. The questions in this section were categorised into 5 parts according to the parameters identified in Chapter 3, Figure 3.2: *nature, integration needs, company size, adoption factors* and *time*. The questionnaire was validated by two MIS managers from an IT manufacturing company in Taiwan. They were asked to identify ambiguous and irrelevant questions, and any for which answers may not be easily available. The questionnaire was then mailed to computer professionals of 500 firms of any size and industry in Taiwan. Enterprises were categorised as SMEs in Taiwan if their paid-in capital is less than NT$60 million (US$1.8 million), or the number of regular employees did not exceed 200. The firms were chosen randomly from the database provided by the Industrial Bureau of Ministry of Economics (MOE) in Taiwan. The respondents were asked: (a) to complete if they are using integration technologies, (b) to complete if they had evaluated integration technologies in the past and chose not to use them, and (c) ignore the questionnaire if the firm does not belong to either category, but to explain the reasons.

A total of 101 responses were received and 68 of them were useable. 40 (58%) responses were from large organisations and 28 (42%) were from SMEs. Fifty nine (87%) of the responding firms are integration technologies users (this includes ERP, EAI, EDI and Web Services), and 53 of these are IT manufacturing/high-technology firms. The remaining 9 of the responding firms are non-users, and 4 of these are IT manufacturing/high-technology firms. The responding firms represented diverse industries, such as manufacturing, IT industry, high-technology industry, services sectors, and merchandising. The survey results were then analysed by descriptive statistical method and are analysed in the following sections.

A.2 Survey Results Analysis

A.2.1 Nature of Organisations

Integration technologies implementation requires capital investment and may involve other expenditure in upgrading the computer and integrating some systems. It seems that large firms should be able to afford such investments more easily than smaller ones, and therefore integration technologies user firms are expected to be the larger ones. According to the data, among the 9 non-users, 8 are SMEs, (see Table A.1). The reasons for not adopting integration technologies are shown in Table A.2. In addition to those reasons, further reasons for not adopting integration technologies were found that: (1) most SMEs do not fully understand what integration technologies (EDI, ERP, EAI and Web Services) are, and (2) some SMEs find it unnecessary to adopt integration technologies as they are satisfied with the current technologies they are using (e.g. Internet is good enough for their daily operations). In this research, the author is particularly interested in the integration technologies adopters (in total, 59 adopters).

Table A.1 User and Nonuser Percentage

	Responses	User Firms	Non-user Firms
SMEs	28	(20) 29.4%	(8) 11.8%
Large	40	(39) 57.4%	(1) 1.5 %
Total	**68**	**59**	**9**

Table A.2 SMEs' Reasons for not Adopting Integration Technologies

Reasons	Responses
Costs	75%
Security	37.5%
Uncertainty	50%
Financial resources	25%
Skills	12.5%
Others	62.5%

Moreover, Table A.3 shows that EAI has not been popular among SMEs compared to other integration technologies. The possible explanation for this is that the high investment cost and complexity associated with EAI might cause concern to many organisations, especially SMEs. According to Charlesworth and Jones (2003), integration technologies need to be "dumbed-down" to effectively communicate the benefits and issues at the most appropriate level within the organisation.

Table A.3 Integration Technologies Adoption

	EAI	EDI	ERP	Web Services
SMEs	0	35%	50%	15%
Large	50.1%	51.3%	90%	38.5%

Therefore, based on the survey results, the researcher suggests that the nature of SMEs might be an obstacle to their adoption of integration technologies. The reasons for this are: (1) the results indicate that cost is still an obstacle to SMEs, as they can not really afford to spend extra money on R&D investment; (2) some SMEs still find it unnecessary to implement integration technologies, as there are not that many employees within the organisation; and (3) most SMEs still lack knowledge about integration technologies compared to large counterparts.

A.2.2 Company Size

The survey results reported in Table A.4 suggest that SMEs and large organisations mange their IS in different ways. The majority of the integration technologies users in large organisations (71.4%) reported that the MIS department is in charge of the companies' information systems. As for SMEs, there are only around 40% which reported this. The remaining 60% indicated that their IS are often managed under managers or outsourced. The possible explanations are that, firstly, the culture of a small enterprise is tied in with the needs, desires and abilities of its owner (Bridge *et al.*, 1998). The owners of SMEs often like controlling their own destiny and doing things differently. Thus, the managers like to manage the IS on their own. Secondly, according to Carter and Evan (2000), due to the lack of financial resources and expertise in IT, SMEs usually do not develop IS on their own. Instead, they rely more on standardised and *off-the-shelf* software packages, and normally seek external support for their IT problems, such as friends, vendors or consultants. Thus, many SMEs like to outsource their systems. This shows that companies of different sizes manage their IS and integration technologies differently.

Table A.4 Information System Management in Organisations

	MIS Dept	Managers	Outsourcing	Others
SMEs	40%	33.3%	20%	6.7%
Large	71.4%	14.3%	9.5%	4.8%

A.2.3 Integration Needs

Table A.5 shows that the reasons that push SMEs and large firms to turn to integration technologies are different. The majority of large organisations reported that integration technologies can provide real-time data which can help them to eliminate: (1) systems heterogeneity, (2) data redundancy, and (3) low data quality. For example, multiple applications store data for the same entity (e.g. orders), but there is often an inability to combine data and take decisions, since there is: (1) data incompatibility, (2) confusion regarding data latency, or (3) communication problems. As for SMEs, the majority reported that external pressure and competition are the main reasons that push them to adopt integration technologies. There are only 2.6% and 7.7% of large organisations which reported this. Thus, it clearly shows that integration needs are different between SMEs and large organisations, and this can influence the ways they approach integration technologies.

Table A.5 Integration Needs Related Factors

Integration Needs	SMEs	Large Firms
External pressure	45%	2.6%
Competition	40%	7.7%
Technical reasons	10%	2.6%
Financial reasons	10%	5.1%
Provide solution to existing problem	20%	12.8%
Managerial reasons	35%	43.6%
Strategic reasons	20%	7.7%
ERP can not fully automate and integrate business process	10%	2.6%
Others	5%	2.6%

Additionally, Table A.3 in Section A.2.2 shows that the newer the technologies, the less likelihood that SMEs will adopt them. For instance, the adoption rate for EAI and Web Services among SMEs is relatively low compared to their large counterparts. This suggests that the more complex and expensive the integration technologies are, the less likelihood that SMEs will adopt them. For large organisations, they will use the integration technologies in a circumstance where the adoption of integration technologies will help them to increase their competitiveness or solve a particular problem. This also shows the different motivations towards integration technologies adoption between SMEs and large organisations.

A.2.4 Time

Table A.6 demonstrates that the timing of integration technologies adoption is different between SMEs and large organisations. For instance, the majority of large organisations reported that they have adopted integration technologies for more than 10 years. As for SMEs, this only applies to around 15% of them. The majority of SMEs lie in between 5 to 10 years. This indicates that SMEs tend to be later adopters compared to large organisations.

Table A.6 Timing for Integration Technologies Adoption

	< 10 Years	5-10 Years	> 5 Years	Very Recently	Planning
SMEs	15%	35%	25%	15%	10%
Large	35.9%	23.1%	10.3%	5.1%	2.6%

Table A.7 shows that the early adoption of integration technologies can help organisations to gain some minor competitive advantages. However, many of the respondents claimed that it is hard to tell whether adopting integration technologies giving them major competitive advantage, but they are sure that not having implemented any of these integration technologies may become a problem for their companies.

Table A.7 Timing and Competitive Advantages

	Test Value = 0					
	T	DF	Sig. (2-tailed)	Mean Difference	95% Confidence Interval of the Difference	
					Lower	Upper
SMEs	6.848	67	.000	.412	.29	.53
Adopted	16.836	67	.000	.809	.71	.90
Competitive advantages	1.000	2	.423	.333	-1.10	1.77
Don't know	2.000	2	.184	.667	-.77	2.10

A.2.5 Adoption Factors for SMEs and Large Organisations

Table A.8 shows that SMEs and large organisations face different problems when integrating their IS. The majority of SMEs reported that due to their lack of technical skills they have encountered many technical problems. As for large firms, they reported that they have encountered many strategic problems when integrating their information systems (around 33.3%).

Table A.8 Problems Faced When Adopting Integration Technologies

Problems Faced When Adopting Integration Technologies	SMEs	Large Firms
Financial problems due to limited resources	35%	10.3%
Technical problems due to lack of expertise's support and technical skills	60%	12.8%
Organisational change	20%	17.9%
Managerial problems	25%	25.6%
Strategic problems	15%	33.3%
No problem at all	0	10.3%
Others	5%	2.6%

Table A.9 Integration Technologies Adoption Factors

Adoption Factors	SMEs	Large Firms
Availability of standards	70%	56.4%
Barriers	20%	7.7%
Perceived industry pressure	15%	2.6%
Business complexity	5%	7.7%
Customer power	35%	5.1%
Internal pressure	10%	2.6%
IT infrastructure	20%	12.8%
Technology characteristics	15%	5.1%
Organisational readiness	20%	10.2%
Extent of organisational change	30%	12.8%
IT infrastructure	10%	12.8%
Security Technical factors	5%	10.3%
Competitive pressures	20%	12.8%
Dependency on partners	25%	7.7%
External pressure	5%	5.1%
IT sophistication	25%	7.7%
Support	20%	17.9%
Perceived financial cost	20%	12.8%
Perceived benefits	40%	35.9%
Perceived technical competence	30%	5.1%
Perceived government pressure	15%	2.6%
Others	0	2.6%

Table A.9 indicates that SMEs and large organisations take decisions for the adoption of integration technologies, mostly focusing on the different factors. For example, there are around 35% of SME respondents reported that customer power influences their adoption decisions, but only 5.1% of large organisations reported this. Another example is that 25% of SMEs claimed that dependency on partners is the factor that influences their adoption decisions, but only 7.7% of large organisations reported this.

A.3 Conclusion

The results here show that SMEs and large organisations focus mostly on different issues when considering their integration technologies adoption. Nevertheless, these issues are further examined in Chapter 3 according to the research aim addressed in Chapter, Section 1.7. Thus, the main purpose of this survey is to investigate issues regarding the adoption of integration technologies in SMEs and large organisations to support the research questions analysis reported in Chapter 3 (i.e. this survey results reported here acts as an exploratory case study investigation).

Appendix B: Technical Issues for Middleware Technology

There are different types of middleware and they are discussed as follows:

RPC

RPC provides the ability to invoke a function within one program and have that function execute within another program on a remote machine. RPCs are synchronous. In order to carry out an RPC, the RPC must stop the execution of the program. This quality is what defines RPCs as "blocking middleware" (Linthicum, 2004). They also require more bandwidth than other types of middleware products because carrying out a remote procedure call requires so much overhead. Despite their simplicity, most RPCs are not well-performing middleware products. To function well, RPCs demand a tremendous level of processing power. Furthermore, many exchanges must take place across a network to carry out a request. A typical RPC may require 24 distinct steps to complete requests in addition to several calls across the network. This level of performance limits the benefits of making RPC calls across slower networks, such as the Internet.

Message oriented middleware (MOM)

MOM uses the notion of messages to communicate between applications, direct coupling with the middleware mechanism and the application is not required. MOM products rely on an asynchronous paradigm. The asynchronous model allows the application to function independently to continue processing after making a middleware service request. The message is dispatched to a queue manger, which ascertains that the message is delivered to its final destination. Messages returning to the calling application are handled when the calling application finds the time.

Distributed objects

Distributed objects are classified as middleware because they facilitate inter-application communication. However, they are also mechanisms for application development, providing enabling technology for enterprise, or enterprise-wide method sharing. In fact, distributed objects are small application programs that use standard interfaces and protocols to communicate with one another. There are two types of distributed objects on the market today: CORBA and Component Object Model (COM).

Database oriented middleware

Database oriented middleware is any middleware that facilitates communication with a database, whether from an application or between databases. Developers typically use database oriented middleware as a mechanism to extract information from either local or remote databases. Database oriented middleware works with two basic database types: Call-Level Interfaces (CLIs) and native database middleware.

Transaction oriented middleware

Transactional middleware such as TP monitors and application servers does a commendable job of coordinating information movement and method sharing between many different resources. However, while the transactional paradigm they employ provides an excellent mechanism for method sharing, it is not as effective as simple information sharing. For example, transactional middleware tends to create a tightly coupled application integration solution, while messaging solutions tend to be more cohesive in nature. In addition, in order to take advantage of transactional middleware, the source and target applications have to be changed.

TP monitors

TP monitors are first-generation application servers as well as transactional middleware products. They provide a mechanism to facilitate the communication between two or more applications as well as a location for application logic. TP monitors are based on the concept of a transaction – a unit of work with a beginning and an end. The reasoning here is that if the application logic is encapsulated within a transaction, then the transaction either completes or is rolled back completely. Transactions have the advantage of being able to break an application into smaller portions and then invoke those transactions to carry out the bidding of the user, or another connected system. Because transactions are small units of work, they are easily managed and processed within the TP monitor environment. By sharing the processing of these transactions among other connected TP monitors, TP monitors provide enhanced scalability.

Appendix C: Integration Technologies Benefits and Barriers Classification

EAI Benefits and Barriers Classification

Themistocleous *et al.*(2001) classified the benefits and barriers of EAI technology according to Chang and Seddon model.

Table C.1 Classification of Application Integration Barriers
Source: Themistocleous *et al.*,(2001)

Dimension	Sub-Dimension	Reference
Operational	• Extra cost for redesign and change business structure, processes • AI has a high cost	• (Edwards and Newing, 2000) • (Duke *et al.*, 1999)
Managerial	• Lack of employees with AI skills • Earlier approaches on AI had proved problematic	• (Markus, 2000) • (Ruh *et al.*, 2000)
Strategic	• Resistance to change • Organisations are reluctant to share their data and processes with business partners	• (Edwards and Newing, 2000) • (Kalakota and Robinson, 1999)
IT Infrastructure	• No plug and play AI solutions • No single AI product solves all integration problems • No single integration technology solves all integration problems • Integration technologies are confusing • Integration solutions are based on a combination of AI products and integration technologies • Lack of knowledge • High complexity in understanding the processes and systems in order to redesign and integrate them • Lack of enterprise architecture • Lack of common definitions and standards • Existing systems have restrictions regarding their integration capabilities • Lack of documentation especially in the case of custom systems • Many existing systems are complex and incompatible • Some AI products and technologies are immature	• (Linthicum, 1999) • (Duke *et al.*, 1999) • (Ring and Ward, 1999) • (Ruh *et al.*, 2000) • (Linthicum, 1999) • (Markus, 2000) • (Edwards and Newing, 2000) • (Ruh *et al.*, 2000) • (Duke *et al.*, 1999) • (Zahavi, 1999) • (Zahavi, 1999) • (Kalakota and Robinson, 1999) • (Duke *et al.*, 1999)
Organisational	• Politics and political impact (e.g. who controls the processes) • Complexity of business processes • Cultural issues • No time for training employees on integration technologies	• (Edwards and Newing, 2000) • (Ruh *et al.*, 2000) • (Edwards and Newing, 2000) • (Markus, 2000)

Table C.2 Classification of Application Integration Benefits

Source: Themistocleous *et al.*(2001)

Dimension	Sub-Dimension	Reference
Operational	• Reduces lost sales • Increases productivity • Achieves customer satisfaction • Reduces cost • Improves data quality	• Edwards and Newing (2000) • Duke *et al.* (1999) • Kalakota and Robinson (1999) • (Linthicum, 1999) • (Ring and Ward, 1999)
Managerial	• Provides more understanding and control of processes • Improves management and supports decision making • Improves planning in supply chain management • Increases performance • Achieves return on investment • Results in reliable data • Increases data analysis • Provides a centralised point of control	• Duke *et al.* (1999) • Edwards and Newing (2000) • Kalakota (2000) • Linthicum (1999b) • Edwards and Newing (2000) • (Zahavi, 1999) • Klasell and Dudgeon (1998) • (Ruh *et al.*, 2000)
Strategic	• Improves planning in supply chain management • Allow organisations to do business more effectively • Increases collaboration among partners • Increased market share • Improves relationships with suppliers	• Linthicum (2000) • (Ruh *et al.*, 2000) • Edwards and Newing (2000) • Urlocker (2000) • (Ruh *et al.*, 2000)
IT Infrastructure	• Results in reusable systems, components and data • Reduces redundancy of applications, data and tasks • Faster and cheaper implementation than bespoke solutions • Offers interfaces-standardisation • Provides flexible, maintainable and manageable solutions • Results in reliable data • Provides process and systems scalability • Provides portability • Reduces development risks • Achieves non-invasive solutions • Achieves process integration • Improves data quality • Supports efficient data sharing • Provides data integration • Provides objects/components integration • Provides real-time integration • Integrates custom systems • Integrates packaged systems • Integrates e-business solutions	• Zahavi (1999) • Klasell and Dudgeon (1998) • Edwards and Newing (2000) • (Morgenthal and La Forge, 2000) • Linthicum (2000) • Zahavi (1999) • Ruh *et al.* (2000) • (Ring and Ward, 1999) • (Ring and Ward, 1999) • (Linthicum, 1999) • Zahavi (1999) • Zahavi (1999) • Linthicum (2000) • Edwards and Newing (2000) • Klasell and Dudgeon (1998) • (Ring and Ward, 1999) • (Themistocleous and Irani, 2000) • (Morgenthal and La Forge, 2000) • Linthicum (2000) • Kalakota and Robinson (1999)
Organisational	• Results in more organised business processes • Allow organisations to do business more effectively • Increases flexibility • Achieves quicker response to change • Achieves process integration	• (Ruh *et al.*, 2000) • Linthicum (2000) • (Ring and Ward, 1999) • Kalakota and Robinson (1999) • (Linthicum, 1999)

Appendix D: Integration Technologies Adoption in SMEs and Large companies Survey

Thank you for agreeing to take part in this survey. The purpose of this study is to investigate the adoption of integration technologies by SMEs taking into account the differences between SMEs and large companies. The survey looks at (a) to what extent SMEs' integration needs differ from large companies? (b) Is the nature of SMEs a real obstacle to integration technologies adoption? (c) What is the relationship between integration technologies and their adoptions in companies of different size? (d) Do SMEs and large companies consider the same factors when taking decisions for the adoption of integration technologies? If not, what are the differences?

The responses received will help in understanding the questions proposed above. Your responses will be treated in the strictest of confidence and no reference will be made to individuals' names, so please feel free to answer the questions as accurately as you can. The questionnaire should not take more than 15-20 minutes to complete, as most questions require you to simply select an answer from the options provided. The results of the study will be used purely for academic purposes.

Participation is voluntary and you are free to withdraw at any time or decline to answer any particular question. If you have any questions regarding the survey or in general, please contact Hsin Chen at: hsin.chen@brunel.ac.uk , a research student at Brunel University who is conducting this study.

Thank you once again!

Questionnaire

Please mark the appropriate box with an 'x' unless otherwise stated.

	Questions
Q1	**What is the number of the company's employees?** ☐ 1-10 ☐ 11-50 ☐ 51-250 ☐ <250 **What is the company's turnover?** ☐ > US$ 5 million ☐ Between US$ 5 and 20 million ☐ < US$ 20 million **How wide is the market area?** ☐ Local ☐ Regional ☐ National ☐ International **What is the company configuration?** ☐ It's member of a group ☐ It's an independent company **Does the company have other geographically distributed offices/branches?** ☐ Yes ☐ No **What is the competitive strategy of the company?** ☐ Diversification ☐ Other **How many company's activities are carried out internally?** ☐ Inbound and outbound logistic ☐ Human resources management ☐ Production ☐ R & D ☐ Marketing, sales and services ☐ IS management ☐ Supplying ☐ Infrastructural activities (administration, finance, quality management ☐ Other, please specify ______________________________
Q2	**Has your company adopted any integration technologies? E.g. EAI, EDI, ERP, Middleware or Web Services?**

☐ Yes (please answer 2.1 below)   ☐ No (please answer 2.2 below)

2.1 If yes, what integration technologies have/has your company adopted? Please tick all the appropriate boxes.

☐ EDI   ☐ ERP   ☐ EAI   ☐ Middleware   ☐ Web Services

2.2 If no, what are the following factors affecting the company's decision for not adopting integration technologies? Please tick all the appropriate boxes.

☐ Cost   ☐ Security   ☐ Maturity   ☐ Support   ☐ Technical factors

☐ Uncertainty   ☐ Technological skills   ☐ Financial resource

☐ Others, please specify _____

Q3	**How does the company manage its information systems?** ☐ Manage by MIS department ☐ Manage by the manager ☐ Outsourcing i.e. external expertise ☐ Others, please specify _____
Q4	**What are the company's integration motivation/needs towards integration technologies adoption? Please tick all the appropriate boxes.** ☐ External pressures ☐ Competition ☐ Technical reasons ☐ Financial reasons ☐ Provide solution to the existing problem ☐ Managerial reasons ☐ Strategic reasons ☐ ERP can not fully automate and integrate business process ☐ Others, please specify _____
Q5	**How long had the company adopted integration technologies roughly?** ☐ < 15 years ☐ 5 – 10 years ☐ < 5 years ☐ Recently, (Please answer section 5.1) ☐ Non applicable

5.1 What are the cause(s) for the late adoption of integration technologies? Please tick all the appropriate boxes.

☐ Not ready and have no ideas   ☐ Not necessary   ☐ Too expensive

☐ Too complex   ☐ Don't know

☐ Others, please specify _____

Upon the adoption of integration technologies in the company, does the company increase its competitiveness?

☐ Yes, a lot   ☐ Yes, a little   ☐ No at all   ☐ Don't know

Do you think that the early the company adopts integration technologies the
better in terms of increasing competitive advantages? In other words, do you agree that *timing* is important in terms of increasing company's competitiveness upon the adoption of integration technologies?

☐ Strongly agree   ☐ Agree   ☐ Strongly disagree   ☐ Disagree   ☐ It doesn't matter

---

Q6

Upon the adoption of integration technologies, does your company encounter any of the following problems? Please tick all the appropriate boxes.

☐ Financial problems due to the limited resources

☐ Technical problems due to the lack of expertise's support and technical skills

☐ Organisational change, management and strategic problems

☐ No problem at all

☐ Others, please specify _____

Q7

What are the following factors affecting the company's adoption decision towards integration technologies? Please tick all the appropriate boxes.

☐ Availability of standards   ☐ Barriers   ☐ Perceived Industry pressure   ☐ Business complexity   ☐ Customer Power

☐ Internal pressure   ☐ IT infrastructure   ☐ Technology characteristics   ☐ Organisational readiness

☐ Extent of organisational change   ☐ IT infrastructure   ☐ Security   ☐ Technical factors

☐ Competitive pressures   ☐ Dependency on partners   ☐ External pressure   ☐ IT sophistication   ☐ Support

☐ Perceived financial cost   ☐ Perceived benefits   ☐ Perceived technical competence   ☐ Perceived government pressure

☐ Others, please specify _____

The End
Thank you very much!!

Appendix E: Interview Agenda

This interview agenda is divided into 3 parts

The questionnaire aims to address the following issues:

- To obtain general company information
- To identify business information in SMEs (e.g. benefits, barriers with integration technologies adoption)
- To identify business information in large companies (e.g. benefits, barriers with integration technologies adoption)

Name:			
Position:			
Company Name:			
Address:			
Telephone:		**Fax:**	
e-mail:			

Sections
Section A – General Company Information
Section B – Business Information in SMEs
Section C – Business Information in Large Companies

<u>Section A</u> – General Company Information

A.1 How many people are employed by your organisaiton?

A.2 How many subsidiaries does your organisaiton have?

A3 Is your organisation a SME or large organisaiton?

A4 What is the current turnover?

A.5 What are the key businesses of your organisation?

A.6 How many customers do you have (approximately):

A.7 How wide is the market area? E.g. local, regional, national or international?

A.8 What is the company configuration?

A.9 Does the company have other geographically distributed offices/branches?

A.10 What is the competitive strategy of the company?

<u>Section B</u> – Business Information in SMEs

B.1 What is the information systems management like in the company? Who is or which department is in charge of managing company's information systems?

....
....
....
....
....
....
....
....
....
....

B.2 How many company's activities are carried out internally?

....
....
....
....
....
....
....
....
....
....

B.3 Has your company adopted any integration technologies? What integration technologies have your company adopted? Who initiated the idea for adopting integration technologies?

....
....
....

....
....
....
....
....
....
....

B.4 What were the main motivations and integration needs for adopting integration technologies?

....
....
....
....
....
....
....
....
....
....

B.5 How long had the company adopted integration technologies approximately? If is recently, what are the causes for the late adoption?

....
....

The causes for late adoption:

....
....
....
....
....

B.6 Upon the adoption of integration technologies in the company, does the company increase its competitiveness? In what ways?

B.7 Do you think that the early the company adopts integration technologies the better in terms of increasing competitive advantages? In other words, do you agree that timing is important in terms of increasing company's competitiveness upon the adoption of integration technologies?

B.8 What business problems did your organisation face before adopting integration technologies?

B.9 Upon the adoption of integration technologies, does your company encounter any problems? For example, limited resources, financial problems or organisaitonal changes etc.

B.10 What was the impact from the adoption of integration technologies? Please explain:

Impact on organisation:

....
....
....
....
....
....
....

Impact on employees:

....
....
....
....
....
....
....
....
....

B.11 What are the factors affecting the company's adoption decision towards integration technologies? 1 means not important, 5 means very important and so on.

Factors	1	2	3	4	5
	Not Important				Very Important
Adopter Characteristics					
Availability of Standards					
Barriers					
Business Complexity					
Competitive Pressures					
Customer Power					
Dependency on Partners/ Trading Partners Readiness/pressure					
Environmental Characteristics					
Evaluation Framework for the Integration Technology and Packages					
External Pressure					
Extent of Organisational Change					
External Environment Characteristics					
IS Innovation Type					
IT Sophistication					
IT Infrastructure					
Internal Environment Characteristics					
Internal Pressure					
Innovation Characteristics/ Perceived Innovation Characteristics					
Organisational Characteristics					
Organisational Readiness					
Perceived Financial Cost/ Financial Resources					
Perceived Benefits (Direct and Indirect benefits)					
Perceived Technical Competence/ Technological Skills Readiness					
Perceived Industry Pressure					
Perceived Government Pressure					
Security/ Control Procedures					
Support/ Organisation Support					
Stakeholders					
Supplier Trust					
Supplier Commitment					
Technical Factors					

B.12 Apart from the above mentioned factors, what other factors you think is important factors affecting the adoption of integration technologies by SMEs?

....

....

....

....

....

....

....

B.13 What was the overall cost for integration technologies adoption? Please explain:

....

....

....

....

....

....

....

....

....

B.14 What are the barriers to integration technologies adoption in your organisation?

Integration Technologies Barriers	Not Significant	Significant	Very Significant
Face operational challenges			
Face difficulty in managing relationships with others organisations			
Lack of business perspective			
Lack of large-scale implementation examples and experiences available			
Lack of security protocols and standards			
Concern over security			
Lack of user-interface encapsulation mechanisms			
Concern over maturity of integration technologies			
Concern over transaction distribution management			
Add complexity to the business transaction protocol implementation			
Lack of system reliability at a moment			
Concern over whether the old generation solutions are agile enough to react to the changes			
Concern over the maturity of Web Services payment methods			
Inexperience in architecting Web services			
Lack of XML-based management protocol			
Increase organisational complexity			
Difficult to change internal organisational culture to embrace Web services			
Others:			
Others:			
Others:			
Others:			
Others:			
Others:			
Others:			

B.15 What benefits are derived from integration technologies adoption in your organisation?

Integration Technologies Benefits	Not Significant	Significant	Very Significant
Reduce operational costs			
Achieve customer satisfaction			
Minimise errors, delay and increase accuracy of data			
Increase productivity through Web			
Improve inventory control			
Quick access to information			
Achieve higher ROI			
Increase revenue			
Reduce process time			
Simplify transaction flow			
Increase business and management efficiency			
Increase competitive advantage			
Increase collaboration among customers, services providers and intermediaries			
Increase business opportunities			
Offer solutions to the problems of legacy systems			
Minimise the cost of ownership and development costs			
Reduce development complexity, times and risks			
Automate business processes			
Provide open standard			
Reduce integration cost			
Reduce integration complexity and speed up application integration			
Permit full scale integration			
Provide real-time service-oriented architecture (SOA)			
Provide multiple connect points for other systems to integrate with			
Offer ease of integration with other pieces of software			
Simplify the design development, maintenance and usage			
Provide platform independence and language independence			
Achieve reusability and flexibility			
Provide stability using a dynamic integrated interface to integrate systems			
Achieve interoperability			
Able to unite all major systems vendors (i.e. vendor neutral)			
Reduce time and cost to launch applications			
Increase flexibility			
Quick response to change and business needs			
Reduce time to market			
Other:			
Other:			
Other:			

Section C – Business Information in Large Organisations

C.1 What is the information systems management like in the company? Who is or which department is in charge of managing company's information systems?

....

....

....

....

....

....

....

....

C.2 How many company's activities are carried out internally?

....

....

....

....

....

....

....

....

C.3 Has your company adopted any integration technologies? What integration technologies have your company adopted? Who initiated the idea for adopting integration technologies?

....

....

....

....
....
....
....
....
....
....

C.4 What were the main motivations and integration needs for adopting integration technologies?

....
....
....
....
....
....
....
....
....

C.5 How long had the company adopted integration technologies approximately?

....
....
....
....
....
....
....
....
....

C.6 Upon the adoption of integration technologies in the company, does the company increase its competitiveness? In what ways?

C.7 Do you think that the early the company adopts integration technologies the better in terms of increasing competitive advantages? In other words, do you agree that timing is important in terms of increasing company's competitiveness upon the adoption of integration technologies?

C.8 What business problems did your organisation face before adopting integration technologies?

....
....
....
....
....
....
....
....
....

C.9 Upon the adoption of integration technologies, does your company encounter any problems? For example, limited resources, financial problems or organisaitonal changes etc.

....
....
....
....
....
....
....
....

C.10 What was the impact from the adoption of integration technologies? Please explain:

Impact on organisation:

....
....
....
....
....
....

Impact on employees:

....

....

....

....

....

....

....

....

C.11 What are the factors affecting the company's adoption decision towards integration technologies? 1 means not important, 5 means very important and so on.

Factors	1	2	3	4	5
	Not Important				Very Important
Adopter Characteristics					
Availability of Standards					
Barriers					
Business Complexity					
Competitive Pressures					
Customer Power					
Dependency on Partners/ Trading Partners Readiness/pressure					
Environmental Characteristics					
Evaluation Framework for the Integration Technology and Packages					
External Pressure					
Extent of Organisational Change					
External Environment Characteristics					
IS Innovation Type					
IT Sophistication					
IT Infrastructure					
Internal Environment Characteristics					
Internal Pressure					
Innovation Characteristics/ Perceived Innovation Characteristics					
Organisational Characteristics					
Organisational Readiness					
Perceived Financial Cost/ Financial Resources					
Perceived Benefits (Direct and Indirect benefits)					
Perceived Technical Competence/ Technological Skills Readiness					
Perceived Industry Pressure					
Perceived Government Pressure					
Security/ Control Procedures					
Support/ Organisation Support					
Stakeholders					
Supplier Trust					
Supplier Commitment					
Technical Factors					

C.12 Apart from the above mentioned factors, what other factors you think is important factors affecting the adoption of integration technologies?

....

....

....

....

....

....

....

C.13 What was the overall cost for integration technologies adoption? Please explain:

....

....

....

....

....

....

....

....

C.14 What benefits are derived from integration technologies adoption in your organisation?

Integration Technologies Benefits	Not Significant	Significant	Very Significant
Reduce operational costs			
Achieve customer satisfaction			
Minimise errors, delay and increase accuracy of data			
Increase productivity through Web			
Improve inventory control			
Quick access to information			
Achieve higher ROI			
Increase revenue			
Reduce process time			
Simplify transaction flow			
Increase business and management efficiency			
Increase competitive advantage			
Increase collaboration among customers, services providers and intermediaries			
Increase business opportunities			
Offer solutions to the problems of legacy systems			
Minimise the cost of ownership and development costs			
Reduce development complexity, times and risks			
Automate business processes			
Provide open standard			
Reduce integration cost			
Reduce integration complexity and speed up application integration			
Permit full scale integration			
Provide real-time service-oriented architecture (SOA)			
Provide multiple connect points for other systems to integrate with			
Offer ease of integration with other pieces of software			
Simplify the design development, maintenance and usage			
Provide platform independence and language independence			
Achieve reusability and flexibility			
Provide stability using a dynamic integrated interface to integrate systems			
Achieve interoperability			
Able to unite all major systems vendors (i.e. vendor neutral)			
Reduce time and cost to launch applications			
Increase flexibility			
Quick response to change and business needs			
Reduce time to market			
Other:			
Other:			
Other:			

C.15 What are the barriers to integration technologies adoption in your organisation?

Integration Technologies Barriers	Not Significant	Significant	Very Significant
Face operational challenges			
Face difficulty in managing relationships with others organisations			
Lack of business perspective			
Lack of large-scale implementation examples and experiences available			
Lack of security protocols and standards			
Concern over security			
Lack of user-interface encapsulation mechanisms			
Concern over maturity of integration technologies			
Concern over transaction distribution management			
Add complexity to the business transaction protocol implementation			
Lack of system reliability at a moment			
Concern over whether the old generation solutions are agile enough to react to the changes			
Concern over the maturity of Web Services payment methods			
Inexperience in architecting Web services			
Lack of XML-based management protocol			
Increase organisational complexity			
Difficult to change internal organizational culture to embrace Web services			
Others:			
Others:			
Others:			
Others:			
Others:			
Others:			
Others:			

Appendix F: Organisations Profile (Organisations involved in the Industry Automation Programme)

- **ACER Inc, Taiwan**

Acer Inc., established in 1976, is a leading manufacturer of notebook, tablet, handheld, and desktop computers. Other Acer products include servers, storage systems, projectors, and displays. The company also provides IT support services. Acer has streamlined its operations in recent years, spinning off its contract manufacturing operations (now Wistron), as well as its consumer electronics and peripherals business (now Benq). It still holds stakes in both companies. Acer now outsourcers its manufacturing. It sells through resellers and distributors worldwide. The Acer Group employs more than 5600 people in 120 enterprises spanning 32 countries worldwide, supporting dealers and distributors in over 100 countries. Acer Group revenues in 2004 were US$7 billions. There are 1500 employees in Taiwan branch.

- **ASUSTeK Computer Inc**

ASUSTeK Computer Inc. is a Taiwan-based global company that is principally engaged in the provision of 3C (computing, communication and consumer) solutions. It has up to 58,000 employees worldwide and 7800 employees in Taiwan branch. The 2004 revenues reached $7.7 billions. The Company's product portfolio consists of barebones personal computers, motherboards, notebook computers, personal computer components, graphic cards, networking products, optical storage products, personal digital assistants and servers. The Company operates overseas via subsidiaries such as ASUS Computer International in the United States, ASUS Computer GmbH in Germany, ASUS Holland B.V. in the Netherlands, ASUS Computer in China, ASUS Computer MEA in the Middle East and ASUS Computer SA in South Africa.

Recently, Asustek introduced the world's lowest cost mini-notebook computer, jointly developed with JVC. Look for the mini-notebook at a store near you - sold, of course, under a number of different brand names: Asustek is a prime outsourcing partner for multi-nationals, as well as one of the most successful Taiwanese companies in establishing and selling brand name products. In fact, this year, Asus became the number one brand name notebook computer maker in terms of sales in Taiwan's domestic market, unseating Acer in its home court. This development could fundamentally change the dynamics among Taiwan's PC makers, bolstering Asus' position with component and parts suppliers. A part of TaiwanHighTech's Corporate Card Series, this document provides a snapshot of Asustek's operations, including company contact information, product lines, contract manufacturing activities and partners, China manufacturing facilities and 2003-2004 estimated and YTD shipments. The card is divided into sections covering Asustek's graphics card, motherboard, notebook and optical disc drive units.

- **MiTAC International Corp**

MiTAC founded in 1982 and headquartered in Taiwan, MiTAC International Corporation [MIC] is ranked as one Taiwan's leading manufacturers of award-winning computer products and has become a major integrated networking solution provider. It has more than 22000 employees worldwide and 2002 revenue is over $US 10 billions. The employees in Taiwan are around 700 people. MiTAC makes a specialty of technology integration, application of wireless communication technology, and Networking solution (including Server, Workstation, and wireless solution applying IEEE 802.11b). Moreover, the company also specialises in the production of quality-designed, user friendly and good stylish IA products such as PDA. Furthermore, MiTAC is also excellent in the manufacture of other high-quality and high-performance computer products including motherboards, desktop PCs, notebooks, LCD monitors, and industrial PCs. Additionally, A specialist team is also set up to work on the development and application of Linux software. The company boasts state-of-the-art, cost-effective manufacturing sites in Taiwan and China as well as nimble, timely build-to -order and configure-to-order [BTO/CTO] centres worldwide.

- **PRIMAX Electronic Ltd**

Primax was established in Taiwan in March 1984 and listed in the Taiwan Stock Exchange in January 1995. The Company focuses on a diversified product portfolio comprising 4 segments:

- Optical-Electronic Products: scanner, phone camera and multifunctional peripheral (MFP).
- Computer Peripherals: mice/pointing devices, gaming controllers, surge protectors and broadband products.

- Paper Handling Equipment: paper shredder and laminator.
- Communication Accessories: mobile phone and telephone accessories.

Primax has 900 employees in Taiwan and over 5,300 employees in manufacturing sites and R&D operations in both Taiwan and China, sales and marketing offices in Hong Kong, Japan, Europe and the United States. The annual turnover for Primax is $1.24 billions. Today, Primax is a leading solution provider for information, electronics and consumer products. Since established, Primax has continued to expand its global OEM/ODM customer base, which includes many famous world-class leading companies.

- **Inventec Corporation**

Inventec Corporation was founded in June 1975. Inventec's Taiwan factories, Shih-Lin and Tao-Yuan, have been equipped for the full-function scope of R&D, safety and regulatory certificate application, purchasing, production, quality assurance, business operation, and customer services. Inventec's employees are over 25,800 worldwide and the turnover is US$3.88 billions. Among 25,800 employees, there are 2000 employees working for Taiwan branch. Inventec corporation's overseas manufacturing facilities extend to Hongqiao and Pudong in Shanghai, China; Houston in U.S.A., Scotland in U.K., and Czech. The overall annual production quantity is seven millions notebook computers and two million servers. Inventec has also set up software-design bases in Tianjin, Shanghai, Nanjing and Beijing to provide our customers with integrated services.

IT success in Supply Chain Management

Inventec Corporation's information from order process, material delivery, production, finished goods delivery through invoice is well integrated.

- In 1996, the direct connections established through EDI with customers.
- In 2000, long term master planning implemented on Supply Chain Planning (SCP) for world wide demand fulfilment
- In 2000, B2B Web platform implemented for e-procurement with vendors
- In 2001, short term factory planning implemented on i2 Factory Planner (FP) for production schedule
- In 2002, 1st E-Book mechanism connected to Beijing Customs for electronic data exchange in customs clearance process

- **TATUNG Co**

Founded in 1918 and headquartered in Taiwan, Tatung Company is a worldwide leader in the design and manufacturing of a vast array of digital consumer products, including consumer PCs, LCD TVs PDPs, network-connected devices, storage-based media players, videophones and home appliances. Tatung also delivers advanced products for business computing, such as Tablet PCs, blade servers and wireless thin clients. For industrial products, Tatung has well-established power and energy businesses. Tatung has 35,000 employees worldwide and its turnover is $4.32 billions.

By capitalising on the advantages of vertical integration, Tatung makes full use of the supply of key components such as flat-panel displays and digital tuners from its many subsidiaries located across the globe. In order to sustain strong, long-term growth, Tatung is particularly focused on the development of advanced technologies and global network of operations. With its overseas branches spreading across 12 countries, including Japan, China, Singapore, USA, Canada, UK, Holland, Indonesia etc, Tatung is in a solid position to deliver products more efficiently and fulfill customer services more effectively.

- **MicroStar Inc (MSI)**

Micro-Star International Co., Ltd (MSI) enjoys a high reputation for its innovations in the construction of Motherboards, Graphics Cards, Optical Storage Devices, Workstations, Servers, Slim PCs, Barebones Systems and IA Products. Since its founding in 1986, MSI has remained at the forefront in providing easy-to-implement, state-of-the-art products and robust computing solutions for our customers. MSI's efforts are focused on quality, customer satisfaction and innovative solutions to meet growing market demands for computing needs.

A global company with sales of US$1.7 billions, MSI serves an international network of distributors and OEM customers in the US, Europe, Asia, Africa, Australia, and Latin America. MSI has over 1700 employees worldwide. MSI was recently ranked number 22 on Legend Magazine's Top 1000 manufacturing companies in Taiwan and ranked number 85 in the recent Business Week Info Tech 100 report, published in June 2003.

- **ADI Corporation**

ADI Corp founded in 1979, provides a complete line of products and services to its local and international clients. Each branch office offers technical support, training, after sale services and trouble shooting facilities supported by highly trained technicians and engineers. To cope with the growing demand for internet services in the recent years, websites are also available on the World Wide Web to provide on-line services and up to date information to its customers. ADI has set up branch offices strategically located around the globe to reach more clients and provide unparalleled services and quality. At present, besides the headquarters in Taipei, ADI has set up branch offices in U.S.A., The Netherlands, U.K., Germany, France, Japan, Hong Kong, and Thailand to strengthen its penetration and international stance. Employing local people to cater different cultures for overseas branches has been the concept and management philosophy of ADI. ADI has 1500 employees worldwide and the capital of US$1.5 millions.

- **SAMPO Technology Corporation**

SAMPO founded in 1936 in Taiwan and it has capital around US$78.8 millions. The Company's product portfolio consists of colour monitor, LCD monitor and LCD TV/monitor. SAMPO has more than 5,500 employees worldwide and over 60 engineers for its research and development. The number of employees in Taiwan branch is around 1650. SAMPO's sales revenue in 2004 was approx US$4.65 billions.

- **Compal Electronics Inc**

Compal Electronics Inc. manufactures computer notebook and monitor products, as well as communication products. The company offers various computer notebook products. It also produces Personal Digital Assistant (PDA) products, including Pocket Personal Computers (PPCs), global positioning system PDAs, and PPC phone products. In addition, Compal Electronics produces wireless products, including code division multiple access handsets. It operates in Taiwan, China, South Korea, the United States, and the United Kingdom. The company was founded in 1984 and is headquartered in Taipei, Taiwan. Compal Electronics I112, Inc. is a subsidiary of Worldwide Logistics Group. In 2003, its total annual revenue has reached US 4.713 billions dollars and its worldwide workforce over 10,000. The number of employees in Taiwan branch is 3800.

- **First International Computer Inc (FIC)**

First International Computer, Inc. was founded by Dr. Ming J. Chien in 1980. First International Computer, Inc. is part of the FIC Global, a successful collection of technology companies which are a dominant force in the industry. Currently the FIC Global encompasses 3 separate areas of the industry: Information Technology, Telecommunications, and System Integration. The subsidiary companies that make up the FIC Global are all thriving market leaders in their own fields and together span the whole spectrum of IT industries. FIC is now a dominant force in the technology market both in research and development, and manufacturing. As Computer, Communication and Consumer Electronics (3C) markets have converged, FIC has adapted and developed, becoming a respected producer of 3C related products. Many new and innovative products have joined the FIC product line and the company is no longer simply known for its award winning range of motherboards. Now firmly established at the top of the 3C market, FIC is determined to continue achieving excellence in the field of engineering and manufacturing services. 2003 revenue is $3.3 billions and employees are over 10,000 worldwide and 1200 in Taiwan branch. Sophisticated e-Glogistics network for efficient supply chain management includes 6 supplier hubs, 10 manufacturing / assembly sites and 7 Branch Offices.

- **Arima Computer Corporation**

Arima Group, not merely a publicly-held OEM / ODM company, has moved beyond to be the leading integrated service provider headquartered in Taoyuan, Taiwan, with the full-ranged professions and core technologies to design, manufacture, and deliver completely seamless integrated customized solution. As what miscellaneous does, Arima meets diverse customer needs with its miscellaneous product lines that incorporate Notebook, Server, Internet Appliance, Set-top Box, PDA, Display, Optoelectronics, Communication Products and any other anticipated in the future. As what global does, Arima enables customers to net the needed supports of Arima products, technologies, and services with the worldwide manufacturing, service and R&D facilities in Taiwan, China, Europe, Japan, and North America. Arima currently has 1400 employees in Taiwan branch and 3800 worldwide. It has annual turnover of US$0.57billions.

Long-term Partnership and R&D Capability are the most precious assets of Arima. By translating integrated services and advanced technologies into business value along with Arima ERP and Supply Chain Management (SCM) system, the company provides customers the abilities to achieve zero inventory & in-time service, save costs and time-to-market, increase profits & competence, and concentrate on their anticipated market needs & customer services that are all key drivers for top-tier business.

- **Compeq Mfg. Co. Ltd**

As the first company to support government's policies in developing high-tech industries, Compeq Manufacturing Co., LTD. is established in Taoyuan Taiwan since August 1973. Compeq has 8,351 employees worldwide and 4500 employees in Taiwan branch. 2001 revenue is US$ 33 millions and 2002 is US$38 millions. Initially, Compeq was dedicated to produce single side and double side PCB. Focusing on improving processes and developing new technology, Compeq are the first PCB supplier that passed the certification from IBM in Taiwan and began to mass produce of 6 layers in 1983.Since then, Compeq is recognized as having outstanding capability to produce multi-layer PCB.

To help tap electronic consumption product market and serve the North America customers, we have established factories in Utah (U.S.A.) for joining advanced product design and local service; On the other hand, due to Mainland China will be global electronic manufacturing service site gradually, also considering manufacturing cost saving niches and potential internal market demands, our Huizhou (China) plant have been established in 1996 and successfully obtained internal market shares in China.

Under the prosperous and booming electronic consumption products and network market, Compeq has entered the market of telecommunications (cellar phone, base station) and network equipment from computer filed (desktop, notebook, server) originally to keep with main trend in electronic products; Otherwise, in order to meet critical requirements for IC packaging substrates, Tayuan plant are built for IC substrates and entering IC packing field meeting the customer demand in related product in 1998. After starting mass production, Compeq has developed the CSP, FC-BGA, Mini-BGA and FC-BGA related product respectively. Now, Compeq is not only the largest professional PCB manufacturer in Taiwan, but is also ranked as number sixth worldwide. To offer the best service for electronic manufacturer, Compeq will continue to develop new generation technology, enhance competitiveness and fully satisfy the market and customer -demands.

Compeq, insisting on the principle of "Highest quality and Customer first", have and continue to spend a lot of effort on improving processes, developing new technology and set the fully quality system to meet customer requirements and have been certified by international institutions, including ISO-9002 and QS-9000. To raise customer service satisfactions level, we have set up sales offices in European, Singapore, Malaysia, Untied States and Mainland China. Through these sales offices, Compeq offers the product design, optimal manufacturing flow, quality requirements and on site service. The sales offices could improve communication during market chances and helps develop a global strategic partner.

Due to electronic product replaced rapid and new technologies are explored, the capability of developing and researches new technology are global competition resources, which can meet product demands from customer and explore new product in market. Therefore, Compeq focus on the efforts of technology development in followings: to meet thin and small trend in electronic product, we have developed the trace width/trace spacing are 25 um and high density interconnection (HDI) technology (1+N+1 & 2+N+2); based on requirement of high reliability for high-end networking equipment, server product, we have developed the high layer count (HLC, currently has been 26 layers), high aspect ratio plating capability and utilizing the low Dk & low Df, high Tg material in PCB. In addition, because of emphasizing on environmental protection policies, Compeq not only treat the solid waste produced in production, but also invest to build first professional PCB waste water treatment plant in 1991 in Taiwan and obtained the ISO-14001 certification in 1997.To satisfy the worldwide environmental product specification, Compeq explore to apply the Halogen Free Material in PCB. In the future, we will follow the environmental protection policies to continue improve in process and product.

Compeq operation principles are focused on prompting technology development and meet customer-demand satisfaction. When facing intense global competition, we are not only devoted to satisfy market and customer-demands, but also through planned actions to let our vision come true and to be a best partner of global electronic manufacturing companies. Compeq Manufacturing Co., Ltd., established in 1973, is the first PCB (Printed Circuit Board) manufacturer in Taiwan that has achieved compliance with the government's industrial high-tech development strategy. The Compeq team is the largest multi-layer PCB manufacturer in Taiwan, and ranked seventh globally. Compeq's PCB manufacturing capability covers Information (Computers), Networking (Hubs/Switches/Routers), Communications (Mobile Phones/Base Stations) and Semiconductors (IC Packaging Base).

- **Twinhead International Corporation**

Twinhead International Corporation (TIC) of Taiwan is a publicly traded company in Taiwan. Twinhead has employees approximately 1200. The turnover is approximately US$8.4 billions. A major manufacturer of portable notebook computers, Twinhead is one of the largest notebook suppliers in the world. Other wholly owned Twinhead subsidiaries include the United States, China, Germany, and the United Kingdom. Because Twinhead is a true manufacturer, not an Original Design Manufacturer (OEM), it is able to offer the most competitive pricing possible. Twinhead has been building notebook computers for some of the biggest names in the computer business and is known throughout the industry as a quality provider to the O.E.M market.

- **Delta Electronic**

Delta is the world's leading switching power supply manufacturer and a major supplier of video displays and electronic components for the computer, telecommunications, networking, and other industries. The company has manufacturing plants in Taiwan, China, Thailand, Japan, Europe, and Mexico, as well as R&D centers and sales and service offices throughout the world. It has over 30,000 employees worldwide and 1500 employees in Taiwan branch. Continuing Delta's vigorous growth of the past decade, Delta Group expects to achieve worldwide sales of US$3.012 billions in 2004. In addition, revenues have increased more than six times since 1994, with a 10-year compound annual growth rate (CAGR) of 18 percent.

Innovation is the focus of Delta's research and development. In recognition of Delta's strength in product design, we have recently received both the Taiwan Symbol of Excellence and the National Award of Excellence. Our design process is based on Product Life Cycle Management (PLM) providing a stringent and accelerated design cycle while ensuring product quality and reliability. Our capability for innovative design is what sets us apart from the competition.

Delta has design teams, engineering teams, and R&D laboratories in Taiwan, Hong Kong, China, the U.S., and Europe. Delta's labs at Research Triangle Park in North Carolina, U.S.A., include the Delta Power Electronics Laboratory, which develops high-efficiency and high-density power conversion products, and the Delta Networks R&D Laboratory, which develops networking products.

Continuous enhancement of our engineering capabilities allows us to develop products with better value and performance. In recent years we have developed high-density and high-efficiency telecommunication power systems, UPSs with advanced interfaces, computer networking components and products with high software content, microdisplay PTVs, and many others.

- **YODI Technology Ltd**

YODI established on 1978 and became CSA qualified manufacturer in 1987. In 1994 YODI has been passed ISO-9002 by RWTUV authentication. YODI is a multinational organisation that traditionally manufactures in the computer application product sector and builds up the factory in 1978. It still has only 30 employees in Taiwan. However, it expands its manufacturing productivity in China, set up two factories located in Dongguan in 1997 and Kunshan in 2002. YODI also holds global markets around the world. YODI is not only a name for computer application equipment wire such as Wire Harness, Computer Application Wire, Photoelectron Application and household electronic Application Wire and also customized design wire products but also, for a whole range of further product areas. Examples are household appliances, and communications technology, HDMI-DVI cable and Coaxial cable. YODI has a range of key customers and also co-operation for more than 20years. The key customers are National/Panasonic, SAMPO, WYSE, Quanix, TATUNG, DARFON, BENQ, TECO and FTI.

- **Tex-Chu Trading Co. Ltd.**

Tex-Chu set up the company since 1978 and became the agent in Taiwan for "Rich bond" cyanoacrylate glue of Florex from Japan in 1980. In 1992 Tex-Chu expands its business into electronic materials in IC components, EMI gasket and conductive fabric tape of Zipper tubing from Japan makes Tex-Chu getting into the EMI field in 1993. And then, those products become our major business for the development of Notebook Computer; it has ISO 9002 certificate in June 1999. The organisation consists of 7 subsidiaries and affiliated companies in Taiwan and China. Now Tex-Chu employs 80 factory workers in Taiwan. Tex-Chu set up the factories in Suzhou in 2002 and Dong Guan in 2004 in China. These business activities of Tex-Chu are divided into four business units sectors namely: (a) PC & PC peripheral: ACER, AOC, ARIMA, ASUSTEK, COMPAL, CLEVO, CHIMEI, FIC, INVENTEC, MITAC, QUANTA,LITEON,ASUS,COMPAL; (b) power supply: AMBIT,

DELTA, LEN CHANG, PHIHONG,POTRANS, POWER MATE, SAMPO, USI, UMEC; (c) communication:AMBIT, ASKEY, GVC, PALMAX, SENAO   and; (d) consumer: ALTEK, E-ONE, KOLIN, PROTON, SAMPO, SINPO, SUNPENTOWN, TATUNG CAR MAKER, KUOZUI (TOYOTA), CMC (MITSUBISHI); and (e) car maker : CMC(MITSUBISHI), KUOZUI(TOYOTA), and YULON(NISSAN).

- **Prohubs International Corp**

PROHUBS founded in 1995 and professional agent which provided digital multimedia and network communication. There are 40 employees in PROHUBS. PROHUBS is a multinational organisation that particularly operates in the semiconductor industry. PROHUBS is excellent agent in a name for equipment of computer application such as electronic components, mobile communications, personal digital equipment, household electronics, semiconductor and material of Photoelectron Application. PROHUBS provides professional services to main semiconductor manufacturing and IC design companies such as SIGMATEL, C-MEDIA, MSTAR, SYMWAVE, INFOTALK, ADIMOS, ENTROPIC, ICPLUS, INFRANT, RDC, ACARD, SST, SIPEX, ZYWYN, POTENTIA, G-LINK, and TMTECH.

- **Chia-Soon Electronics**

Chiao-Soon established in April 197 and began its operation in Taipei City, with the capitalisation of only US$0.06 millions dollars, less than 30 factory workers and 8 cooperating companies. In 1980 when was in economic recovery, the company expanded its operation by getting new machinery and staff. At that time, its factory workers increased to 70 its capitalisation rose to US$0.30 millions dollars and it had over 100 cooperating companies. Its capitalisation was increased again in 1986 to the current scale. Furthermore, in 1987 the company bought the land it is currently situated to build new offices and factories which were inaugurated in December 1991. Chia-Soon Electronics became a UL and CSA certified company in 1988 and 1989, respectively, assisted by the R.O.C. Industrial Technology Research Institute, and joined an ISO-9002 quality assurance system at the end of 1993. In the following December, this company was certified by the Bureau of Commodity Inspection & Quarantine, R.O.C. Ministry of Economic Affairs. Furthermore, on January 20, 1995, Chia-Soon passed the required evaluation to become qualified for the "Central-Satellite Factory System of Sampo Corporation."

Since 1992, Chia-Soon Electronics has been introducing quite a few advanced facilities (Such us: automatic crimping machines) and building new factories in order to upgrade product quality and develop new products to exporting Japan and other countries The company is also committed to increasing production volume, upgrading technological level, improving quality control, attaining high quality processing, enhancing the added value of products, and ensuring factory automation. All of these efforts aim to help Chia-Soon gain a higher profile and status is Taiwan's industry. It is hoped that the central factories will better realize the importance of using parts, developing self-brand products in marketing, and wining trust of foreign clients. Moreover, the central factories should help their satellite factories gain better knowledge of market demands at home and abroad so that both sides can benefit from each other by an even closer cooperative relationship.

- **Micon Technology Corp**

MICON set up the company since 1993. The capital of MICON is US$142,850 in the first year and raised to US$1.7 millions in 2002. There are 20 employees in MICON Taipei. The organization includes 3 main departments and mainly focuses on R&D development in company's strategy. MICON's main customers are Weltrend, Myson Century, Trumpion Microelectronic and TOPRO. MICON has variety products in CRT, LCD monitor and also the agent of IC products. We can divide the serious of main products in to 2 parts: (a) for LCD monitor: LCD MONITOR, CONTROL BOARD and LCD MONITOR DAUGHTER BOARD, TV BOARD and REMOTE CONTROLLER, LCD MONITOR MAIN PARTS and POWER SUPPLY: ADAPTER & AC CORD; and (b) for CRT monitor: MCU (H/W & S/W) and OSD CHIP.

- **Sen-Kung Technologies Ltd**

Sen-Kung set up the company since 1979 and mainly produces PCB Board. It has 60 employees in Taiwan and its capital is US$1.51millions in 2004. The organisation affiliated companies 4 countries. Sen-Kung not only provides very good quality electronic products to the main IT companies and very professional in R&D persuasion but also receive many credibility from the customers. These main products of Sen-Kung are divided into two business units sectors: PCB Board and LCD monitor Board.